THE BAR EXAM
IN A NUTSHELL
Second Edition

By

SUZANNE DARROW-KLEINHAUS
Touro College Jacob D. Fuchsberg Law Center

WEST®

A Thomson Reuters business

Mat # 40774876

© West, a Thomson business, 2003
© 2009 Thomson/Reuters
      610 Opperman Drive
      St. Paul, MN 55123
      1–800–313–9378

Printed in the United States of America

ISBN: 978–0–314–19928–7

TEXT IS PRINTED ON 10% POST
CONSUMER RECYCLED PAPER

In memory of
our beloved Cindy

*

PREFACE AND ACKNOWLEDGMENTS TO THE SECOND EDITION

I have learned a lot in the five years since writing the first edition—most, if not all, has been from my students. Perhaps because of the intensity of the experience, but the time I spend working with students in the crazy weeks before the bar exam are the best of my teaching times. The hours are insane and the pressure is intense—almost as much for the teacher as the student—but the feeling that comes from sharing such an experience is without equal. It's not the same as what happens in a regular classroom. The dynamics and the stakes are so different. Everything is heightened—the highs, the lows, and the "gotcha" moments. For many students, it finally comes together when studying for the bar exam and I get to be there when it does. It doesn't get much better than that—except when I learn that they passed the exam.

The additions to this book were stimulated by learning what my students needed to help them through this challenging time. Consequently, this edition adds some very practical information absent from the first edition: suggestions on how to get a "head start" on bar preparation, guidelines for selecting a bar review course that suits individual learning styles, bar planner checklists for the entire bar preparation period, from the initial planning phases to the actual days of the bar exam, advice on how to manage the mountains of material you cover in bar review courses, and how to learn the law you need to know in a way that you can remember it and use it to answer exam questions. I have also included a greater range of examples from additional jurisdictions.

I owe a tremendous debt of gratitude to the students with whom I have worked so closely in the past couple of years. They have shared their thoughts, ideas, hearts, and hopes with me and I am forever grateful to have had this time with them: Kristina Milone, John Anselmo, Lauren Bernard, Erica Borgese, Wayne Broder, Ross Carmel, James Ciscone, Courtney Davy, Tianna Lyons, Miriam Metwaly, Alisa Sondak, Matthew Zimmelman, Ferron Lien, Anita Gupta, Jessica Terranova, Lindsay Godt, Aimee Alix, Kristen Buttafuoco, Oren Gerber, Kerri Flynn, Tara Hakimi, Tyrone Nurse, Gabriela Pacheco-Castillo, Alexander Sherman, and Maria Stavrakis.

I have also had the delightful and unexpected pleasure of making new friends as a result of writing this book. I have had emails from around the country and around the globe, including Japan and Korea. It has been my pleasure to correspond and get to know Masi Takeda and Thomas Song. I never would have believed that a book about the bar exam would bring me together with such hard-working, fascinating, and talented individuals.

PREFACE AND ACKNOWLEDGMENTS TO
THE SECOND EDITION

Thanks again to Heidi Hellekson, Publisher for the West Law School imprint at Thomson-West. Her receptivity to new ideas and faith in my judgment means more to me than I can say. I endeavor to repay it always with the best work of which I am capable.

My deepest appreciation to Touro College, Jacob D. Fuchsberg Law Center and Dean Lawrence Raful. Thank you for the research support and stipend which allowed me to pursue this project.

If you used Mastering the Law School Exam during law school, you may find some familiar sounding passages in the sections on forensic IRAC. I have adapted these sections into the Nutshell. I have also incorporated some material from Acing the Bar Exam, specifically the sections on getting a "Head Start" on bar preparation and the Bar Planner, as well as the material on de-constructing the bar exam and some of the additional jurisdiction-specific information. Although there has been some "borrowing" of material, much has been re-written to comport with the Nutshell's more conversational style and approach. However, if you find that checklists help you focus on the task at hand, then I would recommend Acing the Bar Exam. It complements the Nutshell with a "checklist approach" to the process of studying for and taking the bar exam. Mastering the Law School Exam and Acing the Bar Exam are Thomson-West Publications.

The Multistate Essay Examination ("MEE") has been "Reprinted by Permission" from the February 2001 MEE. Copyright © 2001 National Conference of Bar Examiners. All rights reserved. The Multistate Bar Examination ("MBE") questions have been "Reprinted by Permission" from the following NCBE publications: Sample MBE February, 1991 (© 1991 by the National Conference of Bar Examiners), Sample MBE 1996 (© 1996 by the National Conference of Bar Examiners), Sample MBE III July,1998 (© 1998 by the National Conference of Bar Examiners) and the 2006 Information Booklet (© 2005 by the National Conference of Bar Examiners). The Multistate Performance Test ("MPT") has been "Reprinted by Permission" from Test 2 of the July 1997, MPT, State v. Devine (©1997 by the National Conference of Bar Examiners).

In New York, the Board of Law Examiners release answers which received scores superior to the average scaled score awarded for the relevant essay. However, the Board is careful to make no representation as to the accuracy of the answers; they are simply considered above average responses. Like New York, the bar examiners in New Jersey, Florida and California publish essay questions and answers after each bar examination administration. The Florida Board of Bar Examiners Study Guide is copyrighted and the selections reproduced here are under

the express written permission of the Florida Board
of Bar Examiners.

SUZANNE DARROW-KLEINHAUS
BELLMORE, NEW YORK

December 2008

*

PREFACE AND
ACKNOWLEDGMENTS

The bar exam looms large in the mind of every law student from the first day of law school and sometimes even before. But it need not. The bar exam is a practical exam that requires a practical approach. It's meant to test the candidate's basic competency to practice law—to see whether the law student has mastered the legal skills and general knowledge that a first year practicing attorney should possess.

Still, the bar exam is a challenge and the candidate cannot simply graduate law school and expect to pass without any additional preparation. But law school was also a challenge and presumably the candidate made it through or he or she would not be taking the bar exam. The truth is that law school prepares candidates for the bar by providing a solid foundation in the skills the bar exam seeks to test and in turning out an individual who knows how to handle the competing demands on his or her time, memory, and energy. When a student has learned how to learn the law, then bar passage is not an obstacle that cannot be overcome, but a requirement for entering the profession which must be met like any other.

First and always, my husband Murray. His love, support, encouragement, and meals have been constant throughout our marriage, and especially throughout the writing of this book. Our family would have starved long ago if it weren't for him.

I owe much to my daughter Meredith who believed in my ability to teach before I did, insisting that I was so much clearer and better at explaining how to write than any of her high school or college teachers that I should be the one who wrote her textbooks and taught her classes. She believed in me so strongly that she sent all of her friends to me for help. My sister, Jessica read the early drafts and made some great suggestions. Together we reminisced about our bar prep days and tried to come up with what we would have wanted to know to make the task even the slightest bit more tolerable. Many thanks to my parents, Bernice and Albert, who taught me so much, but especially my dad, who reminded me when I was tired and disheartened that I should never let go of my dream to teach and to write.

I am truly indebted to all of my teachers life long, including and particularly, my dear friends and mentors, Professors Michael D'Innocenzo and Ruth Prigozy. Their voices are now and for always in my head.

And of course, my students, for whom this book is intended and without whom it would not have been written. The development of "forensic IRAC' would not have been possible without their willingness to open up and let me into their thoughts.

My deepest appreciation to Touro College, Jacob D. Fuchsberg Law Center and especially Dean

Howard Glickstein and Vice Dean Gary Shaw for their unreserved support and unwavering commitment to our students.

I've endeavored to make clear throughout the book that the candidate's best friends during this time are the Bar Examiners. Both the National Conference of Bar Examiners ("NCBE") and the state boards make numerous materials available to bar candidates.

The Multistate Bar Examination ("MBE") questions, the Multistate Essay Examination ("MEE") interrogatory, and excerpts from the Multistate Performance Tests ("MPT") have been reprinted by permission from the NCBE. Any attempt to create a useful manual for bar candidates would been impossible without these materials.

The MBE questions have been "Reprinted by Permission" from the following NCBE publications: Sample MBE February, 1991 (© 1991 by the National Conference of Bar Examiners), Sample MBE 1996 (© 1996 by the National Conference of Bar Examiners), Sample MBE III July,1998 (© 1998 by the National Conference of Bar Examiners) and the 2001 Information Booklet (© 2001 by the National Conference of Bar Examiners).

The MEE interrogatory has been "Reprinted by Permission" from the February, 2000 MEE (© 2000 by the National Conference of Bar Examiners).

The MPT excerpts have been "Reprinted by Permission" from Test 2 of the February 1997, MPT,

In re Hayworth and Wexler (© 1997 by the National Conference of Bar Examiners) and Test 2 of the July 1997, MPT, *State v. Devine* (© 1997 by the National Conference of Bar Examiners).

Like the NCBE, the individual state bar examiners make vital information available to its bar candidates. It's all right there on the internet and I made extensive use of this vital resource. I urge all candidates to do the same. Each jurisdiction administers the exam and determines its own policy with regard to the relative weight given to the scores for each component of the bar exam. As a result, it's the primary source for such basic information as application materials, test locations and accommodations, test dates, admissions issues, test topics, and more. Even more importantly, most jurisdictions include some examples of past exam questions and sample answers.

In addition to the National Conference of Bar Examiners, I wish to thank the bar examiners of New York, New Jersey, and Connecticut for permission to reprint bar examination materials. The reprinted essay selections and sample answers have all been downloaded from the states' web sites, in large part to illustrate the accessibility of these materials to bar candidates.

In New York, the Board of Law Examiners release answers which received scores superior to the average scale score awarded for the relevant essay. However, the Board is careful to make no representation as to the accuracy of the answers; they are simply considered above average responses.

Like New York, the bar examiners in New Jersey and Connecticut publish essay questions after each bar examination administration. In New Jersey, the Board publishes actual answers from candidates that it considers to be exceptional although they are not intended as model answers. The State of Connecticut publishes seven sample answers for each essay question, providing the applicant with an opportunity to see a range of scores. Connecticut's bar examiners identify the scoring system and the candidate can read what was considered a "much below average" response as opposed to a "much above average" response, and everything in between.

A regularly updated list of each jurisdiction's bar admission office phone number and address can be found at www.ncbex.org, the NCBE's official website.

SUZANNE DARROW-KLEINHAUS
BELLMORE, NEW YORK

June 2003

*

OUTLINE

Chapter 6. Learning the Black Letter Law

Page

*

THE BAR EXAM
IN A NUTSHELL

Second Edition

*

CHAPTER 1

ABOUT THE BAR EXAM

A. WHY SHOULD YOU LISTEN TO ME?

If you're like other bar candidates, you've been bombarded with lots of well-meaning advice on how to prepare for the bar exam. You may even have paid thousands of dollars for this advice. So what could another so-called "bar expert" possibly have to tell you that is not already to be found somewhere in the pile of materials growing like Mount Vesuvius on the side of your bed? Simple: I can tell you what you need to know to make all this guidance work for you and not simply overwhelm you. I can share with you what I have learned in the past five years from working with classmates, students, and other bar candidates who failed the bar exam multiple times and then passed after we had worked together. I can spare you what they went through trying to figure out what the exam was all about. Then you can pass the bar exam the first time you take it.

I can't believe it's been 10 years since I sat for the bar exam. The experience is still fresh in my mind—as it remains for all of us who take the bar. I promise that you'll never forget the struggle of studying for and taking the bar exam; I also promise that you'll never forget the moment of joy and exhilaration when you learn that you've passed. And that is what this book is all about—getting you to that moment.

I never thought I would make the bar exam some kind of personal calling. I was just happy that it was over and I could pack away my flash cards, notebooks, and the ton of study materials I had accumulated. But my happiness was short-lived when I learned that my best friends had not passed with me. I was shocked: I knew my friends had studied long hours, like me. I knew that they had gone to all the bar review classes and had taken copious notes, like me. I knew that they had followed the suggested study outlines and written sample essays, like me. So why the different result? I wanted to do something—anything—to help.

I offered to study with them. I had been a good student in law school and one of my essays had been selected as a sample answer in New York. I felt I had something of value to offer. We started to meet weekly at my house and as we sat around the kitchen table, working through essay questions and multiple choice questions together, I was able to see how they approached the problems. From that first afternoon, it became clear to me that while we had gone to law school together, taken exams together, and had even taken the same bar review course together, we went about the process of analyzing and answering the questions very differently. I used IRAC and they didn't. It never occurred to me that using IRAC, the method of legal analysis taught to all law students from the very first day of law school, would make the difference between passing and failing, but it did, and as I was soon to learn, it always makes the difference.

B. YOU MEAN THAT IRAC IS THE SECRET?

As I continued to work with more and more students, it became increasingly clear that the secret to passing the bar exam, if there was a secret at all, was not the amount of time spent in study but the nature of that study and the diligent application of IRAC analysis to all problems, essay and short answer alike. The key to getting multiple choice questions correct and high essay scores was finding the issue in each of the questions and working from there. This sounds a lot easier and a lot harder than it is so a little explanation is in order.

It's easier because you're already acquainted with IRAC: the acronym for the familiar "Issue, Rule, Application, Conclusion" structure of legal analysis. It's more difficult because you're probably not familiar enough with it to use it consistently and correctly to reason through objective, short answer questions as well as essay questions where you are given only a general question and must identify the narrow issue in controversy for yourself. Typically, your understanding of IRAC is limited to the form your professors wanted you to use to write an essay exam. But IRAC is more than a form: it is the essence and structure of all legal reasoning.

The questions on the bar exam and its individual sections are designed to test the fundamental analytical skills you learned in law school together with your mastery of legal principles and basic knowledge of core substance. Over and over again, in one format or another, you'll be given a set of facts and must know enough law to find the legal problem. Your ability to find the legal question in the facts is the single most important element in the analysis because you need to know enough law to find the issue. But you must do more than just find the issue: you must identify it and clearly articulate it, either to yourself for the multiple choice questions or in writing for the essays, before you can go on and correctly answer the question or write an essay that gets you the necessary points.

Your ability to conscientiously and consistently apply IRAC analysis to all the questions will make the difference between passing and failing. While there are certainly a number of other factors involved in the equation, and I will discuss them in the course of this book, I've learned that the one common thread linking all the unsuccessful candidates I've worked with was their failure to use IRAC to analyze the questions. It was not enough that they had mastered the substantive rules of law: they needed to know when a particular rule was implicated by the facts. This was the connection between them and what they had been missing. By failing to identify the issue, they failed to recognize when a particular rule was in controversy. Then it didn't matter whether they knew the rule or not. They never got to apply it because they didn't see the issue. The good news is that once these students integrated IRAC analysis into the course and method of their study, they went on to pass the exam.

C. "FORENSIC IRAC"

As I just explained, the key to answering bar exam questions successfully is to engage in IRAC analysis. Sadly, too many bar candidates neglect to do so—much to their subsequent lament. In these cases, it isn't so much that IRAC analysis is absent entirely, but that its use is flawed or inadequate. The real problem is that these students can't tell the difference between the two: they tend to be so disconnected from their own thought process that they continue to make the same mistakes over and over again, blaming everything from poor study habits to nervousness instead of acknowledging what's right in front of them.

Fortunately, however, IRAC is a process and I've identified several techniques for tracking that process. I've termed it "forensic IRAC" because these techniques are similar to those employed by crime scene investigators, accountants, medical examiners, and any of the "so-called" forensic experts who go back over the trail of evidence to determine precisely how that evidence led to a particular result. While such experts rely on fingerprints, ledger books, and DNA to find their culprit, we use IRAC. We work backward from the incorrect exam answer using IRAC analysis to figure out how and what you were thinking that led you to select that answer choice or write that essay response. It's somewhat ironic that we use IRAC analysis to find the flaw in our IRAC application, but it makes sense given the process of legal thought and the dynamics of the exam.

As you study for the bar exam, you will be writing out lots of exam answers and practicing many multiple choice questions when you study. You need a way to critique your own work and understand what you've done right and where you've gone wrong. The good news is that you can do this kind of self-assessment. All you need are the right tools and you can become your own guide. By learning to apply what I've termed "forensic IRAC" to your own essays and multiple choice answers, you'll be able to identify the flaws in your work and correct them.

While all the questions on the bar exam require an IRAC analysis, different parts of the exam emphasize different elements of the IRAC equation. Consequently, our techniques will vary according to the skills tested by the particular type of question. Forensic principles are outlined for the essay and MBE portions of the bar exam and are included in their respective chapters.

D. WHAT IS REQUIRED OF YOU

The goal of the bar examiners is to test your competency for the practice of law. To pass the bar exam, therefore, you must demonstrate a firm grasp of the "black letter law" and a solid grounding in basic analytical, reading, and writing skills.

These skills include:

- problem solving
- identifying and formulating legal issues
- organizing information
- separating relevant from irrelevant facts
- communicating effectively in writing
- managing time efficiently to complete an assignment

The problem is that these are practical skills and students spend most if not all of their bar prep time studying only substantive law. Success on the bar exam requires mastery of both.

1.   Studying Actively

Your bar review course will provide all the substantive law you need to know to pass the exam. Such courses are carefully constructed to give you the black letter law in all the areas of law tested in your jurisdiction. When you think about it, this is a prodigious effort and best left to the professionals. Don't try to do this on your own.

However, a bar review course does not teach you how to process all the law you'll cover in the course, how to write essays, or how to analyze questions. It assumes you developed these skills in law school. And for the most part, you have. You just have to be sure not to fall into the trap of devoting all of your effort to reviewing notes and memorizing rules without spending enough time working with questions.

Practicing questions is essential for developing your analytical, reading, and writing skills.

What this means is that studying for the bar exam requires "active" studying. Unfortunately, it is all too easy to assume a very passive role at this time—sitting through your bar review course for four to five hours a day and then reading and reviewing and summarizing and memorizing your notes for another four or more hours. Before you know it, the day has gone by, you are exhausted, and you have not done a single question!

While your bar review course will provide a study schedule that factors in practice time with essay and multiple choice questions, my experience has shown that it is not enough for most students. Just imagine going to take your road test and never doing more than read the driver's manual and drive the car around the block a few times. Well, going into the bar exam without doing hundreds (yes, I said "hundreds") of multiple choice questions and a significant number of essays will leave you in the same place: without the license you want.

An example from a past Multistate Bar Exam ("MBE") question illustrates this point nicely.

Peavey was walking peacefully along a public street when he encountered Dorwin, whom he had never seen before. Without provocation or warning, Dorwin picked up a rock and struck Peavey with it. It was later established that Dorwin was mentally ill and suffered recurrent hallucinations.

If Peavey asserts a claim against Dorwin based on battery, which of the following, if supported by evidence, will be Dorwin's best defense?

A. Dorwin did not understand that his act was wrongful.

B. Dorwin did not desire to cause harm to Peavey.

C. Dorwin did not know that he was striking a person.

D. Dorwin thought Peavey was about to attack him.

You could spend hours studying your notes on intentional torts, "know" the elements of a battery, and still answer this question incorrectly if you're unfamiliar with the way the elements are tested on the bar exam. If you're like most law students, you learned the elements of the intentional torts in a rather straightforward manner: you read cases, identified the elements in class discussions, memorized them, and recited them back on the final in the context of an essay.

You can see that the bar exam takes a different approach. Your analysis begins with the basic definition of a battery, but that's only your first step. Then you have to analyze each element with respect to the legal issue posed in the hypothetical. If you fail to identify the issue or miss the signal words in the question, you'll arrive at an incorrect answer choice even though you could probably recite the elements of a battery in your sleep!

Typically, I ask a student to answer this question when we begin working together and use it as a kind of "legal" Rorschach test to evaluate the student's substantive knowledge and analytical skills. I am not surprised when the majority of students choose an incorrect answer. For example, one student selected Answer Choice B, explaining that because a battery is the intentional, harmful or offensive touching of another, if Dorwin did not intend to cause harm, then he could not have committed a battery. "Yes," I replied, "but did Dorwin have to intend harm to commit a battery?" The student thought about it and realized that Dorwin need not have intended harm to be found liable in battery.

Not surprisingly, Choice B was the most popular student answer choice. Why? Because if you read the question quickly and scan the answer choices, you jump to Choice B because it contains the familiar battery language: "desire to cause harm."

Choice B was followed closely by Choice A in student popularity. Once again, Choice A reflects a student's tendency to react to answer choices instead of applying the elements mechanically to the issue in the question. Here, the student explained his answer choice as follows: if Dorwin didn't understand his act to be wrongful, then it couldn't have been "intentional." Just as in Answer Choice B, this reasoning is flawed because the intent element of battery is satisfied not only when the actor intends harmful or wrongful behavior, but if he acts with purpose or knowledge to a "substantial certainty."

Here, Dorwin need not have understood his act to be wrongful to have formed the requisite intent: he need only know what would be the likely consequence of striking Peavey with a rock. Consequently, only Choice C completely negates the intent element: if Dorwin had no idea (no "knowledge") he was striking a person, then he could not have formed the requisite intent to do the act.

A number of students selected Choice D. Interestingly, there were two lines of incorrect reasoning to support this answer choice! In one instance, the rationale was that self-defense would be a valid justification to excuse Dorwin's act. "Where in the facts do you find any basis to believe that Peavey was about to attack Dorwin?" I asked. Each student shook his or her head: "Nowhere," each reluctantly conceded. Once again, students had reacted to an answer choice without analyzing it within the factual context of the problem. If they had, they would have realized that there were no facts in the question to lead Dorwin to believe Peavey was about to attack him. In fact, careful reading of the problem would have ruled this answer choice out completely because the first words in the question tell us that "Peavey was walking peacefully" and it was "without provocation or warning, [that] Dorwin picked up a rock." How much clearer could the bar examiners have been? This leads us to Rule One for multiple choice questions: do not assume facts and do not select answer choices that have no basis in the facts of the problem unless a modifier like "unless" or "if" in the answer choice supplies the needed additional facts.

The other line of reasoning relied on the Mc'Naughton rule regarding the insanity defense to a criminal act. The problem, however, is that this was not a criminal prosecution and candidates who arrived at this conclusion did so by failing to read the facts carefully. We are told in the question stem that "Peavey asserts a claim against Dorwin based on battery" which must mean that it is a claim in "civil" battery; if it had been a criminal battery, then the state would have initiated the action.

I've spent a lot of time with you on this problem because it so accurately reflects the nature of an MBE question. As you can see, it seeks to test your true understanding of a subject and not just your ability to memorize. The problem itself comes from the famous tort case, *Garratt v. Dailey*. Remember Brian Dailey, the little five-year old who pulled the lawn chair from under the plaintiff as she was about to sit down? As the court stated in *Garratt*, "a battery would be established if, in addition to plaintiff's fall, it was proved that, when Brian moved the chair, he knew with substantial certainty that the plaintiff would attempt to sit down where the chair had been.... [t]he mere absence of any intent to injure the plaintiff or to play a prank on her or to embarrass her, or to commit an assault and battery on her would not absolve him from liability if, in fact, he had such knowledge." 46 Wash.2d 197 (1955). You can see how applying this definition of intent makes Choice C the correct response. If Dorwin did not know that he was striking a person, then he could not have committed a wrongful act.

It should be clear from this example how you must reason through an MBE question using IRAC or you'll respond incorrectly to a relatively simple torts question. In each case, you must identify the main issue in the question and then address the mini-issues raised in the answer choices. This requires that you ask yourself what's going on in the problem. Here, you're asked to solve a problem by finding Dorwin's best defense. To do this, you'll have to identify the answer choice which prevents the plaintiff from prevailing. This requires that you identify the elements of the plaintiff's cause of action, determine which defense would be strongest (negates that element), and choose an answer which most closely provides a basis for overcoming that obstacle. When you begin doing MBE questions, this thought process will require effort and a mechanical application of the steps; with sufficient practice, you'll run through these steps automatically.

2.   Letting Go of Your Notes

The only way you really learn the law the way you need to know it is to practice the problems. You won't have any time if you spend it all writing and rewriting your notes, and trust me, you still won't be able to answer the questions! You need to do the questions to learn how the rules work. Sometimes, you just have to let go of your notes to learn the law.

Instead, you will follow the study plans and strategies outlined in this book to turn each study hour into an active one. You'll be shown how to practice the rules in the context in which they will be tested. It is not enough to memorize elements and rules without some idea of how they will be tested. As you will see, the very best way to learn the rules in a way you can remember them is to practice them in the context of questions.

E. WHAT THIS BOOK WILL DO FOR YOU

This book will show you how to balance the need for memorization with the need for application. Since you must do both to succeed on the exam, this book will tell you how to effectively manage your time and the materials so that you can do both.

By now you should realize what this book won't do for you:

- It won't tell you that it is enough to attend all of your bar review sessions and simply memorize rules of law

- It won't tell you to spend all of your time reviewing your notes, rewriting your notes, and making note cards

- It won't tell you to become a robot and place yourself in the hands of others to prepare for what might well be the most important test of your life

But here's what it will do:

- It will show you how to learn the law from "doing" released bar exam questions

- It will show you how to rely on your training to respond to questions with an orderly thought process instead of panicking when you come across an unfamiliar question

- It will show you how to perform "forensic IRAC" on your own thought process so you can identify the flaws in your legal reasoning and correct them

- It will show you how to put together an individualized study program that works for you because it works from your strengths while recognizing your weaknesses

- It will de-construct the bar exam and separate it into its component parts

And finally, this book will teach you how to think under pressure. When you study for the bar exam, you are facing one of the most stressful periods of your life. You may be consumed with thoughts of "what if": what if I fail; what if I have to do this again; what if I don't get the job that I want; what if I disappoint my family, my friends, my teachers, myself. These are very normal fears: we all share them. In fact, a certain level of anxiety is a good thing but too much prevents you from doing your job. And you must be able to do your job of studying the law. You can't afford to lose control because of the pressure. Hemingway referred to it as having "grace under pressure." He wrote about the beauty and purity of line of the bull fighter in the ring facing the bull. The bull fighter's ability to remain focused and in control allowed him to control the bull and hence the outcome of the contest. You need to do the same in your arena.

CHAPTER 2

THE BAR PLANNER

A. THE NEED FOR PREPARATION

It might be just plain common sense to say this but it is true nonetheless: the bar exam requires a major commitment of time and effort to succeed. Bar review courses are structured to lead you through the material, but you must make the effort to learn it. It takes time to memorize black letter law and to practice problems. This part is neither fun nor easy. Still, it is possible to prepare adequately during the usual bar review period of six to eight weeks—*if you devote your time exclusively to bar preparation.* Still, too many bar candidates come to their bar review courses not really ready for them—not ready because they have not made enough time available to study or because they are not ready academically.

In this chapter, we'll consider the essential components of a successful bar preparation plan. Such a plan takes account of two things: first, the lifestyle changes you may need to make to let you concentrate solely on the bar exam for the entire bar review period; and, second, the steps you can take to "jump start" the bar prep process by brushing up on critical skills and targeting key subject areas while still in law school.

B. LIFESTYLE CONSIDERATIONS

1. Making Time to Study

"Making the time" you need to study for the bar exam is the first step in your study plan. You must plan ahead to give yourself enough study time. To a considerable extent, success on the bar exam is a function of the actual time spent in concentrated study. And concentrated study requires a mind free from distraction and worry.

This sounds funny—free from worry—when all you're going to do is worry about the exam, but I mean free from the basic concerns of money, family obligations, living arrangements, and the countless other demands on your time and attention. These major life considerations must be addressed as early as possible so that you won't be distracted when you need to concentrate. It's hard to focus on the elements of crimes and learn the Rule Against Perpetuities when you're worrying about the rent and childcare.

The key is to make these arrangements well before the bar exam period. The optimum period would be eight weeks of uninterrupted, concentrated study time. Certainly candidates have passed the bar exam while relying on less study time, but the stakes are high and you want to do everything in your power to maximize the likelihood that you'll pass the first time around. Whatever your personal situation, you will want to "free up" as much time as possible.

How do you "make" the time you need?

The moment you began law school, you knew the bar exam was lurking—waiting for you at the end—even though you weren't really thinking about it then. But sometime before your last year of law school, the thought should have entered your head—especially if you are a working student or have family obligations or both.

- If you must work, consider taking all of your available vacation time and sick time in the weeks prior to the exam.

  It is preferable to have several weeks of uninterrupted time towards the end of bar review rather than a day here and there throughout this period. The idea is to have concentrated study time when you will most benefit from it—the bar review course will be over and you can devote all of your energies to your studies. When you have to work—even if it is only for a few hours a day—your mind is not fully focused on the law. Inevitably, it is distracted by work obligations.

- If you have friends and family, don't be shy about asking them for help.

  Now is no time to be a martyr and insist on doing everything yourself. Let others help you. They can assist in a variety of ways, making them feel useful and a part of the process. They can baby sit; prepare meals, and run errands.

2. Preparing Your Study Place

During the bar review period, your life will be rather limited and confined. You need to realize that simple fact right now. For the most part, your day will be spent in a bar review course and a study area. Your study area should be that place where you can concentrate for long periods without distraction. By this time, you should know whether that place is at home or the school library. In either case, you'll want to make sure it's fully ready to accommodate your study needs.

Consider, as well, packing away any papers, books, or magazines that might distract you from studying. Clean out your closet and take care of leaking faucets—whatever could possibly keep you from concentrating. You do not want underlying irritations to distract you from your goal.

3. Arranging Your Finances

Once again, you cannot be focused on your studies if you are worried about paying the rent and grocery bills. Whatever your financial situation, you are best prepared for the bar exam if you have made arrangements for all aspects of your financial life during this period so the most you have to think about is getting to the ATM machine when you need cash. Everything else should have been planned for and arranged. Here's how:

- If necessary, take a loan to meet all your basic needs during this time. There are bridge loans available to cover your expenses during the bar review period. Chances are you have taken loans to get you this far in your education; now is not the time to shy away from loans. If you consider the alternatives—as a true lawyer would do—you'll realize that the sooner you pass the bar, the sooner you get your license, the sooner you practice law, and the sooner you earn some money.

- Consider paying all the usual bills that come due during this six-week period before you settle down to your bar studies. Pre-pay the rent or mortgage or anything else that can be paid ahead of time for this period.

- If you can't do this—and most of us can't—then prepare all the paperwork and then just mail things out as they come due. This should obviate the need to go through all of your usual time-consuming bill-paying procedures.

- If you can delegate this task to another, then do that. The less you have on your mind, the more room you have for the law!

4.   Advising Friends and Family

You'll need the people in your life to realize how critical this time is for you. You may not be available to them in the same way you may have been in the past. If you prepare your family and friends for your unavailability during this time, they will be more understanding when you have to refuse invitations because you must study.

Most importantly, the people in your life can be understanding of your situation—if you let them know what you are doing, how long it will last, and what it requires from them. Get them on board with what you are doing and it will be easier on all of you.

Child-care arrangements

If you are a parent—of children of any age—you'll need to plan for them. Of course if your children are younger, this probably means making actual child-care arrangements. Do this as far ahead of time as possible and have a back-up plan in place as well.

However, even if your basic child-care needs are met, you must plan for time to be with your children. They need you and you need them. This time may be as little as half an hour every morning before you leave for bar review or an hour after dinner. Or it may be able to wait for the weekend if your children are older. But whatever the case, factor this time into your study schedule.

5. Caring for Your Health

If possible, get a complete physical exam before you begin your bar review course. Now is the time to see to basic medical needs. Have your vision checked. While you read a lot during law school, you'll be pushing it to the limit during bar review. You want to make sure that you're using the right prescription. Also, go to the dentist. Don't wait. Toothaches don't go away. They get worse and you can't study when you're in pain.

During bar review, plan to take vitamins, exercise, get enough sleep, and watch what you eat. While now is not the time to go on a killer diet or give up smoking, you must take care of your basic health. You can put off any promises to quit smoking and give up chocolate until after the bar exam. Now is not the time to add any more stress to your life!

C.   GETTING A "HEAD START"

Whether it is a question of time to prepare or if you have one or more of the recognized "risk factors" associated with bar passage—one of which is "time"—you might want to consider beginning your bar preparation earlier than the traditional bar review period. The good news is that you have options. For example, since the ABA's approval of bar courses for credit, law schools are beginning to make such courses available to its students. This would give you the option of beginning your bar preparation time during your last year of law school and jump start the bar review period. You have other choices as well and may want to consider getting a head start on your bar preparation as outlined below.

Still, it is important to realize that even if you had all the time in the world, there are limits to how much information you can retain and how long you can maintain the level of intensity required during the preparation period. In many respects, it might well be a good thing that the bar prep period is finite. You just couldn't keep it up much longer!

The traditional bar review course begins around the time of your law school graduation and continues for the next six or eight weeks, ending a week or so before the bar exam. It provides all the law you need to know in a structured, cohesive package. This insures that you will cover all the law necessary to succeed on the exam. This is the route followed by most bar candidates—and it is usually sufficient to do the job. However, it is not the only way to go, nor is it suited to all candidates. In a number of instances, there is much to recommend a "head start."

As you'll learn in a subsequent chapter, a bar review course is just that—a review of the law. While it covers all the basic black letter law you need to know, a bar review course assumes a great deal about you. For example, it "assumes" that:

- you have a basic knowledge of most of the substantive law and the review course is just review

- you know how to study and juggle the competing demands on your time

- you know how to combine memorization with application

- you know how to take multiple-choice exams

- you know how to write essays in the format and structure of legal analysis

If you have weaknesses in any of these areas or if you have one or more of the recognized "risk factors" associated with bar passage, then you may want to use your last year of law school to begin your bar preparation. Here a word or two about "risk factors" is in order before we proceed: such factors are based on statistics of groups of past bar takers and you are an individual. Statistics do not decide whether you'll pass the bar exam—only you will do that. Nonetheless, if you find you have one or more of the traditional risk factors (as identified in the following questions), there are steps you can take to compensate by beginning your bar preparation in the last year of law school.

1. Would You Benefit From Early Preparation?

If you answer "yes" to any of the following questions, then you should strongly consider beginning your bar preparation before graduation.

a. Do you have serious gaps in your knowledge base?

Since you cannot retain all the black letter law you need to know for the bar exam *too* many months beforehand, you must focus on only those subjects which will be the most efficient use of your time.

How do you know which subjects to target for an early intervention?

1. What are the specific topics tested on your bar exam?

    You need to know exactly what will be covered on your bar exam. The state bar examiners identify the specific subject areas tested on their bar exam. This information is often found in the Rules for the state's Board of Bar Examiners. Use the link to Bar Admission Offices from the NCBE website at www.ncbex.org to locate the website for the jurisdiction(s) in which you plan to be licensed.

2. Are you weaker in some of the tested areas than others?

Everyone has strengths and weaknesses, but now is when you must be completely honest with yourself—only you know what you know and what you don't know, which courses you did well in and those where, let's just say, your performance was less than stellar (anything with a grade in the "C" range or below).

In addition to specific courses, look for trends in performance. For example, how do you perform in:

(i) transaction-based subjects?

In Contracts, Business Organizations, and Property, problems tend to be long, factually dense, and feature numerous communications between multiple parties. Here, you might find difficulty in organizing exam answers or missing issues and facts because of long, complicated fact patterns.

(ii) statute-based subjects?

In Sales, Evidence, Civil Procedure, and Trusts and Estates, problems require skill in working with and applying statutory rules of construction. Also, these areas combine procedural with underlying substantive issues, thus requiring multiple levels of analysis. If you have had difficulty in any of these subjects, then you need to work on your reading and analytical skills as well as developing a more thorough understanding of the black letter law.

Make of list of these subjects:

_____

_____

_____

_____

_____

3. Compare the list of bar-tested subjects (which should include the six multistate subjects) with your personal subject list and highlight the subjects that appear on both lists.

4. Select four or five subjects from this list and write them here. By narrowing your focus to only a few subjects, retention of the material until the bar exam is more likely.

_____

_____

_____

_____

Although you've already identified the subjects that warrant your attention, some subjects are "worthier" than others. In choosing from this pared down list, ask:

(i) Is it an area that is heavily tested on the bar exam?

Not all topics are accorded equal treatment on the exam. Some are tested more heavily than others. For example, there are 33 or 34 multiple choice questions on each of the six MBE subjects and, in some jurisdictions, these subjects are tested on the essay questions as well. Concentrating your study time in any of these areas would be highly productive.

(ii) Is it a subject that I will be learning for the first time during bar review?

Although it is not possible to eliminate all the new material you may encounter, it is best to minimize what you need to "learn for the bar" and focus instead on "reviewing for the bar."

After using these criteria to further narrow your list, two or three subjects should remain:

_____

_____

_____

b. Do some types of exam questions pose more difficulty for you than others?

In considering this question, ask:

1. Did you score lower on objective, multiple-choice exams than essay exams in law school?

If so, then you are going to want to devote more practice time to working with MBE questions.

2. Alternatively, did your professors make the comments "conclusory," "lacking analysis," or "sketchy on the law" in your exam books? If so, then you are going to spend more time working on your essay writing skills.

c. Do you have something less than "ideal" study habits?

1. Did you have major difficulties juggling your workload of balancing four or five subjects during the course of the semester?

2. Did you find yourself struggling at the end of each semester to finish your outlines and without sufficient time to write out essay questions or practice multiple choice questions?

3. Did you have trouble setting study goals and maintaining a realistic work schedule?

d. Do you have any of the traditional "risk factors" associated with low bar passage?

Admittedly, the bar exam is a challenge and candidates do fail. This is not a secret: jurisdictions publish their pass rates so these numbers are readily available. What is not so readily available, however, are the reasons candidates fail the bar exam. While the explanations tend to be as varied as the candidates themselves, some factors are identifiable and thus useful for our purposes.

If you find yourself answering "yes" to any of the following criteria, you should strongly consider incorporating one or more of the suggested options for beginning your bar preparation period during your last year of law school.

1. Academic standing: Do you have a low law school GPA? Do you rank in the bottom 20–25% of your graduating class? Did you have a low LSAT?[1]

   Research shows that the strongest predictor of bar passage is law school GPA: the higher the law school grade point average, the greater the likelihood of passing the bar exam. Still, you are not doomed to failure if your law school grades are less than spectacular. Grades are not destiny. But they should tell you something: you need to take your preparation efforts seriously—*very* seriously. And you should begin them *before* the traditional bar review period.

2. Did you not take many of the bar-tested courses in law school, or if you did, were your grades in the "C" range?

3. Will you have to work or have primary care of your family (or both) during the bar review period?

4. Are you a non-traditional student? That is, are you an older student, a part-time student,

1. See, e.g., Denise Riebe, *A Bar Review for Law Schools: Getting Students on Board to Pass Their Bar Exams*, 45 Brandeis L.J. 269, at 284 (2007).

or have more economic and familial responsi-
bilities than the typical full-time law student?[2]

5. Are you not planning to take a bar-review
    course?

    Almost all students take a bar review course
    and I strongly recommend that you find the
    time and the money to do so. Some law schools
    offer bridge loans to get you through this
    period. After all the time and money you have
    spent on your education, this is not the time to
    economize. The longer it takes you to pass the
    bar exam and get your law license, the longer it
    will take you to start earning a salary.

6. Do you perform poorly on essay exams?
    Multiple-choice exams?

    Recognizing specific test-taking weaknesses
    early enough in the preparation process allows
    you to devote extra time to practice in areas
    you need to improve.

7. Are you or a close family member facing a
    health or personal crisis?

    It's pretty easy to see that the bar review
    period takes all of your emotional and physical
    energy. Illness or any significant life crisis—

    2. See, e.g., Linda Jellum & Emmeline Paulette Reeves, *Cool
Data on a Hot Issue: Empirical Evidence That a Law School Bar
Support Program Enhances Bar Performance*, 5 Nev.L.J. 646
(2005).

either personal or that of a loved one—can seriously detract from your ability to focus and study. If this is the case, you have several options, depending on your circumstances. You might seek professional help, emotional support, or consider whether this is the best time for you to take the bar exam.

8. Do you have excessive fear or anxiety about test taking?

As we discussed, there is a real basis for anxiety about the bar exam and it is natural to be anxious. But it cannot be the kind of anxiety that prevents you from focusing on your studies. This kind of fear can sabotage your efforts and stand in your way of succeeding. If you find the suggestions in this book insufficient to overcome your fears, then you might want to consider getting professional help.

2. How Should You Proceed if You Want to Begin Your Bar Preparation Early?

a. Does your law school offer an early bar preparation program?

If your law school provides this opportunity, take it. Look for the following possibilities at your school:

1. Is there a course identified as bar preparation, whether for-credit or not? Increasingly, law schools are providing students with bar preparation courses during the third year. Since the name of the course may not tell you what to expect, be sure to consult with the Registrar or Academic Dean at your school.

2. Is there a course in state law or state procedural law you can take? Many schools offer classes that teach state-specific law such as New York Practice, Florida Law, Texas Oil and Gas Law. Typically, such courses provide a solid foundation in the substantive and procedural law tested on the state-based portion of your bar exam.

3. Are there workshops about the bar exam? Even if formal classes are not offered, many schools provide information about the bar exam. Look for the following:

☐ Advisement sessions about the bar application process.

☐ Lectures previewing the components of the bar exam, sometimes offered by professional bar preparation experts at a small or no-fee. They may just require your attendance, but to be of any real value, count on giving it your full and active participation.

☐ Informational visits from members of your jurisdiction's bar examining committee.

b. Can you create your own "informal" bar review program by carefully selecting classes?

If your law school does not offer a formal bar preparation course, you should consider creating your own by using other resources available to you:

1. Does your school offer a course in Remedies?

If so, this course is an excellent vehicle for reviewing the substantive law in several areas—Torts, Contracts, and Civil Procedure. Typically, these were first year courses and looking at them again from the vantage point of your third year will let you see things you did not see earlier while reviewing the substantive material at a time much closer to the bar exam.

2. If you have not already done so, do you still have time to take courses in such heavily tested bar subjects as

☐ Evidence?

☐ Trusts and Estates?

☐ Business Organizations?

☐ Family Law?

☐ Sales?

☐ Negotiable Instruments?

☐ Criminal Procedure?

These are just some of the possibilities. Many schools do not require these courses for graduation, but if you can take courses in the areas tested on your state's bar exam, it makes sense to do so. You do not need to sacrifice the electives you want to take—just try to balance them with the courses that will help you prepare for the bar exam as well. Besides, these "so-called" bar prep courses are usually basic law courses and should be part of every law student's legal education.

3. Does your school have an academic support department?

If so, you can meet with the academic support professional and work together on setting up an independent study program—one that is tailored to your individual strengths and weaknesses.

c.   Can you pursue an early bar preparation program on your own?

This requires a bit more effort on your part, but it is very doable. Begin by identifying and working with the two or three subject areas most worthy of your attention based on the considerations outlined in section a. You will strengthen your substantive knowledge in these areas and transfer the skills gained from reading, analyzing, and answering questions in one subject area to others when you begin your formal bar review.

Use the study guidelines outlined in a subsequent chapter for learning the substantive law in these areas. You can work with the subject matter outlines from your bar review course—these are usually given to you as soon as you sign up to take the course and are probably sitting somewhere in your room. If you don't have access to these materials, then use commercial outlines. After reviewing the black letter law, you are ready to move on to practice the questions.

Follow the approaches in the chapters on the essays, the MBE, and the Multistate Performance Test, to do the following:

1. Work with released essay exams from your jurisdiction to develop your essay writing skills.

2. Practice answering MPTs if your jurisdiction includes this component on its bar exam.

3. Develop your multiple-choice test-taking skills by:

   ☐ Using the Subject Matter Outlines from the Bar Examiners to target study areas.

   ☐ Studying the black letter law and then practicing the questions in that area by working with released MBE questions.

d. Does your bar review course allow you to attend its lectures twice?

For example, if you are planning to graduate in May and sit for the July bar exam, then you would take the bar review course offered the previous December—which is the course typically taken by candidates sitting for the February bar exam. In this case, you would be taking a bar review course *before* graduation from law school.

Since some bar review courses offer candidates a repeater course if their first attempt at the bar exam is unsuccessful, it can't hurt to ask if you can sit through the course prior to your actual bar course period. This can be very helpful:

1. Attending the bar review classes in advance would let you devote the entire bar review period to studying your notes and practicing problems instead of sitting in lectures.

Of course you would be juggling regular classes and bar review classes at the same time, but this would only be a few weeks. Most bar review courses begin in December as soon as finals are over and end by the second week of February.

2. It would be enormously beneficial to hear the material twice if you are an auditory learner.

D. CALENDAR COUNTDOWN

Since preparing for the bar exam involves a number of tasks over a period of time, the most practical approach is to calendar the activities. This allows you to keep track of what you have done and what you may still need to do—and to do so at a glance.

The following pages provide checklists to guide you through the phases of the bar preparation process. The time frames are not definitive and tasks may overlap so use them as a general guide. If you are getting a bit of a late start, don't despair. Most of the early tasks can be made up along the way. Of course there are some you can't make up—such as the "jump start" program outlined above—but for the most part, you will be in fine shape if you follow the suggested guidelines. Extremely time-sensitive tasks are marked with a clock so can't miss them. There is really only one critical deadline you can't afford to miss: registering for your bar exam. You will want to verify and comply with this date as soon as possible.

The following Bar Planner lists take you through the entire bar preparation period, from the initial planning phases to the actual days of your bar exam. ***The "countdown" is to the start of your bar review class.*** As you work your way through each stage, you will most likely find your own points to add to the list.

Bar Planner Lists

9–12 Months Ahead

4–6 Months Ahead

3 Months Ahead

3–4 Weeks Ahead

During Your Bar Review Class

　　First 4 Weeks of Bar Review

　　Next 2 Weeks of Bar Review

　　Final 2 Weeks of Bar Review

The Days of the Bar Exam

After the Bar Exam

9–12 MONTHS AHEAD

☐ Are you familiar with the bar exam and the bar review process so you know exactly what to expect?

    ☐ Procedurally? (the application and licensing process, bar review courses, and the bar review period?)

    ☐ Substantively? (the content and subjects tested on your bar exam?)

◉ Would you benefit from a "head start" on bar prep?

☐ Now that you are close to completing your law school education, are you sure you want to practice law?

    ☐ If not, and you are considering another path, is it necessary to take the bar exam?

    ☐ Even if you are planning a career where your law license is not essential, would it be beneficial to have it nonetheless? If so, then continue.

☐ Assuming you plan to take the bar exam, is now the best time for you to do so?

    ☐ Are there family or health issues that require your full attention?

    ☐ Are there financial issues you cannot overcome at this time?

☐ Would the July or February bar exam be a better "fit" for you?

☐ Have you decided where you will be practicing law?

☐ Are you planning to take a bar examination in more than one jurisdiction? If so, it is your responsibility to determine the requirements of each jurisdiction and whether or not it is feasible for you to take a concurrent examination.

☐ Have you located the contact information for your chosen licensing jurisdiction(s)?

☐ Have you contacted your licensing entity to learn the following?

    ☐ Your state's admission information with respect to:

        ☐ Requirements for Admission?

        ⊛ Character and Fitness?

        Resolve any "character and fitness" matters well before you seek admission.

    ☐ Your state's registration requirements for the bar exam with respect to:

        ☐ Application packet and forms?

        ☐ Application fees?

        ☐ Filing deadlines?

        ☐ Dates of the bar examination?

        ☐ Test center locations?

⊘ Test accommodations?

Since each jurisdiction has its own policy and procedures with respect to test accommodations, you must verify that policy well in advance of your test date to allow sufficient time to comply with any requested documentation.

☐ Does your jurisdiction require the Multistate Professional Responsibility Exam ("MPRE")? If so,

  ☐ What is the required passing score?

  ☐ When must you pass it in relation to the bar exam?

  ☐ If you have not already taken the MPRE, when do you plan to take it?

    ☐ March   ☐ August   ☐ November

  ☐ What is the application deadline for the MPRE administration you will take?

    Date: _____

☐ Have you selected a bar review course?

☐ Have you considered your finances to ensure that you have enough to cover your living expenses during the bar review period?

  ⊘ If finances are an issue, can you borrow the money you need?

☐ If you are a working student,

  ☐ Can you take time off during the bar review period by using accumulated sick and vacation time?

☐ Can you take time off without pay?

⊙ If finances are an issue, can you borrow the money you need?

☐ Have you set up your bar calendar to record all information about your bar application, bar review, and bar licensing activities? Have you noted:

    ☐ Filing dates?

    ☐ Exam dates?

    ☐ Bar review schedule?

Notes:

_____

_____

_____

_____

_____

_____

_____

_____

_____

_____

_____

_____

_____

_____

_____

4–6 MONTHS AHEAD

☐ Have you selected and registered with a bar review course?

☐ If you are pursuing an early bar preparation program, are you:

   ☐ Working with released essay exams from your jurisdiction to develop your essay writing skills?

   ☐ Practicing MPTs if your jurisdiction includes this component on its bar exam?

   ☐ Developing your multiple-choice test-taking skills by:

      ☐ Using the Subject Matter Outlines from the Bar Examiners to target study areas?

      ☐ Studying the black letter law and practicing questions in that area by working through released MBE questions?

☐ Have you started to fill out your bar exam application?

   ☐ Have you considered whether you need to request a Change in the Test Center Location?

   ☐ Do you have the option to type your bar exam?

   ⊚ Have you completed and filed your request for test accommodations if you require them?

Notes:

3 MONTHS AHEAD

☐ Have you completed and submitted your bar application?

   ☐ If you are a re-applicant, have you verified the filing deadline since it may differ from first-time applicants?

    Have you requested test accommodations if you require them?

☐ Have you made hotel reservations near the Test Center?

☐ Have you scheduled any necessary medical exams?

   ☐ Doctor?

   ☐ Dentist?

   ☐ Vision exam?

Notes:

_____

_____

_____

_____

_____

_____

_____

_____

_____

3–4 WEEKS AHEAD

☐ Have you finalized your bar review preparations with respect to:

    ☐ Financial arrangements?

    ☐ Living arrangements?

    ☐ Childcare?

☐ If you are planning to study in your home (as opposed to the library), have you readied your study area?

☐ Have you decided whether to take the morning or evening session of your bar review course?

☐ Even if you are not working and can attend day sessions, would you benefit from evening sessions?

☐ Have you spoken with family and friends to let them know what you will be doing during the bar review period, how long it will last, and what it may require from them?

☐ Have you made travel arrangements for the days of the bar exam?

⊗ Have you made hotel reservations near the Test Center?

☐ Have you visited the drug store, supermarket, office supply store, etc. to purchase basic supplies and personal necessities?

☐ Have you planned a day (or weekend if you have the time and resources) to do something you really enjoy *before* your bar review class begins?

☐ Have you planned to do something *after* the bar
    exam so you have something to look forward to
    when the exam is over?

Notes:

_____

_____

_____

_____

_____

_____

_____

_____

_____

_____

_____

_____

_____

_____

_____

_____

_____

_____

_____

DURING THE BAR REVIEW PERIOD

First 4 Weeks of Bar Review

Goal: To define a workable routine and maintain it

☐ Have you set a realistic work schedule that allows for

    ☐ Lecture time?

    ☐ Review time?

    ☐ Practice time?

    ☐ Relaxation time?

☐ Have you defined realistic study goals based on your strengths and weaknesses?

☐ Are you varying your study activities sufficiently throughout the day to maintain your concentration level?

☐ Have you set up a daily work schedule to include time for

    ☐ Attending your bar review class?

    ☐ Reviewing the material covered in each class?

    ☐ Consolidating your notes?

    ☐ Working through practice questions?

        ☐ Approximately 15 to 20 MBE questions?

        ☐ One or two essay questions?

        ☐ One MPT per week?

    ☐ Taking mini-study breaks and exercising?

☐ Have you set up a weekly schedule that includes
    one afternoon or evening away from your stud-
    ies?

The following are suggested study schedules:

Assuming you take a morning bar prep course:

7:30–9:00 a.m.	Shower, breakfast, dress, and travel to bar review class.
9:00–12:30/1:00	Bar review course.
1:00–2:00	Lunch break. Take pup for a walk.
2:00–4:00/4:30	Thorough review of notes from morning's session; make flashcards for black letter law; consolidate notes.
4:30–5:00	Break—exercise, call a friend (if you still have any!).
5:00–6:30	Work through 15 to 20 MBE questions in the subject you have just studied.
6:30–7:30	Dinner break.
7:30–9:30	Work through another group of 15 to 20 MBE questions, one to two essays from a released bar exam, or an MPT, depending on your study needs.
9:30–11:00	Review materials for next day's bar review session; review notes from one subject covered earlier in the bar review period.
11:00/12:00	Relax. Watch *Law and Order*. Pass out.

Assuming you take an evening bar prep course:

7:30–8:30 a.m.	Shower, breakfast, and dress.

8:30–10:30/11:00	Review notes from the previous evening's class. Make flashcards for law.
11:00–11:30	Break—go for a walk or any kind of exercise.
11:30–1:00	Work through 15 to 20 MBE questions in the subject you have just studied.
1:00–1:30	Lunch break. Take pup for a walk.
1:30–3:00	More multiple choice practice, one to two essays from a released bar exam, or an MPT, depending on your study needs.
3:00–3:30	Take a break; have a snack.
3:30–5:00	Review materials for next day's bar review session; review notes from one subject covered earlier in the bar review period.
5:15	Leave for bar review class.
6:00–10:00	Bar review class.
10:30/11:00	Home at last.
11:00/12:00	Relax. Watch *Law and Order.* Pass out.

Note: Evening review classes eliminate a regular dinner hour. Have a snack before class or pack a sandwich to eat during class. Learn which works best for you and make sure you have healthy snack foods available.

DEFINE YOUR INDIVIDUAL STUDY SCHEDULE

Create a schedule that works for you:

Time	Activity

STUDY SCHEDULE

Week of: _____

Day	Study Subjects	Time/Task
Monday		
Tuesday		
Wednesday		

Day	Study Subjects	Time/Task
Thursday		
Friday		
Saturday		
Sunday		

DURING THE BAR REVIEW PERIOD

Next 2 Weeks of Bar Review

Goal: To avoid burnout and boredom and maximize retention of the black letter law

☐ Is the study schedule you set at the beginning of your bar review course still working for you by

    ☐ Keeping you engaged so you can focus?

    ☐ Allowing adequate time to review your bar review notes and practice questions?

    ☐ Ensuring sufficient time for study breaks?

    ☐ Enabling you to memorize the black letter law?

If your answer to any of the above is "no," then consider ***revising your schedule***:

    ☐ Vary the sequence of your study activities

    ☐ Change your study location

Or consider ***revising your approach***:

    ☐ Alternate your review materials to take up the topic in another form—anything that keeps you interested and adds to your understanding of the subject

        ☐ Read a different outline from your bar review materials

        ☐ Go back to your law school outline

        ☐ Consult a hornbook

☐ Shift the balance of study vs. practice time to allow more time for practicing questions

☐ Are you acclimating yourself to the "time zone" in which you'll be taking the bar exam by getting up in the morning and beginning your studies at the same time in which you'll be taking the bar exam?

☐ Are you going to sleep at a reasonable hour so you have enough rest?

☐ Are you finding your stress level starting to increase and interfere with

  ☐ your ability to concentrate?

  ☐ your ability to sleep?

If so, consider:

  ☐ Revising your study goals to make them more consistent with what you can realistically achieve each day

  ☐ Varying your routine

  ☐ Increasing your study breaks to a minimum of 10 minutes for every 90 minutes of study

  ☐ Including a regular exercise period every other day, even if it is only a 30 minute walk

  ☐ Scheduling an entire afternoon or evening away from your studies

  ☐ Making sure that you are eating properly

☐ Have you identified your strong and weak subject areas so you can target your study efforts effectively?

☐ Have you been reviewing subjects covered earlier in the bar review period, selecting a different one each day?

☐ Have you been steadily increasing the number of questions you practice each day in sufficient numbers to complete the following by the bar exam:

    ☐ All the released MBE questions and hundreds more for a total of at least 2000 questions?

    ☐ A minimum of three MPTs and more if you have a problem with timing?

    ☐ Most, if not all, of the released essay questions available in your jurisdiction?

☐ Have you received your Admission Ticket from the bar examiners?

☐ Have you received your Test Center Assignment?

☐ If possible, have you visited the Test Center location?

    ☐ Will it be a big room?

    ☐ Will it be noisy? If so, will you need earplugs?

    ☐ Will there be distractions?

    ☐ Will there be somewhere for you to go on your lunch break?

    ☐ Will you need to bring all of your own food? If so, be sure to bring something high in protein and easily digested!

☐ If you'll be traveling to the test location on the days of the exam, have you planned a trial run to know exactly where you're going and how long it will take to get there?

☐ If applicable, have you checked the Security Policy for your Test Center to verify

 ☐ The required form of personal identification?

 ☐ What personal items you may or may not take with you to the test site?

 If you are typing your exam, have you loaded it with the proper software and verified its operation?

Notes:

_____

_____

_____

_____

_____

_____

_____

_____

_____

_____

_____

_____

DURING THE BAR REVIEW PERIOD

Final 2 Weeks of Bar Review

Goal: to solidify your knowledge of the black letter law and improve your timing

☐ Have you confirmed your hotel reservations?

☐ Have you packed what you need to take with you?

   ☐ For staying at a hotel?

      ☐ Your most comfortable clothing?

      ☐ An alarm clock (or will the hotel give you a wake-up call)?

      ☐ Snack foods?

   ☐ For taking to the test site?

      ☐ Test Admission Ticket?

      ☐ Personal Identification?

      ☐ A watch?

      ☐ Adequate supply of pencils, pens, highlighters?

      ☐ "Quiet" food?

☐ Have you taken a complete, simulated exam, either with a bar review course or on your own?

   ☐ Was your timing within range for the MBE? the MPT, the essays?

   ☐ Were your scores within range?

☐ If you simulate a portion of the exam on your own, are you able to

　☐ Complete 17 MBE questions in 30 minutes; 34 MBE questions in an hour?

　☐ Complete an essay in the time allotted for your jurisdiction?

　☐ Complete an MPT in 90 minutes?

☐ If you do not take a complete, simulated exam, have you taken a complete MBE exam of 200 questions?

☐ Are you now practicing MBE questions in random order instead of one subject at a time as in earlier weeks?

☐ Have you been reviewing subjects covered earlier in the bar review period, one each day, to keep them fresh in your mind?

☐ Based on the results of simulated exams, can you identify where to focus your attention for the next two weeks:

　☐ By specific subject areas?

　　☐ MBE subjects?

　　☐ Jurisdiction-specific law?

　☐ By specific exam components?

　　☐ The essays?

　　☐ The MBE?

　　☐ The MPT?

☐ Now that your bar review course has ended, have you increased your study time and directed most of the additional time to ***practicing*** questions?

Notes:

_____

_____

_____

_____

_____

_____

_____

_____

_____

_____

_____

_____

_____

_____

_____

_____

_____

_____

_____

_____

THE DAYS OF THE BAR EXAM

☐ Have you put your books away the night before the exam and tried to relax by watching television or a movie?

☐ Have you set your alarm or left a wake-up call with the hotel?

☐ Are you dressed in layers so you will be comfortable during the exam whether it's warm or cold in the exam room?

☐ Have you packed snack foods and lunch?

☐ Are you planning to get to the test site approximately 30 minutes before the starting time, yet stay away from the crowd?

☐ If you will be with friends, have you agreed not to talk about the exam, either before or after the exam?

☐ Will you listen carefully and follow all instructions from the test proctors?

☐ When you are told to begin the exam, will you allocate your time for each question and set a timetable on scrap paper?

☐ When a session is over, will you leave the test site promptly and go home or to your hotel?

☐ Will you try and get a good night's rest between the days of the exam, knowing that you have done everything possible to prepare for this exam?

Notes:

_____

_____

_____

_____

_____

_____

_____

_____

_____

_____

_____

_____

_____

_____

_____

_____

_____

_____

_____

_____

_____

_____

_____

_____

AFTER THE BAR EXAM

☐ Have you made plans to:

    ☐ Get together with friends?

    ☐ See family?

    ☐ Have some fun?

    ☐ Do something you were not able to do during bar review?

☐ Do you find you need some time to simply de-compress? If so, this is perfectly normal and you should give yourself time—

    ☐ to be absolutely alone

    ☐ to "veg out" in front of the television

    ☐ to do absolutely nothing

☐ Do you find yourself reliving the exam or re-thinking your answers?

Invariably, you will find yourself thinking about the exam. It will be difficult, but you must stop yourself. You have no idea how you did on the exam and thinking about it won't change the results. It will only drive you crazy! Instead, as soon as you find your mind wandering in this direction, stop yourself and do something—listen to music, call a friend, watch a movie—anything to redirect your thinking.

☐ Do you find that you are physically exhausted yet have trouble sleeping?

If so, you are most likely overtired from the weeks of concentrated study and it will take time to get back to a normal routine. Consider exercising every day—even if it is only walking for half an hour.

☐ Do you find that you are have difficulty staying focused on even simple activities?

This too is a result of the hundreds of hours you have just spent in preparation for the exam. Because of the intensity of the effort, it will take time for you to feel normal again!

☐ If you have received the Application for Character and Fitness from your jurisdiction, have you begun to fill it out?

Notes:

CHAPTER 3

PROCEDURAL MATTERS

A. SELECTING THE STATE FOR YOUR BAR EXAM

Typically, the matter of where you will "sit" for the bar exam is determined by where you received a job offer or where you want to live. Often you know the answer to this question—or have a pretty good idea—before you graduate and so selecting the state in which to apply for bar admission is not a major consideration.

Sometimes you are not so sure—maybe you attended an out-of-state school and are considering a move away from your hometown or perhaps you received a clerkship and will be in a temporary location for a year or two. In any case, you need to select a licensing jurisdiction and you need to do so carefully. Since the expenses involved in taking the bar exam are high—physically, emotionally, and financially—you want to make the right choice.

B. TAKING MORE THAN ONE BAR EXAM

Some candidates choose to sit for more than one bar exam. Usually, this is based on not knowing for sure where they will finally settle or believing that it increases their employment opportunities. Sometimes this makes sense if you know (or there is a strong likelihood) that you will be relocating in the near future since it is usually best to take the bar exam while the habits of studying and the black letter law are fresh in your mind.

However, before you commit to taking more than one bar exam, consider the costs involved—and not just the additional application and licensing fees and time and energy spent in studying for and taking the exam, but the expenses associated with maintaining that license. Each jurisdiction has its own annual or biannual license fees and Continuing Legal Education ("CLE") requirements. So plan carefully—if you do not intend to practice law in another jurisdiction, think long and hard before making that commitment.

The Case of Concurrent Exams

Since the MBE is given on the same day in every jurisdiction, it is possible for applicants to take a concurrent bar examination in a state which gives their essay or local section on a different day from your primary jurisdiction. For example, in New York, the essay or local day is Tuesday whereas in New Jersey it is Thursday so you can sit for both bar exams in both jurisdictions during the same exam period.

It is your responsibility to determine the requirements of the other jurisdiction and whether or not it is feasible for you to take a concurrent examination. While it might seem like an excellent opportunity to take two bar exams simultaneously because you take the MBE only once, you should nonetheless consider the following:

- the added expense of application fees and subsequent licensing and CLE costs

- the physical burden of an additional day of exams

- the study time involved in preparing for another jurisdiction's exam

As you should realize, the most critical factor in making this decision is whether you can afford the time to prepare for two exams. While this is your call, you must consider whether your time is better spent in concentrating on learning the substantive law of one jurisdiction or splitting your efforts between two. Even if you can rely solely on multistate or common law for one of the exams, you still need to become familiar with the essay structure of the other jurisdiction. Weigh these factors carefully before you make your decision.

C.   LEARNING WHAT YOUR STATE REQUIRES FOR ADMISSION

Bar passage is only one of a number of jurisdictionally-set criteria you must meet before gaining admittance to the practice of law. While you are probably aware that each state determines the composition and scoring of its own bar exam, you might not realize that there are other requirements for admission besides exam passage. These include age, education, and moral character requirements. We'll discuss the specifications of the bar exam in the next chapter and we'll consider these other requirements here.

The Licensing and Application Process

Naturally, the primary source for this information is your individual licensing entity. Make sure you check licensing requirements early in the preparation process to ensure that you are fully compliant—or can become compliant—before you seek admission. Pay close attention to the following:

- **Application deadlines**: pay careful attention to all deadlines. In some cases additional fees are imposed if you miss a deadline; in other instances, you may be out of luck and there is no second chance. Note all applicable deadlines in your Bar Planner.

- **General education requirements**: general requirements include college work requirements and, in some cases, high school requirements.

- **Legal education requirements**: there are requirements for law school (i.e., ABA-accredited, provisionally accredited, or otherwise authorized by statute) or, in some cases, work-study alternatives such as supervised study in law offices or the courts.

- **Moral character qualifications**: these are typically satisfied by a passing score (as determined by the jurisdiction) of the Multistate Professional Responsibility Exam ("MPRE") and satisfaction of a Professional Responsibility course in law school.

- Other "moral character and fitness" requirements may include:[3]

  ☐ Compliance with court ordered child or family support obligations

  ☐ Letters of reference

  ☐ Character and fitness interviews in addition to passing scores on ethics exams

  ☐ Conditional admission where there are issues of substance abuse, mental instability, debt, or criminal history

While this list is not exhaustive and varies widely among jurisdictions, it indicates that states consider more than just a passing score on a bar exam before the privilege of a law license will be granted. I strongly recommend that if you have so much as an outstanding parking ticket, you pay it as soon as you finish reading this chapter.

D.   TEST ACCOMMODATIONS

If you had special accommodations during exams in law school, then you will want to have them for

3.   Check with your individual jurisdiction for the most recent requirements. You can also refer to Chart II: Character and Fitness Determinations in the *Comprehensive Guide to Bar Admission Requirements* on the NCBE website at www.ncbex.org/comprehensive-guide-to-bar-admissions/.

the bar exam as well. However, each jurisdiction has its own policy and procedures with respect to test accommodations. Be sure to verify that policy well in advance of your test date to allow sufficient time to provide any requested documentation.

E. TEST CENTER LOCATION

I firmly believe that there is nothing more frightening than the unknown. That's why I insist on practicing the types of questions you're going to see on the exam. It eliminates the surprise on test day. Therefore, I also insist on checking out the test site itself. You need to know what to expect. Will it be a big room? Will it be noisy? Will there be distractions? Will there be somewhere for you to go on your lunch break? Will you need to bring all of your own food? I worked with one student who was so psyched out by having to take the exam in a large conference center with over 5000 other students that she requested another location from the state's bar examiners. They were able to accommodate her request and she took the exam at a less populated site where she felt considerably more at ease.

Not every jurisdiction offers multiple test locations but you may also have this option. Also, you need to know where your exam will be held in case it is necessary to make hotel reservations.

1. Request for Changes

Some jurisdictions allow changes in assigned test locations but typically only in rare instances and require a showing of good cause. Be sure to comply fully with all requirements for such requests—be especially careful to check the date for submission of such requests.

2. Admission Tickets

Typically, you will receive your seating assignments about two to three weeks prior to the date of the examination. Depending on your jurisdiction, seat assignments may be mailed to you or made available for printing directly from the website.

Seating assignments are often used as a means of identification throughout the grading process (on MBE answer sheets and essay booklets) so it is extremely important for you to follow all directions regarding these tickets.

3. Security Policies

At some point prior to the date of the bar examination, you should consult and carefully review the security policy in effect in your jurisdiction, noting the following:

- What you will be allowed to take with you to the exam site (you will probably have to part from your cell phone)

- What you will need for personal identification

F. USING YOUR LAPTOP

Increasingly, jurisdictions are offering their candidates the opportunity to type the essay portion of their bar exam. This option is usually time-sensitive and sometimes done as a lottery among candidates so pay close attention to all directions. Also, there is special software you will need for your computer, usually at an additional cost.

CHAPTER 4

THE BAR REVIEW COURSE

No one does it alone. Do not even attempt to do so. The commercial bar review course is essential to your success because it will provide all the law you need to know in a structured, cohesive package. These courses serve another important function as well: they provide much needed emotional guidance and support as you go through the tedious preparation period. They provide a structured study environment and insure that you will cover all the law necessary to succeed on the exam.

Do you learn by listening? By writing? By a combination of both? Can you study on your own or do you need a daily regimen of classes and assignments? While most law students have made the commitment to a bar review course before the end of law school, it is probably not too late right up until the classes begin and you should strongly consider choosing one. You'll be glad you did.

A. SELECTING THE RIGHT COURSE

One would think that three years of law school (four if you were a part-time student) would be enough to prepare you for the bar exam. It is and it isn't: on the one hand, your law school education has taught you the fundamentals of the legal system and "how to think like a lawyer." On the other hand, chances are your law school professors did not focus on imparting the "black letter law"—even though you learned a lot of substantive law—but rather on developing your analytical abilities and understanding of legal process. Successful performance on the bar exam, however, requires both an expertise in the reasoning skills you developed in law school and a comprehensive knowledge of core substance.

Here's where a bar review course plays an integral role: it puts together a master template of all the law tested in your particular jurisdiction. It structures and sequences the material, providing a comprehensive and organized approach to study. But it's no substitute for what you learned in law school and you'll need both to succeed on the bar exam.

When it comes to selecting a bar review course, there's no such thing as "one size fits all." There are lots of options and you will want to select a course that best suits your learning style, time availability, and pocketbook. Do you learn by listening? By writing? Can you study on my own or do you need a daily regimen of classes and assignments? As you proceed, remember that your goal is to find a course or combination of courses that prepare you for the entirety of your exam, both its substance and its structure.

Where do you learn about bar review courses? The answer is pretty simple: you learn about bar review courses from all the usual sources. First, you can do your preliminary research on the web and then check out each program by calling and speaking with a representative. Ask to see sample study materials and a course schedule. Second, you can speak with recent law school graduates. Ask what they liked and disliked about the programs they took and whether they thought they received adequate preparation for the bar exam. Third, you can ask your school's director of academic support or dean of students. Typically, these people are familiar with the various bar review courses offered in your area and can help you make an informed decision.

1.   Selecting the Right Program for Your Learning Style

Your individual learning style is a critical factor in the choice of a bar review course. If you are an auditory learner, then you learn primarily by *hearing* the information. In this case, you'll want to choose a lecture course over one which requires you to write extensively. A course that provides tapes as well as the usual course outlines would be very helpful to you as well.

On the other hand, if you are a visual learner, then you learn primarily by *seeing* the material. Here, you will want to choose a course that requires you to write—of course there will be lecture, but it will be geared primarily to having you record what you hear. Your course materials should include lots of tables and charts, and if not, creating such materials yourself will be essential.

Another area of concern is whether you require a structured learning environment or are a self-regulated learner. If you need discipline, then the structure of a traditional bar review course that requires daily attendance with a schedule of study activities should be your primary choice. In contrast, if you are primarily a self-learner, capable of setting your own study goals and schedule, then consider a home study program. Some of the traditional courses include a home study option for those unable to attend regularly scheduled sessions. This is also a viable option if you must work during the bar review period or would have difficulty reaching one of the bar review locations. But choose this option carefully—it only works if you are highly motivated and dedicated.

2.   Supplemental Bar Courses

Depending on your own strengths and weaknesses, you might want to consider one of the add-ons to supplement your basic bar review course. Typically, these are specialty courses designed to provide additional assistance in particular areas of the bar exam, most notably in essay writing and MBE preparation. Once again, the options are numerous and you can choose from in-class or home study versions.

3.   A Matter of Timing

Not only is it important to find a course that suits your learning style, it is equally important to take that course at the right time, i.e., the right time of year and the right time of day.

a. Would a July or February bar exam be a better "fit" for you?

It is usually best to take the bar exam as close as possible to law school graduation while the habits of study and the retention of substantive knowledge are at their peak. However, if you found it difficult to concentrate for spring semester exams because you had "spring fever," then you will find it incredibly challenging to study for almost three months in the summer. For some, it's easier to study during the winter months, when the days are short and you don't mind being indoors. After the excitement of the holidays, there are few, if any, distractions. In this case, you might consider sitting for the February exam—if it is offered in your jurisdiction.

b. Would a day or evening bar review class be a better "fit"?

Typically, bar review courses offer day and evening sessions. Don't rule out taking an evening session just because you are available during the day—a day session is not always the most productive use of your study time. If you are a "morning person," you might be better off taking an evening bar review course and leaving your days free to study.

On the other hand, if you are a "night person," then your most productive hours are in the evening and the last thing you want to do is use them to sit through lectures. Also, if you took evening courses in law school and became used to an evening schedule, then it may make sense to continue this arrangement. However, you will probably need to reset your body clock toward the end of the review period so that you are wide awake for the actual bar exam!

Once you've made your choice, stick with it. Don't alternate class sections unless you need to make up a missed class. You want to get used to a regular work schedule. While it may seem strange to you now, you'll find comfort in a familiar routine. Even if you fought the predictability of a routine existence all your life, give up the battle for the next two months and let your body and mind have what it needs to function at its best. Eat regularly, sleep regularly, exercise regularly, and study regularly. And don't forget to take breaks regularly.

B. WHAT TO EXPECT FROM YOUR COURSE

If you were expecting the type of lectures you had in law school about legal policy, principle, and theory, then you are in for a bit of a surprise. A bar review course is all about imparting the black letter law. As I mentioned earlier, such courses do an excellent job of providing comprehensive coverage for the topics tested in your jurisdiction.

However, a bar review course does not teach you how to process all the law you'll cover in the course, how to write essays, or how to analyze questions. It assumes you developed these skills in law school.

And for the most part, you have. You just have to be sure not to fall into the trap of devoting all of your effort to reviewing notes and memorizing rules without spending enough time working with questions. Practicing questions is essential for developing your analytical, reading, and writing skills. An effective study schedule includes time for both.

CHAPTER 5

DE–CONSTRUCTING
THE BAR EXAM

A. KNOW YOUR BAR EXAM

Each jurisdiction sets the format for its own bar exam. It determines the type of questions and sets its own policy with regard to the relative weight given to each section of the exam in calculating a bar passage score. To this extent, each state's bar exam is unique and you'll want to know everything there is to know about the make-up of your particular bar exam. Still, bar exams tend to be more similar than different in several respects. For example:

Bar exams are licensing exams that seek to test for minimum competency.

The methods of testing typically include objective questions and essay questions.

There is a state-based component that tests the candidate's knowledge of local law.

There is a national component from the National Conference of Bar Examiners.

B. IT'S TIME TO MEET THE BAR EXAMINERS

Bar review courses pretty much lead you to believe that you must read everything, learn everything, and do everything they tell you in the way that they tell you or you'll fail. The result is that you can end up feeling overwhelmed. This is neither productive nor necessary. Instead, you should trust the bar review course to give you all the law you need to know but look to the bar examiners and your own strengths and weaknesses to tailor a study program that puts you in control and not the other way around.

But I can hear you now: "what do I know about making my own study plan? Shouldn't I just leave it to the experts?" Yes, you should, but not without considering all of the experts.

- Aren't the bar examiners "experts" on the bar exam?

- Aren't you an "expert" on how you study and how you learn?

- Aren't you the "expert" when it comes to knowing your strengths and weaknesses?

Shouldn't you at least consider the voices of these experts as well as the bar review experts? Just ask yourself the following questions:

- Who is creating the exam and who is grading it?

- Are all the topics accorded equal treatment on the exam?

- Are some topics tested more than others?

- How are the topics tested in essays?

- Am I more familiar and comfortable with some areas of the law than others?

The bar examiners give you the real scoop on the bar exam and any information they provide should figure prominently in your collection of study materials. This is true of both national and state bar examiners. Now let's see what they have to tell you. The next chapter will show you how to use what they tell you to design your own study plan.

The National Conference of Bar Examiners ("NCBE")

The NCBE develops the national bar exams and provides them to the participating jurisdictions who administer them. The NCBE creates four tests which may be included as part of a state's bar exam.

1.   The Multistate Bar Exam ("MBE")

The MBE is part of almost every jurisdiction's bar exam. It is administered by participating jurisdictions on the last Wednesday in February and the last Wednesday in July of each year. The state-specific portion of the bar exam is given either the day(s) before or the day(s) after the MBE. There are a few states that offer the MBE only once a year so it is essential to consult your individual jurisdiction for precise information. A regularly updated list of each jurisdiction's bar admission office address and phone number can be found at www.ncbex.org.

The MBE is a six-hour examination, consisting of 200 multiple choice questions. The exam is divided into two periods of three hours each: one in the morning and one in the afternoon, each containing 100 questions. Applicants are asked to choose the *best* answer from four alternatives. Since your score is based on the number of correctly answered questions, you're advised to answer every question. Even if you have no idea as to the correct answer, it's still appropriate to guess because you're not penalized for incorrect answers.

Each jurisdiction sets its own policy with respect to the relative weight given to the MBE score. If you have any questions with respect to the use made of your MBE score in calculating your overall bar passage score, you must direct such inquiries to your individual jurisdiction and not the NCBE. A regularly updated list of each jurisdiction's bar admission office address and phone number is available from the NCBE website.

The NCBE website is a comprehensive resource for current information on the MBE. It provides:

- A detailed description of the MBE

- Subject matter outlines indicating the scope of coverage for each subject with a breakdown by percentage of questions from each category

- Representative sample questions

- MBE Study Aids are available for purchase and include released questions from past administrations of the MBE.

a. The MBE Annotated Preview ("MBE–AP")

The MBE–AP is delivered online. The 100 questions represent the same content distribution as seen on a full-length MBE. According to the NCBE, "you can take the exam in either timed or untimed sittings, and you will receive feedback on your answers, including annotations and a customized score report that can help you identify strengths and weaknesses in your knowledge of the six MBE subject areas."[4]

Taking the exam one question at a time allows you to consider the annotated answers in close proximity to reading the test question. After the exam is taken once, you may choose to take the entire exam again or retake only the questions answered incorrectly. The NCBE expects that in addition to using the MBE–AP to gain experience and familiarity with the MBE multiple-choice format, many examinees will also use it as a learning tool for substantive content.

b. What subjects are tested

Multiple choice questions are used because they allow the examiners to test a wide range of topics. The MBE includes questions from six subject areas:

- Constitutional Law

- Contracts (including Article 2, Sales)

- Criminal Law (including Criminal Procedure)

---

4. *See* National Conference of Bar Examiners, NCBE Study Aids Store, www.ncbex2.org/catalog/ (last visited August 29, 2008).

- Evidence
- Real Property
- Torts

The questions are presented in a completely random manner so both the subject matter and the complexity of the question varies from one question to the next. This means that you might go from answering a Contracts question to a Property question and on to an Evidence question. You'll also have to figure out the subject for yourself since you're not told which area is being tested for any question.

As of September, 2008, there are 190 scored questions[5] consisting of 33 questions each on Contracts and Torts and 31 questions each on Constitutional Law, Criminal Law, Evidence, and Real Property. Of the 33 Contracts questions, approximately 25% of the questions are based on provisions of the Uniform Commercial Code, Articles 1 and 2. Of the 31 Criminal Law questions, approximately 40% of the questions are based on Criminal Procedure issues arising under the 4th, 5th, and 6th Amendments.[6]

5. On each administration of the exam, 10 of the 200 questions are used by the NCBE for question evaluation purposes and are not included in calculating the candidate's MBE score.

6. The NCBE provides subject matter outlines indicating the scope of coverage for each of the topics covered on the exam. There is an outline for each of the six MBE subjects. Not only is each potential test topic identified within each subject, there is also a breakdown by percentage of how many questions will be taken from a particular category. For example, of the 33 Real Property/ Future Interests questions on the MBE, only 25% (8–9 questions)

The MBE is challenging for even the best students. It's a challenge because there are so many questions and so little time. It's a challenge because it tests knowledge of the substantive law, reading comprehension and reasoning skills, the ability to work quickly and efficiently, and the capacity to remain focused and functioning over a long period of time.

Still, a candidate need not expect to walk into the bar exam knowing every single rule of law and its fine distinctions—this is not only impossible, it's not necessary. Considering that a candidate can pass the bar exam even though almost 80 out of 200 questions have been answered incorrectly depending on the weight accorded the MBE in a particular jurisdiction,[7] it is evident that a candidate is not expected

come from Real Property contracts and mortgages. The likelihood that there will be more than four or five actual mortgage questions is extremely unlikely. On the other hand, it is very important to know that of the 34 Torts questions, approximately one-half of them will be negligence questions which represents almost 8.5% of the entire MBE.

7. Only six states and the District of Columbia require candidates to achieve a "set" passing score for the MBE, i.e., Kentucky, Oklahoma, Rhode Island, South Carolina, Vermont, and Wyoming. Out of 39 states identifying scoring standards, only South Carolina sets an automatic failure based on an MBE scaled score of less than scaled 110. If a candidate achieved a scaled score of 110, then that candidate conceivably answered less than 50% of the MBE questions correctly. See National Conference of Bar Examiners, Comprehensive Guide to Bar Admission Requirements, www.ncbex.org/fileadmin/mediafiles/downloads/Comp_Guide/CompGuide.pdf (last visited August 29, 2008).

to know every rule to be found "minimally competent" to practice law.

2.   The Multistate Performance Test
("MPT")

The MPT has been adopted by thirty-two jurisdictions as part of their bar exam.[8] Participating jurisdictions select from the two ninety-minute problems
provided   by   the   NCBE   for   each   exam
administration. It is administered by participating
jurisdictions on the Tuesday before the last Wednesday in February and July of each year. Like the
MBE, each jurisdiction determines its own policy
with regard to the relative weight given to the MPT
and grades the exam.

Just as it publishes released MBE questions, the
NCBE makes previously released MPTs available on
its website. Additional MPTs and Point Sheets
(points sheets are the scoring guidelines suggested
by the NCBE in preparing the question) can be
ordered from the MPT Study Aids Order Form at the
end of the MPT Information Booklet. You will want
to practice as many MPT problems as possible to
sample the various tasks you might encounter on
the exam.

The MPT tests fundamental lawyering skills: the
ability to read and follow directions, synthesize and
apply law from cases, separate relevant from irrel-

---

8.   NCBE,   www.ncbex.org/fileadmin/mediafiles/downloads/
Comp_Guide/CompGuide.pdf (last visited August 29, 2008).

evant facts, and complete an assigned task in the allotted time. Here you are given both the legal issue and the law because the goal is to test your proficiency in the basic skills developed in the course of a legal education and not the ability to memorize.

Designed very much like a closed-universe memo assignment, the MPT consists of a client "File" and a law "Library" and you are asked to complete a typical assignment for a first year associate. Examples of such tasks include the following:

- Writing an objective memorandum

- Writing a persuasive memorandum of law or trial brief

- Writing a client letter

- Drafting a will or contract provision

- Drafting an opening or closing statement to the jury

3. The Multistate Essay Examination ("MEE")

The MEE is administered by participating jurisdictions on the state day of their bar exam. It consists of a set of thirty-minute essay questions where participating jurisdictions typically select six of the seven questions prepared by the NCBE.[9] You must check with your jurisdiction to find out whether it administers the MEE. Also, you'll want to

9. *See* NCBE, www.ncbex.org/multistate-tests/mee/ (last visited August 29, 2008).

know how many MEE questions there will be and whether you are to apply the common law or state-specific law.

Beginning July, 2007, new test specifications were introduced and jurisdictions are able to choose from nine questions instead of seven. Some questions may include issues in more than one area of law. The areas of law that may be covered include the following:

- Business Associations (Agency and Partnership; Corporations and Limited Liability Companies)

- Conflict of Laws

- Constitutional Law

- Contracts

- Criminal Law and Procedure

- Evidence

- Family Law

- Federal Civil Procedure

- Real Property

- Torts

- Trusts and Estates (Decedents' Estates; Trusts and Future Interests)

- Uniform Commercial Code (Negotiable Instruments; Secured Transactions)

Here, too, the NCBE provides candidates with the opportunity to work from previously released questions. Several examples are included in the MEE Information Booklet and five years of MEE Study Guides are available online. Additional questions are available for purchase at the NCBE Online Store.

The MEE Study Guides contain questions and model analyses that are "illustrative of the discussions that might appear in excellent answers to the questions. They are provided to the user jurisdictions for the sole purpose of assisting graders in grading the examination."[10] This information may be given to graders to guide them in grading essays, but it is given to you to prepare for writing them.

4.   The Multistate Professional Responsibility Exam ("MPRE")

The MPRE is a multiple-choice examination consisting of sixty questions and is required for bar admission in all but three jurisdictions. Passing scores are established by each jurisdiction and currently vary between 75 and 86.[11] For the most current information regarding passing scores and exam policies, you must check with the jurisdiction to which you intend to apply for admission.

The exam is given three times a year in August, November, and March. It tests the law governing the

---

10.   *See* NCBE, THE MULTISTATE ESSAY EXAMINATION 2008 INFORMATION BOOKLET, *available at* www.ncbex.org/uploads/user_docrepos/MEE_IB2008_01.pdf.

11.   *See* NCBE, www.ncbex.org/multistate-tests/mpre/ (last visited August 29, 2008).

conduct of lawyers, including the disciplinary rules of professional conduct as stated in the ABA Model Rules of Professional Conduct, the ABA Model Code of Judicial Conduct, and other controlling rules and judicial decisions. For this reason, many students like to take the MPRE when they have completed the course on Professional Responsibility or Legal Ethics given in their law school.

However, it is not necessary to take a course before taking the MPRE. In fact, even if you have taken a course, it might not cover the same material as is tested on the MPRE and not necessarily in the same detail. So in either case, you'll want to do the following:

• Check with your bar review company. Most bar review courses include an MPRE component and offer a review session to coincide with the administration of the MPRE.

• Use the materials available to you from the NCBE.[12] Use its subject-matter outline identifying the scope of the exam and the MPRE Study Aids which include actual and simulated MPRE questions.

It makes sense to take the MPRE sometime during your third year of law school to complete this

12. *See* NCBE, www.ncbex.org/uploads/user_docrepos/ MPRE_IB2008.pdf (last visited August 29, 2008). A wealth of information is at your fingertips: application procedures, sample questions, and guidelines for taking the exam are available in the MPRE Information Booklet.

hurdle before sitting for the bar exam. Just be sure when checking the MPRE requirements for your jurisdiction, that you take the exam within the time frame specified. Not only does each jurisdiction set its own passing score as previously noted, but it establishes its own policy for when the exam must be taken with respect to the bar examination.

C. STATE–BASED COMPONENTS

Like the NCBE, the individual state bar examiners make vital information available to its bar candidates. It is your primary source for such basic information as application materials, test locations and accommodations, test dates, admissions issues, and more.

Unfortunately, it's easy to overlook this primary source of inside information when you have so many bar review guides competing for your attention. But if you fail to consult this incredibly valuable resource, here's what you would be missing:

- a comprehensive and detailed list of the topics tested on your particular bar exam

- the exam schedule

- specific exam-taking instructions

- grading and scoring information

- guidelines for answering an essay question

- past examination questions and sample answers

1. The Subjects to be Tested

The state bar examiners identify the specific subject areas tested on their bar exam. This information is often found in the Rules for the state's Board of Bar Examiners. By knowing the scope of the exam, you can narrow the universe of what you need to know. Even if you can eliminate only one or two topics, it makes a difference.

a. *Florida*

Like most other jurisdictions, Florida provides information regarding the precise subject matter of its bar exam.[13] It advises its candidates that Part A of the exam consists of six one-hour segments where:

> "One segment will include the subject of Florida Rules of Civil and Criminal Procedure and the Florida Rules of Judicial Administration Rules 2.051, 2.060, and 2.160. The remaining five segments, each of which will include no more than 2 subjects, will be selected from the following subjects including their equitable aspects:
>
> Florida Constitutional Law
>
> Federal Constitutional Law
>
> Business Entities, including Corporations and Partnerships
>
> Wills and Administration of Estates

13. *See* Florida Board of Bar Examiners, Rules of the Supreme Court Relating to Admissions to the Bar, Rule 4–20, www.floridabarexam.org/ (last visited August 29, 2008).

Trusts

Real Property

Evidence

Torts

Criminal Law

Contracts

Family Law

Chapter 4, Rules of Professional Conduct,

Chapter 5, Rules Regulating Trust Accounts, of the Rules Regulating The Florida Bar"

b. New Jersey

New Jersey provides candidates with the following information in its Admission to the Bar Booklet, section C, the Bar Examination, subsection 4, New Jersey Essay Questions:

"The second day of the examination consists, in part, of seven 45–minute essay questions drafted by the New Jersey Board of Bar Examiners that are designed to examine candidates' abilities to reason, analyze, and express themselves in a lawyer-like manner. The questions are based upon the subjects of contracts, criminal law, real property, torts, constitutional law, evidence, and civil procedure.

An essay question may cut across two or more of the basic subject areas. In addition, these questions may be framed in the context of fact situa-

tions involving, and interrelated with, the following subjects: agency; conflicts of law; corporations;
equity; family law; partnership; Uniform Commercial Code Articles 2 (Sales), 3 (Commercial
Paper), and 9 (Secured Transactions); wills,
trusts, and estates; zoning and planning; and
disciplinary rules. Accordingly, familiarity with
the basic principles and concepts of those subjects
may help the candidate in answering the
questions."[14]

c. *New York*

New York follows the same approach in identifying tested subject areas. However, in addition to
identifying the general subject areas covered on the
exam, it has recently released a content outline to
indicate the examination's potential scope of
coverage. The outline is comprehensive and follows
a similar structure to the NCBE's subject matter
outlines for coverage of the MBE.[15]

Candidates are informed that:

"The New York portion is based on both procedural
and substantive law. It may deal with the six
subject matters covered on the Multistate Bar
Examination (MBE)—Contracts, Constitutional
Law, Criminal Law, Evidence, Real Property, and

14. *See* New Jersey Board of Bar Examiners, www.
njbarexams.org/barbook/aic4.htm (last visited August 29, 2008).

15. See New York Board of Law Examiners, www.nybarexam.
org/CONTENTOUTLINE08–08–08.pdf (last visited August 29,
2008).

Torts (including statutory no-fault insurance provisions). In addition, the questions may deal with

Business Relationships

Conflict of Laws

New York Constitutional Law

Criminal Procedure

Family Law

Remedies

New York and Federal Civil Jurisdiction and Procedure

Professional Responsibility

Trusts, Wills and Estates, and

UCC Articles 2, 3, and 9

More than one subject is tested in a single essay question. Except for questions involving federal law, the New York essay and multiple choice questions are based on the law of New York."[16]

d. *California*

The California bar exam has a reputation for being one of the most difficult bar exams to pass. I am not interested in discussing whether that reputation is deserved, or even if it's true—my only concern, as should be yours—is how to pass it. And

---

16. *See* New York Board of Law Examiners, www.nybarexam. org/barexam.htm (last visited August 29, 2008).

California does a lot to help you in this effort, if only you choose to follow its advice.

The State Bar of California's website is easy to navigate and provides lots of useful information. A good starting point is the "Scope of the California Bar Exam." Here you will find a list of the 13 subjects from which you may be expected to answer questions. You will also find a subject matter outline detailing the scope of coverage for each of the individual subjects. In addition, there are instructions from the bar examiners regarding some of the subject areas, including how and where to target your studies. For example, you are told to direct your study to specific provisions of the UCC and the California Probate Code.

Further, and even more important for your studies, you are told that when answering questions that have issues concerning the Federal Rules of Evidence and the California Evidence Code, you should "be prepared to compare and contrast the differences between the Federal Rules and the California Evidence Code, especially where the California rules of evidence have no specific counterparts in the Federal Rules."[17] You are given similar instructions with respect to issues concerning the Federal Rules of Civil Procedure and the California Code of Civil Procedure.

17.   *See* the State Bar of California, Scope of the California Bar Exam, at www.calbar.ca.gov/calbar/pdfs/admissions/ex1000900. pdf (last visited August 29, 2008).

This information is invaluable because it tells you exactly what the California bar examiners want you to discuss when answering these questions. Your job is to follow such instructions to the letter.

2. The Exam Schedule

An essential part of the preparation process is being familiar with the format and length of the exam. In addition to helping you structure your practice sessions, knowing what to expect goes a long way toward lessening your anxiety on bar day.

While commercial bar review courses provide some of this information, your state bar examiners provide precise details. If you want to know exactly what to expect on bar day—down to the last detail— check with your bar examiners.

For example, Connecticut advises its candidates as follows:

"The Connecticut Essay Examination is a 12– question, essay-style examination. Each question should be answered in 30 minutes. Questions 1—6 are distributed in the morning and questions 7—12 in the afternoon. *Applicants must answer the questions in order. Questions are collected every hour: Questions ##1 & 2 in the first hour; Questions ##3 and 4 in the second hour, etc.* If you finish a pair of questions early, you may go on to the next question. Detailed instructions will be provided the morning of the examination. Bring plenty of black pens."[18] *[italics added]*

Here, even though all the questions are distributed at the beginning of the test session, you are required to answer the questions in order and you are not free to use your time any way you choose. If you were not familiar with these instructions, you could easily go astray since it is not the usual or ordinary test practice to collect questions every hour.

New York is equally explicit in its information to candidates but does not set the order in which you must answer the questions; this part is up to you:

"In the morning session, which begins at 9:00 A.M. and ends at 12:15 P.M., applicants must complete three essays and the 50 multiple choice questions in three hours and 15 minutes. Although applicants are free to use their time as they choose, the Board estimates an allocation of 40 minutes per essay and 1.5 minutes per multiple choice question."

"In the afternoon session, which begins at 1:30 P.M. and ends at 4:30 P.M., applicants must complete the remaining two essay questions and the MPT in three hours. Again, although applicants are free to use their time as they choose, the

18.   *See* State of Connecticut Judicial Branch, Connecticut Bar Examining Committee, Taking the Connecticut Bar Examination at www.jud.state.ct.us/CBEC/examinfo.htm#How (last visited August 29, 2008).

National Conference of Bar Examiners developed the MPT with the intention that it be used as a 90–minute test. Therefore, the Board recommends that applicants allocate 90 minutes to the MPT and 45 minutes to each essay."[19]

3.   Grading and Scoring

Each jurisdiction has its own formula for calculating a passing score and makes this information available to candidates. The NCBE also includes information on each jurisdiction's grading and scoring policy in its *Comprehensive Guide to Bar Admission Requirements*.[20]

While you need not concern yourself with understanding the fine points of the procedures bar examiners use to scale and equate scores, you should know the relative weights accorded each section of your bar exam. This allows you to apportion your study time with respect to where it will yield the most return: for example, if the written portion of your bar exam is weighted twice that of the MBE, you want to be sure to spend considerable time developing your essay writing skills.

It is also important to know whether your jurisdiction sets a minimum passing score for individual

19.   *See* New York Board of Law Examiners at www. nybarexam.org/ (last visited August 29, 2008).

20.   *See* NCBE, Comprehensive Guide to Bar Admissions, Chart VII: Grading and Scoring at www.ncbex.org/fileadmin/ mediafiles/downloads/Comp_Guide/CompGuide.pdf (last visited August 30, 2008).

components of the exam. For example, an applicant with a scaled MBE score of 110 or less automatically fails the bar exam in South Carolina.[21] However, the number of jurisdictions with individual passing scores are very few, seven to be precise,[22] and the overwhelming majority consider a combined score in calculating bar passage. In New York, for example, there is no passing or failing on any one portion of the exam and its bar examiners write that "a poor performance on one section of the examination may be offset by a superior performance on another section. Passing or failing is determined only on the basis of the applicant's total weighted scaled score."[23]

4.   Guidelines for Answering an Essay Question

Not only do bar examiners provide a list of subjects to be tested so you'll know exactly what to study, many provide guidelines so you'll know exactly how to answer their questions. They give you the details you need to know to write point-earning essays. Let's consider two jurisdictions.

---

21.   *Id.*

22.   *Id.* In addition to South Carolina, the jurisdictions which require individual passing scores include: the District of Columbia, Kentucky, Oklahoma, Rhode Island, Vermont, and Wyoming.

23.   *See* New York Board of Law Examiners, www.nybarexam.org/barexam.htm (last visited August 29, 2008).

a. New Jersey

In its Complete Bar Book, the New Jersey Board of Bar Examiners directs its candidates to write "lawyer-like" responses that "approximate the work product of a practicing lawyer." To help in this effort, they offer the following advice:[24]

1. Read and re-read the problem carefully to familiarize yourself with the facts and circumstances. Do not assume additional facts unless directed to do so.

2. Make sure you understand the directions that appear in boldface type at the conclusion of the problem. Adhere to those instructions and plan your response accordingly. Before you begin to write your answer, outline and organize your response.

3. Do not use a "scattershot" approach; rather, structure your answer before you begin to write so that your essay will demonstrate your ability to analyze legal problems and to provide an organized, logical and coherent written response.

4. When appropriate to the format of the question, discuss all sides of issues and do not let your disposition of an issue preclude discussion of other issues presented. When appro-

24. *See* The New Jersey Board of Bar Examiners, the Complete Bar Book, Suggestions on Answering Essay Questions, at www.njbarexams.org/barbook/barbook.pdf (last visited August 30, 2008).

priate, discuss procedures and remedies, as well as legal rights and liabilities.

5. Allocate enough time to compose a clear and concise response. The writing ability exhibited by your response will affect your grade.

b. Oregon

Similarly, Oregon's State Board of Bar Examiners provides its candidates with an information booklet containing answers to questions about the entire bar admission process, including several questions relating specifically to the essay examination. Consider the following three questions:

What types of questions should I expect?

What is expected in an answer?

Must my answer be voluminous?[25]

As you can see, Oregon's bar examiners have anticipated the questions every candidate has about the bar exam. They are the same questions you had in law school. Here they are answered for you in scrupulous detail. For example, with respect to what the examiners are looking for in exam answer, they write:

"A frequently voiced complaint is that the essay questions present too many issues to permit full discussion within the time allotted. While the examiners do not seek superficial answers, they

25. *See* Oregon State Board of Bar Examiners at www.osbar. org/_docs/admissions/Q & A.pdf (last visited October 20, 2008).

likewise do not expect law review articles. ***The purpose of the bar examination is to test the minimum legal competence, not to identify and rank the best legal scholars.*** In this respect, the bar examination differs from law school examinations."[26]

c.   Texas

The Texas Board of Law Examiners provide an incredibly comprehensive set of guidelines tailored to each of the tested subject areas. For example, in its "Comments on Civil and Criminal Procedure Evidence/Questions," the Examiners write not only what not to do, but exactly what you should do:

READ THE QUESTION, UNDERSTAND THE "CALL" OF THE QUESTION *BEFORE* YOU ATTEMPT TO ANSWER IT.

For example, a question typically may ask the student, "Explain whether there is any proper basis for your objection *and* the proper method through which any error is preserved."

The response that "I would object with a *Batson* motion stating that the opponent … struck a particular race [from the panel]" without more, answers only *part* of the question. The student did not explain the proper *method* through which error is preserved, i.e., explain that before the jury is empanelled, one must offer the objection and demonstrate to the court the suspect pattern of

26. *Id*.

strikes. The burden then shifts to opponent to show a race neutral reason for strikes.

E.g., "Explain whether there is any prohibition regarding the discussion of liability insurance *and* whether the trial court's ruling is reversible error (emphasis added). The answer should include the proposition that while (1) there is a general prohibition against mentioning liability insurance before the jury (2) the mere mention of insurance is not reversible unless it caused the rendition of an improper verdict (i.e. "harm")."[27]

While the Texas law examiners refer to these as "comments," you can see that they are much, much more: they speak directly to content and provide direction for both the scope and substance of your answers. If you plan to take the Texas Bar Exam, you should go to the Law Examiners' website, select the Examiners' Comments menu from the Main Menu, and print the Comments for each and every subject. As you study each topic, you will work with this information to guide your every step.

d. Connecticut

Connecticut's Bar Examining Committee is straightforward in its advice to candidates. Its website offers concrete advice on "Taking the Connecticut Bar Exam," including how to answer a Connecticut bar examination essay question. It also offers

27. *See* Texas Board of Law Examiners, at http://www.ble. state.tx.us/Comments/comments_main.htm (last visited August 30, 2008).

some practical advice on "what not to do": consider the following two suggestions:

"Do not anticipate trick questions or attempt to read into the question hidden meanings or facts not clearly expressed."

and

"Unless specifically called for in the question, it is not necessary to engage in an academic discussion of the applicable law or its historical basis and ramifications."[28]

Naturally, jurisdictions vary widely in approach and the level of detail they provide to candidates. Still, there is a wealth of information available to assist you in your preparation and this resource should figure prominently in your study plan.

5.   Past Examination Questions and Sample Answers

Released exams should be your primary source for practice essays. While your bar review course includes a good number of simulated practice tests and essay writing exercises, there is no substitute for the real thing—nor is there any need.

Most jurisdictions make their past exam questions available to you from their website—some even provide sample answers, either student essays or suggested analyses. In a few cases, you are told where you can access these materials. For example,

28. *See* Connecticut Bar Examining Committee, www.jud. state.ct.us/CBEC/examinfo.htm (last visited August 30, 2008).

the Arkansas State Board of Law Examiners advises candidates that "previous exam questions and answers are available from the Arkansas Supreme Court Library, the Law School Library at Fayetteville, and the Law School Library at Little Rock."[29] However, Arkansas now makes the top examination paper in each subject available from its website (dating back to February 1996) so a visit to the Supreme Court or a law school library is no longer necessary. If information about past exams is not available online from your jurisdiction, then contact the licensing entity directly. This is no time to be lazy!

It is impossible to overemphasize the value of working from released bar exam essays. There is no greater authority on the bar exam than the writers and graders of the exam themselves and when they provide their questions and answers, they are doing what they can to make the test process as transparent as possible.

Consider what the following jurisdictions provide in addition to past exam questions and answers:

a. Alaska

The Alaska Bar Association provides past exam questions with grader's guides. Grader's guides are answers written by the examiners for the purpose of

---

29. See Arkansas State Board of Law Examiners, Arkansas Bar Examination Requirements and Information at http://courts. arkansas.gov/opp/ble_exam_essay.html (last visited August 30, 2008).

guiding grading of the exam—as the word itself indicates. While not available for every administration of the bar exam, Alaska provides "benchmarks" answers for a great many of them. "Benchmarks" are actual applicant answers which are selected by the graders as being representative of points on the grading scale, with 5 being the highest, and 1 being the lowest.[30] These answers offer a window into the grading process and let you see the basis on which graders distinguish between answers.

b. *Florida*

Florida provides its candidates with a Study Guide. It contains general essay examination instructions, essay questions with selected answers, and sample multiple choice questions with an answer key. The essay answers were written by candidates who passed the exam and received high scores.

The Study Guide is updated with the essay questions from the last administration of the bar exam twice annually. When last viewed, there were eight Guides online for a total of nine complete exams.[31]

30. *See* Alaska Bar Association, Resources: Past Exam Questions and Grader's Guides, February 2006 Alaska Bar Exam: Questions, Grader's Guides and Benchmarks http://www.alaskabar.org/INDEX.CFM?ID=6280 (last visited August 30, 2008).

31. *See* Florida Board of Bar Examiners, Frequently Asked Questions, "Does the Board offer any Study Materials?" Study Guide, at www.floridabarexam.org (last visited August 30, 2008).

c. California

The State Bar of California provides an extensive array of past examination questions and selected answers for both the essays and the performance tests.[32] There are two candidate answers for each question, thus showing a range of possibility in answering the question.

d. Texas

Texas provides its candidates with an abundance of study materials. In addition to general comments by subject, Texas bar examiners provide specific, detailed comments on past exams, indicating the common problems they encountered in grading the essays.[33] These critiques are very specific as to substance, identifying what was answered correctly and, where incorrect, exactly how the answers were deficient.

For example, the following paragraph is a short excerpt from the comments to Question 1 Wills and Administration from the February 2008 Bar Examination:

"Among the less successful answers to this question many examinees seemed to focus on paternity as the major issue. Some incorrectly concluded that Tim was a pretermitted child and did not

32. *See* The State Bar of California at www.calbar.ca.gov/state/calbar/calbar_home.jsp (last visited August 30, 2008).

33. *See* Texas Board of Law Examiners at www.ble.state.tx.us/Comments/comments_main.htm (last visited August 30, 2008).

seem to understand the significance of an insurance policy that otherwise provided for Tim. This made it difficult to reach a correct conclusion as to how the estate should be distributed. Others incorrectly assumed that Bill's role as Executor of the will was a conflict of interest with respect to his taking the estate as the sole beneficiary of the will. This also led to difficulty in reaching a correct conclusion as to how the estate should be distributed."[34]

34.   *See* Texas Board of Law Examiners, www.ble.state.tx.us/ Comments/comments_0208.htm#crim (last visited August 30, 2008).

CHAPTER 6

LEARNING THE BLACK LETTER LAW

A. UNDERSTANDING THE PROCESS

I'm going to assume that you've followed my advice and selected a bar review course. I'm also going to assume that you're like the rest of us and after you've completed your first week of the course, you're in a panic because:

(A) you're feeling overwhelmed

(B) you're afraid that you're never going to be able to learn it all

(C) you're scared that you're going to fail

(D) all of the above

These feelings are absolutely normal. There would be something wrong with you if you didn't have them. There is a real basis to your anxiety. You have a lot of black letter law to learn and your future is riding on the outcome. Allow yourself to feel anxious but don't let yourself panic. Some anxiety is good and serves a purpose because it motivates you to work. Panic, on the other hand, only eats up valuable time by taking you away from your studies. Instead, you're going to accept the fact that the next two months will be a something of an emotional roller coaster and then you're going to get on with the business of studying.

111

B. STUDYING THE LAW

The key to managing your anxiety is to have a study plan that puts you in control of your time and the material. However, before you can define your study schedule, it's important to know "what" and "how" to study for the bar exam.

First, you need to internalize the law. A solid knowledge of the black letter law is required to answer bar exam essays and objective short answer questions. Preparing for the bar exam simply by attending lectures and reading through bar review outlines, even if read several times, does not allow for the type of internalization of the material necessary to respond to these questions. "Knowing the law" means that you internalize the material in such a way that you truly "own" it. This is not the same as thinking you know something because a term or concept seems familiar. There's a big difference between recognizing something because you've seen it before and really knowing it. The bar exam requires you to know the rules with precision and specificity: it also requires a solid understanding of those rules.

Second, you must sharpen your basic analytical, reading, and writing skills. You can easily fall into the trap of devoting all your time and energy to memorizing rules without ever developing your practical sense of how the law works. You'll be amazed at how many answers to questions depend as much on your understanding of general legal principles as on your knowledge of specific rules.

This requires that you "actively" engage in the process by working through thousands of multiple choice questions and hundreds of essay questions. Yes, I wrote "thousands" and "hundreds"—this was not a typographical error. You need to do as many questions as possible to really learn the rules by working with them in a factual context. There is no substitute for this part of your preparation.

1.   Memorizing the Law

Memorization is essential to success on the bar exam. As you proceed through your bar review course, make it a priority to memorize basic definitions and the elements of rules. Here are some suggestions:

- Focus on basic vocabulary for each subject area.

- Create your own condensed study outline of key concepts in each subject area.

- Make your own flash cards.

  Remember when you were in grade school and had to learn the multiplication tables? You used flash cards and repeated the tables over and over again until you knew them cold. The same principle applies here.

- Create a short hypothetical for each rule.

  Play around with the facts of the hypothetical. Ask yourself whether the change affects the outcome. Apply different rules to the same scenario. What if you apply the common law to this set of facts? What if you apply the rule in your jurisdiction? Same result or different result? This type of practice provides the context you need for understanding as well as memorizing the rules of law.

• Wherever possible, "de-construct" a rule statement and reword it according to an "if, then, unless" construction.

Examples:

☐ *If* a minor enters into a contract, *then* it is voidable at the minor's option, *unless* it is a contract for necessities.

☐ *If* a material mistake is made by both parties at the time the contract is made as to a basic assumption, *then* the contract is voidable by the adversely affected party, *unless* he bears the risk of the mistake.

☐ *If* a partner acts on behalf of the partnership, *then* the partnership is bound *unless* that act is beyond the usual or ordinary business of the partnership.

2. The Who, What, and When of Practicing Questions

Studying to learn the material is one activity; practicing with it is quite another. Memorizing rules from flash cards and outlines won't guarantee that you'll recognize them when they're tested in a fact pattern. Instead, you must learn the rules in the context in which they're likely to appear.

There is a method to learning from practice exams and you may be surprised to discover that it's not just about sitting down and answering the questions. That's what you'll do on bar exam day but not when you're studying. The difference is between answering the questions and using the questions to learn.

One of the most important things you can keep in mind as you study is that the only test that counts is the one you take on exam day. All the rest is preparation.

3. Whose Questions to Practice

Just as you studied from your professor's old exams to prepare for law school finals, you'll review released exams from the National and your state's bar examiners when you study for the bar exam. While your bar review course includes a good number of simulated practice tests and essay writing exercises, there is no substitute for the real thing. It is essential that you become familiar with the structure, style, and content of the test questions you can expect to see on bar day. Since the ultimate authority on the bar exam are the bar examiners, their questions should be the primary source for your practice questions.

4. What Questions to Practice

While you must practice questions in all subject areas tested on the bar exam, you can focus your energies in two ways: where you need the most work and where it will do you the most good. How do you know which subjects require the most work? All subjects are not created equal—not with the bar exam and not with you. This means that you can target your energies where you need them the most.

If you answered the questions in Chapter 2 to determine whether you would benefit from an early bar preparation program, then you have already identified your subject strengths and weaknesses. If you have not answered these questions, then do so now. Be sure to identify the subjects you like better than others as well as those which come easier to you. If you excelled in certain subjects in law school, it's likely to be the same on the bar exam. Here's where you can "save" some study time and "spend" it on the more difficult subjects.

While I would not ordinarily suggest "writing off" any subject, I strongly recommend that you consider doing so with the one or two sub-topics that you just can't seem to master. After making a good faith effort to learn the topic, if even the most diligent efforts yield minimal efforts, then it's time to give yourself a "pass" and move on. Just make sure that the topic is a very small part of your bar exam—at most two or three objective questions or a sub-issue on an essay. The time you save on this subject can be redirected to where it will do more good.

Can you identify which type of question poses more of a difficulty for you? Once again, if you answered the questions in Chapter 2, then you know the answer to this question. If you did not answer those questions, then answer these now: did you score lower on objective, multiple-choice exams than essay exams in law school? If so, then you are going to want to allocate more practice time to working with MBE questions. Alternatively, did your professors write the comments "conclusory," "lacking analysis," or "sketchy on the law" in your exam books? If so, then you will want to budget more time for working on your essay writing skills.

5.   When to Practice Questions

You should begin practicing exam questions as soon as you begin your bar review class. Don't make the mistake of waiting until you think you know enough law: first, you'll never think you know enough law; second, once you've attended a class and reviewed your notes on a topic, you're ready to go to work. Working with rules as you learn them by applying them in the context of new factual situations is the most effective way to learn whether you truly understand them while you still have time to find answers to questions that naturally arise as you practice the material.

6.   Why to Practice Questions

The reason to practice questions is to learn from them. While you may find this difficult to believe, *you've learned as much as you are going to learn from your notes after you've read them once or twice*. You've got to put them aside and move on to the questions to apply what you've learned to actual problems. This is the only way to find out what you know and what you don't know.

When your studying is "question-driven," it will lead you back to any gaps in your knowledge of the rules.

The more I work with students, the more I realize that they don't know what it means to study from questions. Instead of learning from them, students are constantly testing and grading themselves. Certainly the instinct to "answer" the question and see if you've gotten it "right" is instilled in the educational process early on, but here it's more of a hindrance than a help.

This approach doesn't work because while you may have "answered" questions, you've not learned to "analyze" questions. And you must know how to reason through a question to arrive at the correct answer choice. Not only is this process essential to arriving at the correct answer, but you must be aware of how you've reasoned through a problem so you can go back and examine that thought process should you make an incorrect choice.

What you need to do is *learn how to learn* from the questions.

How do you learn from "doing questions"?

- By looking up the rule to help you work through analysis of an MBE question: this is learning through repetition and reinforcement.

- By going back to your outline and reviewing your notes to help you write an essay answer if you are not certain of the complete rule: this is learning in context.

C. LEARNING LAW FOR THE MBE

Learning the law for the MBE, a short-answer, objective exam, is not the same as learning the law for the essays. It requires not only that you memorize the rules of law but that you fully understand them. If you don't know the rules with precision and specificity and truly comprehend how they fit together, you won't be able to find the issue in the facts, apply the rule, and select the best answer from among the four answer choices in the span of the 1.8 minutes you have for each question.

Such an understanding of the law usually comes only with real experience—but in the fictionalized world of the MBE, even real life wouldn't prepare you adequately for the way that the bar examiners like to test the rules, the elements of rules, and the exceptions to the rules. In this case, the only meaningful way to prepare for the MBE is to practice from actual, released MBE questions. Anything else is, as they say, "close, but no cigar."

1. Individual Propensities

While the Bar Examiners accord every subject on the MBE substantially equal weight in terms of the number of questions per subject, you'll quickly find that not every subject is equal with you! I've yet to find a candidate, myself included, who was equally competent in every MBE topic. For one thing, there are some subjects that you just like better than others. You probably did well in these classes in law school and the same is likely to be the case on the bar exam. But then there are the other topics, that for whatever reason, you didn't like, couldn't understand, and simply never figured out. Maybe it was future interests, the Rule Against Perpetuities, third-party beneficiaries, intergovernmental immunities, or consequential damages. It doesn't really matter which topics they were–only that there were some that were more difficult for you. Now here they come again on the bar exam, dressed up and configured in ways that even your law professor might not recognize.

a. When you know too much

When I started practicing questions, I was astonished to find that I was having difficulty with Contracts questions. It had been my favorite subject in law school and I even considered myself something of an "expert" in the area. I had been a Contracts Teaching Assistant and a Research Assistant for a Contracts professor. I was certainly humbled when I answered question after question incorrectly during my practice sessions. I started to panic. If this was the result in my supposedly "strong" subject, what chance did I have with respect to the others?

For me, it turned out that I knew the subject *too* well–I knew the exception to the exception and remembered the very language in cases. I was eliminating answer choices because they were not as precise as the holdings in cases. Here was my undoing. I knew too much! The bar examiners were not testing the material to this degree of exactitude.

Or to put it another way, while it might have been appropriate and even critical to know the material with this degree of specificity for my professor's exam and for practice in the field, it was by no means what the bar examiners were seeking. They wanted me to know the general rules and the basic exceptions. I was making the problem more complex than it actually was because of my own sophisticated knowledge of the subject. Fortunately, I figured this out through practice and increased my percentage of correct answer choices when I stopped making the questions more complex than they were and relied instead on a general but thorough understanding of the rules. It was actually a comfort to realize that the bar examiners did not expect me to be an "expert" on the law but simply competent.

b.   When you'll never know enough

On the other hand, there were some topics that eluded me in law school and eluded me still when I prepared for the bar exam. My first option, one which I heartily embraced until I saw that it wasn't at all practical, was simply to write off the offending subject. So what if I couldn't quite fathom the Rule Against Perpetuities? There weren't going to be many questions on this one topic. Then I started to conclude similarly with respect to questions in other areas that caused me difficulty: Future Interests and Character Evidence, to name but two. Suddenly I realized that while I could afford to give up a sub-topic here and there, I couldn't eliminate whole areas or I'd never pass the bar exam. I desperately needed a new strategy.

First, I decided that I would try to be as prepared as possible by making a good faith effort to review every topic. However, I also decided that this did not require that I make myself crazy when I found that even my most diligent efforts yielded minimal results. It just didn't make sense to devote hours of precious study time to a single topic which I none-theless continued to answer incorrectly.

Realizing that I didn't need a "perfect" score to pass the Multistate, I allowed myself a "pass" on my most troublesome topic. For me, it was the Rule Against Perpetuities. It simply had to go. While even the mystery of recording statutes had yielded to my efforts, I had no such luck with RAP. I felt much better about my decision after I happened to look at the Real Property subject outline in the Information Booklet and found that even the Bar Examiners had placed the Rule Against Perpetuities in a class by itself. It wasn't listed with Future Interests: it had its own place under "Special Problems."

2.　Subject–Specific Strategies

In all fairness, Future Interests and the Rule Against Perpetuities are difficult areas of the law. Not only are they conceptually complex topics, but they present long and factually dense questions. However, once I'd met my quota for concessions, I knew that I'd better figure out a way to handle other troublesome topics as they came along.

In trying to understand why certain topics presented a challenge, I realized that it wasn't simply a matter of the law. There's something about Property and Contracts questions, and Evidence ones as well. Once I started to consider these areas objectively, and not just through the haze of my own prejudices and idiosyncracies, I was able to detect a legitimate basis for my difficulties and a way to resolve them.

a. Why Contracts and Property present a challenge

While Contracts might have posed a difficulty for me initially because I knew too much, this subject continued to present a challenge. And I was having the same problem with some of the Property questions, quite aside from the Rule Against Perpetuities. After careful application of the forensic principles, I determined the source of the difficulty. It turns out that Contracts and Property questions share some significant characteristics—characteristics which have nothing to do with the rule of law but everything to do with the construction of the questions.

Typically, these questions are longer and feature a series of transactions between parties. Sometimes, a fact pattern can fill half of the page. And a long fact pattern generally means a greater likelihood for error—in mixing up parties, in missing significant language, and in just plain losing focus.

By realizing the source of the difficulty, I compensated for it and so can you. When a series of transactions are involved, it's essential to read the call-of-the-question first and use it to narrow the scope of the problem. Let it focus your attention on the relevant parties, cause of action, or the issue you're called upon to resolve. When you know what you're looking for, it keeps you centered as you work your way through the fact pattern. You're able to distinguish relevant from irrelevant facts, keep track of transactions, and follow the relationships between parties. And if the fact pattern contains several transactions or takes you through a series of property transfers, then by all means sketch it out in the test booklet. There's no need to keep it in your head and every reason not to!

Once you're aware of the dangers lurking in long fact patterns and how to guard against them, you're often rewarded with questions that are not nearly as difficult legally as they are to wade through factually.

b. Why Evidence presents a challenge

Evidence questions present quite a different matter. While these questions tend to be shorter and take less time to read, they nonetheless require more time to answer because they involve several levels of analysis. Each analytical step takes time and presents a possibility for error. Still, there's something to like about Evidence questions. They're shorter, so you can keep your focus. They require a no-nonsense direct application of the Federal Rules of Evidence. The MBE follows *only* the federal rules so don't make the mistake of applying the local rule or the common law.

No matter how it is presented, an Evidence question is pretty much always the same question: is this evidence admissible or inadmissible? Identify the theory operating behind the evidentiary proffer and apply the federal rules rigorously to the facts of the question.

After considering the threshold questions of admissibility including relevancy and the balancing test of probative value and undue prejudice, if you find the evidence admissible, then consider

- What form is it permitted to take?

- Who can admit it?

- When can it be admitted?

c. *Statute-based questions*

Criminal Law questions

Questions that work with a statute are a means of testing your ability to follow "the letter of the law." Such questions are a "gift" because you don't have to worry about identifying which rule of law to apply to the issue—the bar examiners are giving you the rule with the statute.

Read and apply the statute to the facts. The shortest distance to the correct answer choice is a simple, direct application of the elements of the statute to the facts in the problem. Also, pay particular attention to the issue of "intent." While it's easy to identify the "act" the criminal defendant committed, it's not so obvious to discern the "intent." That makes it a favorite test topic with bar examiners. Consequently, you should make learning the intent requirements for the different crimes a top priority when you study Criminal Law topics.

Constitutional Law questions

Statutes operate a bit differently here than in Criminal Law. Here, they're used as a vehicle to test your knowledge of federal and state powers. You'll be given a statute and asked whether it's valid. This translates to whether it's a valid exercise of the relevant state or federal power. Focus on learning the enumerated powers of Congress, the typical bases of state regulatory authority, and the limits on such authority. Pay particular attention to the Constitutional requirements of due process and equal protection, and the commerce clause.

d. Torts: Keep Negligence and Strict Liability "strictly" separate

Torts questions on the MBE are relatively "nice," rule-based questions. If you know the black letter law and apply the elements of the rules to the facts in the question without deviation, you should do well. So what are the "sticking points?"

Negligence accounts for one-half of the 34 MBE questions so you must really, truly know the categories of negligence, its elements, and the defenses. It's usually your job to figure out whether it's a negligence claim or defense from the facts of the question because the bar examiners don't tell you.

You may find language of strict liability in the fact pattern and the answer choices although the issue in the question is one of negligence. What should you know?

- Remember that the major difference between negligence and strict liability is one of "intent." An actor can be held liable in strict liability even though he did not intend to bring about the undesirable result and even though he behaved with the utmost care.
- Be alert to words in the fact pattern that refer to "intent" and "care" and evaluate such language carefully against the stated cause of action. For example, if you're told that an actor "carelessly knocked a lighted Bunsen burner into a bowl of chemicals," or acted with "all reasonable care," but the suit is based in strict liability, then whether the actor was careless or careful is purely irrelevant.

D. LEARNING LAW FOR THE ESSAYS

One of my students expressed to me a very common concern and one we need to discuss. It was a paralyzing fear of never being able to know what she thought would be "enough law"—and that even if she could remember the law, she would never know it as perfectly as she thought she should. She said, "If I don't have the right words in my head—the exact ones that I have in my notes from bar review—then I can't write an answer!"

This kind of thinking is dangerous and self-destructive. It prevents you from doing what you need to do. It is indeed possible to get lost in the details and lose sight of the big picture. And for many of you, the most challenging part of studying for the bar exam will be dealing with the tremendous volume of material from your bar review course. Between the notes you take in class and all the other study materials, there is an overwhelming amount of law to learn. And you must learn it. The problem is that you will try to memorize it in the very words in which it is presented to you and you will not be able to do so. This will lead to incredible frustration. And with good reason. You are trying to do the impossible. ***You cannot expect to memorize every sentence of your notes.*** Don't even try. That's because the material is not given to you in a form that you *can* remember. It is your job to craft it into sensible paragraphs of law that you can remember and use to write the rule sections of essays. We'll talk about writing rule paragraphs in the chapter on essay writing, but for now, you need to know that a good part of studying for the essay portion of the bar exam will involve creating "paragraphs of law" for as many of the tested issues as possible.

1. "Paragraphs of Law"

Writing rule paragraphs as part of your studying will let you learn the law in a way that you can remember it because you will have framed it in your own words. Putting the paragraphs together by building from the general rule to the exception and defining all legal terms of art allows you to pre-write large sections of your bar exam for the most frequently tested subject areas. It also "trains your brain" to think this way so that on the bar exam you will formulate such paragraphs for any area of law by working from what you know about how the law works. Consequently, you will no longer be paralyzed with fear of not remembering every word in your notes. You will "own the words" because now you are their creator.

2.   Sample Paragraphs

Although we will write rule paragraphs in a subsequent chapter, it will be useful to see some examples here so you can understand the concept. As you will see, a paragraph of law takes a large and complex area of law and summarizes it. It identifies what is essential by focusing on core doctrine.

Anticipatory Repudiation

An anticipatory repudiation occurs when one party to a contract expresses the intent, either through words or conduct, that a promised performance will not be forthcoming. An express repudiation must be a clear, positive, unequivocal refusal to perform. The statement must be sufficiently absolute and certain so as to be reasonably understood that a party will not or cannot perform. Mere expressions of doubt as to willingness or ability to perform are insufficient. A repudiation may also occur through conduct. Here, the party voluntarily does something to put the promised performance out of his or her power to perform. Upon repudiation, the aggrieved party has several options. It may either wait a reasonable time for performance or treat the repudiation as a present breach and resort to its remedies, even as it urges the repudiating party to perform. In either case, the aggrieved party may suspend its own performance—whether it chooses to treat the repudiation as a breach or wait a reasonable time before doing so.

Avoiding a contract based on Infancy

Under the common law, a minor has the capacity to incur only voidable contractual duties until the beginning of the day before the person's eighteenth birthday. The general exception is a transaction for necessaries. Typically, contracts for food, shelter, clothing or other such basic items necessary for the maintenance of life are found to be necessaries. Even if the minor has entered into a contract for a necessity, she is liable only for its reasonable value and this liability is deemed in restitution and not on the contract.

Upon reaching majority, the contract can be ratified or disaffirmed. Ratification is the infant's manifestation of intent to be bound by the agreement and ends the infant's power to avoid the contract. It can be by words or conduct such as performance of the contractual obligation or accepting the other party's performance under the contract. Alternatively, an infant may *disaffirm* the contract, the whole, not merely parts, by words or conduct, either before or after a reasonable time upon reaching majority.

Fourth Amendment

Under the Fourth Amendment, a person has the right to be free from unreasonable searches and seizures by the government. A search is unreasonable absent a warrant based on probable cause and signed by a detached and neutral magistrate. Evidence obtained in violation of the Fourth Amendment is inadmissible at trial as "fruit of the poisonous tree" pursuant to the Exclusionary Rule.

However, there are exceptions to the warrant requirement. A police officer who has probable cause to make an arrest can make a warrantless search incident to a lawful arrest. Here, an officer can search not only the suspect's person, but also areas within the suspect's "wingspan." If the suspect is arrested in an automobile, the "wingspan" includes the passenger compartment. Also pursuant to a lawful arrest, a police officer can make a warrantless search of an automobile if he has reason to believe it contains contraband. The police officer can then search any containers found in the car that might contain the contraband. The rationale is that one has a lesser reasonable expectation of privacy in one's automobile.

Frustration of purpose

Where the bargained-for performance is still possible, but the purpose or value of the contract has been totally destroyed by some supervening event, such frustration of purpose will discharge the contract. The purpose that is frustrated must have been a principal purpose in making the contract and recognized by both parties at the time of contract. The object must be so completely the basis of the contract that without it, the transaction would make little sense.

Parol Evidence Rule

The Parol Evidence Rule determines the provability of a prior or contemporaneous oral agreement when the parties have agreed to a written agreement. The first question is whether the parties intended the writing to be a final embodiment of their agreement. If the parties had such an intention, the agreement is said to be "integrated," and the parol evidence rule bars evidence of prior negotiations for at least some purposes. If the parties had no such intent, the agreement is said to be "unintegrated," and the parol evidence rule does not apply. If the writing is a final expression of the parties agreement and complete with respect to all of its terms, it's a total integration and can't be contradicted by any type of evidence nor supplemented by consistent (non-contradictory) additional terms. A partial integration is final as to the terms it contains but not complete as to all the terms so it may be supplemented by consistent additional terms, but cannot be contradicted.

Unconscionability

Under the common law, an unconscionable contract is one that is manifestly unfair or oppressive—a contract which no one in his right senses and not under a delusion would make. The contract must be unconscionable at the time of its making. In determining whether a contract is unconscionable, the court looks to see whether it is procedurally and substantively unconscionable. The procedural aspect is one characterized by an absence of meaningful choice so the court looks to the relationship between the parties to determine if there was unequal bargaining power, a lack of opportunity to study the contract and inquire about the terms, and whether the terms were non-negotiable. The substantive aspect is one which looks at the terms of the contract to see if they are unfairly one-sided. A one-sided agreement may be found where one party is deprived of all the benefits of the agreement or left without a remedy for the other party's breach or there is a large disparity between the prevailing market price and the contract price.

E. FACTORS TO CONSIDER IN PLANNING YOUR SCHEDULE

Although we considered the components of a successful bar preparation plan in Chapter 2, here we will consider it in greater detail. Besides, repetition is essential to the learning process so a little redundancy on this topic could not hurt.

A schedule is essential for making sure you study "actively" by covering all the necessary material with the right mix of class time, study time, and practice time. Typically, your bar review course will provide a daily and weekly schedule of study activities. However, this is only a general guide and you'll probably need to make some changes to make it responsive to your needs. You'll want to define a personal study schedule, one that takes account of when you study, the way you study, and what you need to study.

1. What is Your Study Personality?

Your study personality is an important factor in planning a schedule that works for you. For many students, getting started in their study program follows one of two possible directions, each one based in large part on the student's own personality. The first is the "gung-ho" approach. Here the student plunges wildly into the fray, vowing to study 14 hours a day, complete every bar review assignment, read every outline, and do at least 100 multiple choice questions a day. While there is much to be said for enthusiasm, this poor schnook won't survive a week at this frantic pace. Not only is this kind of schedule impossible to maintain, it's guaranteed to lead to burn-out.

The second approach is what I call the "Scarlett O'Hara" philosophy. In this case, the student can't bear to think about the reality of the bar exam and believes that there's always tomorrow to get serious about studying. So what if a bar review class or two is missed. What's the big deal? There's always the DVD backup for missed sessions. The problem with this mind-set is that there's no time to waste. You can no more "ease into" bar review than you could "ease into" law school. Each day counts; there's no making up for lost time.

My advice is to strike a balance between the overly aggressive approach and the overly complacent approach. You can do this by setting realistic goals for yourself. If you know that there's no way you're going to get through 50 or 100 multiple choice questions a day, don't set such an unreasonable goal. Why set yourself up for failure? You must be able to sustain the effort over the entire review period, up to and including the bar exam itself. It's no good if you burn out too soon. Besides, as we'll discuss in the next chapter, the objective in practicing multiple choice questions is not the "doing" of numbers but the learning of law and analysis.

2. Know Your Weakness: Is it Essays or Multiple Choice?

Identify which particular type of question poses more of a difficulty for you. Consider your academic career: have you typically scored lower on objective tests than essay tests? Are you like me and when it comes to choosing between two answers, it seems I always make the wrong choice? If so, then you're going to want to devote more of your study time to learning how to analyze objective questions.

Alternatively, if your professors consistently found much to be lacking in your essays, then you're going to consider spending more time on developing your essay writing skills. I'm not suggesting that this is the time to learn to write for law review, but you can learn to write quality essays that rack up the points on the bar exam. In fact, most of my work with repeat candidates has been in this area and the results have been impressive. As we'll be discussing shortly, the essay portion of the bar exam is where you have the greatest opportunity to influence the outcome. Consequently, it's the part of the exam where this book can be of the most value to you.

3.   All Subjects Are Not Created Equal

Here is where you can use expertise in certain subjects to your advantage by allocating your study time accordingly. While you must cover all the topics tested on the bar exam, you do not need to study them all with equal intensity. How do you decide where to spend your time? For the MBE, use the subject outlines to identify which sub-topics within each subject tend to be more difficult for you. You will want to devote more of your study time to these subjects than to the ones where you have a pretty solid understanding. Here is where you will adjust your study schedule: if your bar review course devotes but one lecture to contract remedies and this is your weak spot, then you'll spend more time with it than the review course might allocate and make up the time in an area where you are stronger.

Do you find some subjects easier to learn than others? Since the MBE does not treat all topics equally in terms of their significance on the exam, neither should you. Why spend precious study days on a topic that is particularly difficult for you when it might be at most one or two questions on the bar exam? This is penny wise and pound foolish. Here's some information to help you decide where to focus your efforts:

- If mortgages happen to be your most dreaded topic, it's unlikely that you'll see more than four or five actual mortgage questions since of the 33 Real Property/Future Interests questions on the MBE, only 25% (8–9 questions) come from real property contracts and mortgages.

- On the other hand, it's very important to know that of the 34 Torts questions, approximately one-half of them will be negligence questions. With 17 questions, which represents almost 8.5% of the entire MBE, you can't afford to treat negligence issues lightly when you study.

4.   Avoid Burnout and Boredom

If you found it difficult to maintain your focus for the typical two-week final exam period, then you will find the six-to-eight week bar review period a true challenge. A few weeks of the relentless routine of going to bar review class, reviewing your notes, and practicing questions will make you feel as if you are reliving the same day, much like a scene from the movie "Groundhog Day." Here's what to do:

- Maintain a realistic work schedule, one that allows for lecture time, review time, practice time, and relaxation time.

- Once you've decided whether to attend a morning or evening bar review session, stay with your choice. Avoid alternating sessions unless you must make up a missed class.

- If you find yourself losing momentum and stuck in a study rut, then it's time to make some revisions. Consider changing your study location. If you've been studying in the same spot in the library, you might consider moving to another floor in the library. Or you might try studying at home. Sometimes a change in venue works wonders.

- Consider varying the sequence of study activities. If you always review your notes right after the bar review lecture, try beginning your study sessions with working through MBE questions. Or try writing out an essay. Answering questions requires that you study "actively" as opposed to the passive process of reading notes.

- Study from different materials. Not only can your notes lose their appeal after the second read, but they can also lose their ability to engage your mind simply because you're familiar with them. It's like listening to a song on the radio. The first time you hear the song, you pay attention and listen carefully. The next time you hear it, you pay less attention because you've heard it before. Your mind drifts and you think of other things. Well, the same is true when you study. You think you're studying but you've stopped paying attention because it's already familiar to you. What you need to do is change to new study materials. Take up the topic in another form—read a different outline from your bar review materials, go back to your own outline from law school, or consider a hornbook—anything that keeps you interested and adds to your understanding of the subject.

F.   WHAT TO INCLUDE IN YOUR STUDY SCHEDULE

Your study schedule must include sufficient time to attend bar review lectures, review and consolidate your lecture notes, practice exam questions, review notes from previously covered subjects, and take breaks. You'll also need an occasional evening or afternoon off. Leave any one of these out of the equation and you will feel its absence.

The question is how much time to allocate for each of these tasks in planning your schedule. While there are no hard and fast rules, consider the following general guidelines.

Bar review classes generally meet five days a week for about four hours a day. Depending on your course, there may be some weekend sessions or longer days, but this is the exception. You may want to revise your schedule on a weekly basis to keep in sync with your bar review course. It should take between two and three hours each day to review and digest the notes from that day's session of your bar review lecture.

Practicing MBE questions should take about 1 ½ to 2 hours of your day. Add another hour or two for practicing essay questions. This time can vary based on how long you spend with multistate questions. Some days you will want to spend all your time with MBE questions and then other days will get the benefit of uninterrupted essay practice time. You should also factor in one MPT per week for approximately two hours. You will also want to consider about 45 minutes to an hour each day to review notes from a previously covered subject.

G.   A DAY IN THE LIFE

While one schedule won't suit all, I still think it's valuable to give you an example of a typical day. I'll describe what mine was like—not because you must necessarily adapt it as your own, but because it's an example of one that worked. It is similar to the sample study schedules that appear in Chapter 2 but the one that follows is based on taking an evening bar review course because that is what I did. If you are taking a day course, then your hours will be reversed and you might want to go back and review the sample in Chapter 2.

Consider using the the blank forms in Chapter 2 to create your own daily and weekly study schedules. Be as specific as possible about allocating your time and activities.

The following was an average day for me:

AM

7:30–8:30   Eat breakfast, read newspaper, shower, and dress

   Note: This would vary. Three or four times a week I added a 30–minute exercise period to my routine. Exercise is very important during this time of intense concentration. If you already exercise, keep it up. If you don't, then start. All you have to do is take a brisk walk. Even if it's only 30 minutes every other day or so, it will make a significant difference in how you feel and how you work.

8:30–10:30   Review notes from the previous evening's class.
Make index cards for rules of law.

Note: It would take about two hours to read and review the approximately 20 pages of notes taken from the previous evening's four hour class.

10:30–11:00   Coffee break; take pup for a walk

11:00–1:00   Practice multiple choice questions in the area of law I had been reviewing.

Note: I would answer a question or the group of questions based on a fact pattern and then check my answers. Even if I answered correctly, I would read the explanations. If I got the answer wrong, I would go back to the question and go through it again to determine where I had erred: was it in the reading of the question? Did I not know the rule? I didn't move on to another question until I was satisfied that I understood what was going on in that question and why I had gotten it wrong. If necessary, I would return to my outline or consult a hornbook on the topic in question. This meant that sometimes I covered only 15 or so questions in a two hour period. But after this time, I felt comfortable that I had really learned something.

1:00–1:30   Lunch. Phone calls. Laundry.

1:30–3:00   More multiple choice practice.

Note: As the weeks went by, I would vary my work during this time to include essay reading and writing. Depending on the requirements of your jurisdiction, I would alternate this period to accommodate the different parts of the exam.

3:00–4:00   Watch *General Hospital*. Fold the laundry.

    Note: Some things are sacred. You don't have to give up everything.

4:00–5:00   Review syllabus to identify what would be covered next in bar review class.

            Review index cards to work on memorizing elements of rules of law/ review subject studied earlier in the course.

    Note: I would focus on one subject at a time and alternate between subjects to make sure that I kept reviewing the material that I had learned earlier.

            Give pup dinner and take her for a walk.

            Have a snack.

5:15   Leave for bar review class

6:00–10:00   Bar review class

    Note: Evening review classes are difficult because they pretty much eliminate any regular dinner hour. But you can't afford not to eat or to eat improperly. Sometimes I would have a snack before class or I would pack a sandwich and eat during class. Figure out which works best for you and make sure you have some healthy snack foods available.

10:30   Home. Talk to husband.

11:00   Relax. Watch *Law and Order*. Pass out.

In looking at how I spent my days, I see that I didn't do much of anything but study. If you ask whether I ever went to the supermarket or cleaners or post office, the answer is "no." But then again, I never went to these places: my husband always took care of such matters. For my part, I continued to do some general household stuff, but the day went by so quickly that there just wasn't time for anything else.

I found studying for the bar to be all consuming. I would become so immersed in my studies that I found it difficult to switch gears and didn't feel like doing anything else. Don't be surprised if you find yourself feeling this way too. It's the natural result of focusing so intently and, for the most part, it's what you need to be doing—and what you should be doing during this time.

However, this is not to say that my routine never varied. Of course it did. Also, during the first half of the bar review period, I would take an afternoon or evening off at least once a week. I would do something enjoyable or just get out of the house: I would go shopping, visit my parents, take care of errands, and go out to dinner with my husband. I would try to relax but I know I wasn't great company because I was always preoccupied. If I wanted to take a break, I found it best to simply watch TV or go to a movie. In fact, movies were the best diversion because it was the only time I would be able to stop thinking about the law I had been studying. I highly recommend regular movie breaks.

H. DEFINING YOUR INDIVIDUAL
STUDY PLAN

The boldface periods are the hours engaged in actual "study." Vary these times by subject area and task according to your needs. Be sure to spend enough time in an area until you feel comfortable with your knowledge level before moving on to another subject. However, don't expect to know everything—this is not possible, nor necessary—but you should feel a level of competency in answering questions before you take up another topic. If you adhere to your schedule, you will have time to review each subject several times during the bar review period.

Day	Study Subjects	Time/Task	
Monday	Contracts	7:30–9:00	Shower, breakfast, dress, and travel to bar review class
		9:00–12:30/1:00	Bar review course
		1:00–2:00	Lunch break
		2:00–4:00/4:30	**Review and consolidate notes from morning's bar review class**
		4:30–5:00	Break—go for a walk with your dog, exercise
		5:00–6:30	**Work through 20 MBE questions**
		6:30–7:30	Dinner break

Day	Study Subjects	Time/Task	
		7:30–9:30	**Work through 15 to 20 MBE questions, one to two essays, or an MPT**
		9:30–11:00	**Review materials for tomorrow's bar review class; study law from a previously covered subject**
Tuesday			
Wednesday			
Thursday			
Friday			
Saturday			
Sunday			

CHAPTER 7

BAR EXAM ESSAYS

A. WRITING IS A DIALOGUE

Before we discuss specific strategies for writing successful bar exam essays, let's talk about writing in general: I'm sure a good number of you have been very successful in law school and a large part of that success can be credited to your ability to communicate effectively in writing. For you, doing well on the essay portion of the bar exam will be a simple matter of gaining familiarity with the types of essays on the bar and their structure. But for those of you for whom essays posed a bit more of a challenge, I want you to know that you too can do well on bar exam essays. There is a method to scoring points and this is what I am going to share with you.

If you think about it, you'll realize that the essays are your **opportunity to converse** with the bar examiners. With every word you write, your goal is to tell the grader that you are prepared to take your place in the profession—that you are ready to meet with clients, analyze their problems, and represent them in court.

How do you convey this message? By using the **language of the law** in the format and structure of legal analysis. This is the only way to demonstrate your competency to join the bar. Presumably, after reading hundreds of cases, you sound something like a lawyer. When a grader reads your essay, there should be "a scintilla of evidence" to show that you've attended law school.

B. HERE'S YOUR CHANCE TO INFLUENCE THE OUTCOME

Every state or jurisdiction includes an essay component as part of its bar exam. Some jurisdictions consider the ability to write so essential that greater weight is given to the written portion (essays combined with the Multistate Performance Test "MPT") than to the Multistate Bar Examination "MBE" in calculating the overall bar passage score—anywhere from doubling the scaled written score to counting it as much as two-thirds.[35] While there is a wide range in scoring formulas, you can count on the essays to be at least equal in weight to the MBE with a good likelihood that the total written portion will weigh even more.

This should be welcome news. It means that the written portion of your bar exam presents the greatest opportunity for you to influence your score because:

35. For example, the MEE/essay/MPT is weighted two-thirds in Idaho; the written portion is 65% of the total score in California; the essays are weighted 60% in North Carolina; scores on the written portion (MPT and essay) are scaled to the MBE and the scaled written score is doubled and added to the scaled MBE score in Ohio. *See* NCBE, Comprehensive Guide to Bar Admissions, Chart VII: Grading and Scoring at http://www.ncbex.org/fileadmin/mediafiles/downloads/Comp_Guide/CompGuide.pdf (last visited August 30, 2008).

You are the one in control of the question when you write. Unlike a multiple choice question where you have to match up your analysis of the problem to fit one of the answer choices, here you have some flexibility. While there are limits determined by the issues set up in the facts, you can take a slightly different path and still accrue significant points.

You can write your way to bar passage—especially when what you write represents a substantial portion of your overall score.

C. WRITING SUCCESSFUL ESSAY ANSWERS: WHAT IT TAKES ACCORDING TO THE BAR EXAMINERS

Bar examiners have the same expectations when reading an essay as did your law professors: one that demonstrates your ability to engage in legal thought and analysis. They are very clear about what they expect from you in an exam answer:

- An answer that evidences "your ability to apply law to the given facts and to reason in a logical, lawyer-like manner from the premises you adopt to a sound conclusion." The State Bar of California Committee of Bar Examiners.

- Neither a "right answer" nor a "bottom line" answer but a well-reasoned argument based on an analysis of the relevant issues and an application of the law to the facts followed by a legal conclusion.[36] New York Board of Law Examiners.

- "The ability to reason logically, to analyze accurately the problem presented, and ... demonstrate a thorough knowledge of the fundamental principles of law and their application." Florida Board of Bar Examiners.

- A demonstration of "your ability to analyze legal problems and to provide an organized, logical and coherent written response." New Jersey Board of Bar Examiners.

Consequently, as you review sample candidate answers, you will find examples of answers that reach opposite conclusions yet have been selected as above average answers. You should pay particular attention to such examples because it's tangible proof of what we've been saying all along—that it's the reasoning that counts and not the bottom line conclusion.

D.   OUTLINING THE APPROACH

While the substantive law and the essay format differs between jurisdictions, what does not is what the bar examiners are looking for when grading an

36.   The ability to reason in a logical, lawyer-like manner is so important that you can get credit for your analysis even if you arrive at the incorrect conclusion. The New York Board of Law Examiners advise that "[a]ppropriate credit is given in the grading of essay answers for well reasoned analyses of the issues and legal principles involved even though the final conclusion itself may be incorrect."

essay. Because of this shared expectation, the process outlined below will allow you to prepare successfully for a bar exam in any jurisdiction.

Always keep in mind that exam writing is a dialogue with the reader. Here, the bar examiner begins the conversation with the question. Your role is to segue to the answer and continue the conversation.

The following are the steps you'll take for writing "bar-right" essays:

1.   Know Your Audience

You must know your audience to write for your audience. Bar exam graders read a large number of essays and evaluate them according to strict criteria. They know what they are looking for and the easier you make it for them to find it, the more points you will accrue. Generally, you can count on writing clear, concise, and focused exam answers which conform to the basic structure of legal analysis—in other words, IRAC, but more about that later. This may require you to make certain adjustments in your style and presentation if you are more accustomed to broad, generalized discussions.

Just as you studied from your professor's past exams to prepare for law school finals, you'll review released essays from your state's bar examiners. Released exams should be your primary source for practice essays. While your bar review course includes a good number of simulated practice tests and essay writing exercises, there is no substitute for the real thing.

Most jurisdictions have made their past exam questions available to you from their website—many even provide sample answers, either student essays or suggested analyses. If released bar questions are not accessible online, then contact the licensing entity directly. It is well worth the extra effort to find out if questions are available. If your jurisdiction uses the Multistate Essay Exam ("MEE"), then contact the NCBE directly for sample questions.

2.   Know Exactly What is Tested and How

As we discussed in an earlier chapter, your jurisdiction provides general information about bar admission requirements, exam dates, and the application process. However, it also provides vital information about the bar exam itself, specifically, its composition and subject coverage. Check for the following:

- The components of the exam

  Know the mix of the elements and the weight accorded to each. There is usually a combination of the MBE, essays, and the performance test. Some jurisdictions include their own multiple-choice questions based on state law as in New York and Florida.

- The number of essays

  Know how many questions you can expect. The number of essays determines your timing.

Knowing what you'll see on your bar exam lets you practice answering questions of similar length and complexity.

- Taking law school exams should have taught you that questions answerable in 30 minutes are significantly different from questions to be answered in an hour. Shorter questions typically involve only one area of law and are more focused; longer questions combine areas of law and present more issues, thus requiring greater organization on your part.

- Subject coverage

  You must know the law to write the law and the first step is to identify what you need to know. Some jurisdictions test only the multi-state law; others include their own common law, statutes, and constitutional law as well. While it might seem as if you're facing the entire legal universe, you're really not since the depth of coverage tends not to be as detailed as a law school exam—but this is something you need to determine.

  You can identify the boundaries of your bar exam by checking with your local bar examiner. Your jurisdiction typically provides a list to bar candidates of the state-specific subjects to be tested. Some provide rather detailed outlines of the covered subject matter which should be used as a checklist to guide your studies.

- Form of questions

Each jurisdiction has its own distinctive essay style. Some will lead you to the issues they want you to discuss and others will leave it open and require you to "issue-spot." Some include both styles in the course of the exam, but not in a single essay. Thorough preparation will let you know what to expect.

You'll find that bar essays conform to one of two general essay styles:

(1) *Single issue: outcome specific*

These tend to be structured, focused, and narrow—quite unlike the long, issue-laden narratives you've seen on law school exams. If you've not had experience answering this type of question, you'll need to practice.

For example, in New York, the essay question asks you to come to a conclusion by answering a particular question:

> *Was the court correct in granting the motion for summary judgment / for the injunction / to admit the testimony?*

> *Can the defendant successfully assert the defense of justification?*

This type of problem is challenging because the precise issue is not identified for you: the issue is not "whether the court was correct or incorrect" but whether the legal theory the court relied upon in coming to that decision was correct or incorrect. Identifying the particular legal theory in controversy requires a multi-step analysis of the facts. It's essential to think through the problem and articulate the precise issue in dispute before writing to produce an essay that is focused instead of one that rambles and follows a "kitchen sink" approach.

Further, this type of question requires that you *not* raise opposing arguments. While typical law school exams are structured for you to see and argue both sides of an issue, this is not the case here. You are required to reach a conclusion and argue specifically for that result. Any time you spend identifying potential counter-arguments is a waste of your time and a loss of potential points.

(2) *Multi-issue: focused response*

These questions are harder to characterize since they seem open-ended and conclude with such familiar interrogatories as "discuss the rights and liabilities of all parties" or "analyze fully." Even these general questions are unlike typical law school exams in that the bar questions are focused and limited in the actual number of issues tested in a single essay.

The challenge lies in your ability to cover the relevant possibilities with the requisite level of detail without going astray. Once again, organizing your answer around the issue and sub-issues is the key to a focused, concise answer.

For example, MEE questions typically ask you to "explain" your answer to a specific question but the "explanation" required is not an extensive dissertation of the law but a concise and succinct discussion of the relevant legal principles as they relate to the issues presented by the question. Consider Question 6 from February 1998:

> *"On what basis, if any, can the injured persons hold Transport liable for tort claims resulting from the HotTrucks accident? Explain."*

While the call-of-the-question contains the usual language indicating an open-ended query *"on what basis, if any"* and *"explain,"* you can't be deceived into a general listing of possible causes of action. You would be casting too large a net and "fishing" instead of writing the targeted, focused analysis required by the facts of the problem. ***Only practice with reading and writing such questions would allow you to proceed to the relevant discussion.***

Whether your state's bar essays are narrow and focused or present more of an open-ended inquiry, you must answer the question asked and only the question asked. In some jurisdictions, the bar examiners will ask you to come to a conclusion. What's critical when you're asked to provide a conclusion is that you take a position and argue it. Unlike a typical law school exam, here you are not supposed to argue in the alternative and present both points of view. In conclusion-based jurisdictions, you're suppose to be an advocate and demonstrate how you marshal the facts to the law.

3.   De-construct Exam Questions and Sample Answers

a.   *De-constructing exam questions*

You might be wondering how "de-constructing a question" differs from "reading a question." Generally, your focus when reading a question is to determine what is required of you to answer it. You are concerned with the information relevant to your task—evaluating whether the defendant committed felony murder, whether the statement was admissible, whether a contract was formed, and so forth.

But when you are studying and trying to learn from the questions, your purpose in de-constructing a question is to analyze its organization and content for patterns and consistencies. This kind of scrutiny lets you see:

- How different areas of the law are combined in a single essay

Unfortunately, bar essays do not come with neat little labels to let you know which is the Contracts essay and which is the Torts essay. Further, most questions combine areas of law in a single essay—

quite unlike what you've experienced in law school where you knew exactly what to expect because exams were class-specific.

Still, there is a natural connection between certain topics and with preparation, you will become familiar with the questions and able to recognize the issues. Although it is not likely you'll find more than two substantive topics in a single essay, you may find ethics or procedural issues woven into any of the questions.

The following are the more common substantive combinations you can expect to see:

- [ ] Contracts with Business Associations (Corporations, Agency, Partnership) Remedies, Damages

- [ ] Torts with Agency principles and Conflict of Laws, Damages

- [ ] Criminal Law with Criminal Procedure or Evidence or any combination of the two

- [ ] Family Law with Property or Trusts and Estates or any combination of the two

- [ ] Constitutional Law with Criminal Law or Evidence or any combination of the two

- [ ] Civil Procedure: in some jurisdictions, this topic may present as its own question (for example, New Jersey) but procedure issues are more likely to be integrated with substantive ones.

- How procedural issues are combined with substantive issues

Bar examiners are adept at weaving procedural questions with substantive issues in ways you might hardly notice—that is, unless you were looking for them. Of course, sometimes procedural questions are "open and notorious" such as,

> *"Al duly filed a notice of removal in federal district court to remove the action to that court, and Dot promptly moved in federal district court for remand of the action to the state supreme court. The court (1) granted Dot's motion. After issue was joined, Al moved, upon proof of the foregoing pertinent facts, for summary judgment dismissing the complaint on the separate grounds that ....."* (New York July 2001 Question 4)

Here it's obvious that you must evaluate the procedural standard for summary judgment before discussing the underlying substantive law. However, it's not so obvious when procedural matters are woven into the fabric of the facts as sub-issues. Some jurisdictions are so subtle in the presentation of procedural questions that unless you're completely familiar with the style and substance of its questions, you could easily overlook the procedural question.

Consider the following interrogatories from past New York bar exams:

1. *"Apple **moved to dismiss** Willie's complaint ..."* (New York July 2003 Question 4)

and

2. *"Harold **brought a separate action** against Wilma ..."* (New York February 2005 Question 3)

with

3. *"Move–It Inc. **moved to dismiss** the action on the grounds that (a) **as a matter of law**, it could not be held liable in strict product liability for the cost of repairing the conveyor system ..."* (New York February 2002 Question 1)

and

4. *"Frank **moved to dismiss** Sean's complaint as to him for **failure to state a cause of action** and the court (1) granted the motion"* ... (New York February 2004 Question 4)

Examples 1 and 2 do not present procedural questions even though the language may seem suggestive. Without more information, there is no procedural standard to evaluate. On the other hand, Examples 2 and 4 refer to a standard with respect to the motion and now you have work to do.

• How issues present in the facts

As you found with law school exams, certain facts give rise to certain legal issues. The more essays you read, the more familiar you will become with seeing causes of action in the context of the facts in which they arise.

• How bar examiners use vocabulary to signal issues, most notably adverbs and adjectives

Bar examiners are incredibly efficient at using a single word or short phrase to convey enormous meaning. Only careful reading of essay questions—lots and lots of essay questions—will allow you to recognize key words and phrases. It's not that the words are unusual or even buried in the text, but they are easy to overlook in the heat of the exam unless you know to look for them.

For example, consider the phrases "walking peacefully" and "without provocation or warning." Such phrases convey enormous meaning. Consider a Criminal Law problem where you're told the plaintiff was "walking peacefully" or the defendant acted "without provocation or warning." You'll know that a claim of self-defense is not viable because it is not grounded in the facts.

Another good example of a loaded phrase is "public place." Just think of the possibilities for Property and Constitutional Law questions. Here a single word can make all the difference in your analysis.

The same is true for such words as "written" and "oral" and all the possible phrases used to convey their meaning. Consider e-mails, telexes, and letters for writings; think of telephone conversations for oral discussions. These words figure prominently in Contracts and Property questions. Learn to look for them.

- How bar examiners use vocabulary to identify non-issues

Bar examiners are similarly adept at using language to signal non-issues. Only the careful, observant reader will know not to discuss such matters, saving time and effort for the real issues.

For example, when the hypothetical contains such phrases as,

"Signed and duly acknowledged"

"Proper written consent"

"Duly executed"

"Duly commenced"

it's your signal **not** to discuss the matter. For example, if you are told that "the will was duly executed," then the issue is not a problem with one of the elements required for execution. Accept what the bar examiners are telling you and move on to address the real issue in the problem.

• How topics tend to repeat

Working through past exams lets you see how often particular topics are tested. While I am not suggesting you will be able to predict the precise questions you will see on your exam, it's very likely you will be able to control the surprise factor and on bar day, the questions will seem distinctly familiar.

b.   *De-constructing sample answers*

Now that you have de-constructed exam questions, it's time to de-construct exam answers—an equally important part of your preparation. Here, rather than studying past exams to see what *you* can expect from the bar examiners, your goal is to learn what *they* expect from you.

By examining each part of a sample answer, you will learn:

- How important a statement of the issue is to the development of the answer

- How much rule you need to write to address the issue

- How a complete and concise statement of the rule differs from a treatise-like discussion

- How to incorporate "distinctions" into your statements of the rule, both state and federal, and statutory and common law

- How analysis of the facts differs from a recitation of the facts

In addition to observing the heavy dependence on IRAC construction in candidate answers and bar examiners' grading sheets, you will discover such other critical information as:

- The need to state the "obvious"

For example, in working with a Sales question, many a bar candidate neglects to make such a basic statement as

> *"This was a contract for the sales of goods because computers are goods."*

but such a sentence is essential to a solid analysis because it completes the nexus between your statement of law that the Uniform Commercial Code governs transactions involving sales of goods and your facts which discuss the sale and delivery of some computers.

Equally obvious, equally necessary, but equally absent from too many answers is a reference to the particular jurisdiction when stating the controlling law

> **"Under Florida law**, *a Settlor can create a trust by....*"

> **"Under New York's** *Domestic Relations Law,....*"

- A credit-worthy answer may have reached the "wrong" conclusion

As you review sample candidate answers, you may find examples of answers that reach opposite conclusions. This is proof that it's the reasoning that counts and not necessarily the bottom line conclusion. Certainly, the correct answer gets the most points but it is possible to get points if your argument is based on law and grounded in the facts.

- The heavy reliance on signal language to lead the reader through the steps of an IRAC analysis

> **"The issue is whether** ....*, when* ....."

> **"Under the** *[statement of the controlling law: common law, federal rule, state-specific statute etc.]*"

*"**Here**,* the [buyer accepted the goods ***because***
...........]"

*"**Therefore**, ..."*

- The use of "because," "since," "as," and "when"
  in the analysis section of the essay to connect
  rule with fact

4. Follow a Formula: Write IRAC

It should be clear from the de-construction process
that your answers will follow a basic IRAC structure
and it's okay to be obvious about it. There's no need
to worry that you're boring the grader. He or she will
be very grateful to find the issue in your essay so
easily. Also, there's no need to try and impress the
grader with your originality. Save the sparkling
prose for your law review articles and proceed
swiftly through your paces on the bar.

IRAC allows you to organize your response and
remain in control, whether addressing a narrow
issue-driven essay or a general question. With slight
variations to account for the type of questions in
your jurisdiction, you can make IRAC your blueprint
for answering any essay question.

This is the where most books would leave you to
your own devices. After describing the basics of
IRAC, you'd be given some hypotheticals and told to
practice the process by writing out answers. However, a vital piece in the process is still missing—
that is, how to do it. It's one thing to tell you to write
an answer—and quite another to show you how it's

done. Sometimes, you need to be shown exactly what to do.

a.   *Writing the issue*

Begin your sentence with *"The issue is whether."* It's okay to be obvious.

- *Use the "whether, when" construction*

The "whether, when" construction leads you to connect the legal question with the specific facts in controversy. When you use this approach to formulate an issue, you avoid overly general statements and provide a path to follow in your analysis. This leads to an essay that connects the rules with the questions presented rather than one that rambles and follows a "kitchen sink" approach.

Begin with,

> *"**The issue is whether**"*

then identify and state the legal conclusion you want the court to reach,

> *Ben **committed a battery**, (or a **contract was formed**, or the **court can assert personal jurisdiction** over the non-resident defendant)*

and connect to the facts in controversy which determine the outcome,

> *when he threw the vase at Amy and hit Jill (or when the acceptance contained additional terms, or when the defendant rented office*

space and opened a checking account in the forum state)

You end up with the following issue statements

*"The issue is **whether** Ben committed a battery **when** he threw the vase at Amy and hit Jill instead."*

*"The issue is **whether** a contract was formed **when** the acceptance contained the additional term of charging interest on late payments."*

*"The issue is **whether** the court can assert personal jurisdiction over the non-resident defendant **when** the defendant rented office space and opened a checking account in the forum state."*

b. Stating the rule of law

After your identification of the issue, your statement of the rule of law is probably the single most important part of your exam essay. First, it lets the reader know that you have identified the legal problem and second, it shows that you know the relevant law. And in writing the relevant law, be sure to write the law of your jurisdiction. Even if you could answer the question using the common law, if there is a state rule on point, you want to be sure to apply that law. Never forget that you are seeking admission to practice in a particular jurisdiction: you want the bar examiners to know that you know the applicable state law.

Writing the rule consists of two parts: first, writing enough of the rule, and second, writing the rule in a logical order.

1.   Write enough rule

The major problem, and where candidates fail to get as many points as they can and should, is that they do not write enough law and they do not do it in a complete, concise, and coherent manner.

By now I'm sure you're asking yourself:

- What is enough rule?

- How do I know how much rule to write?

- Isn't there such a thing as too much rule?

The answer is simple: the whole rule is enough rule to provide the context to analyze the facts. The rule and the facts are inextricably linked. Your analysis of the facts will not make sense unless you have first identified the rule which determines the relevance of those facts. You must use the facts of the problem to guide your discussion of the law.

2.   Write the rule in its logical order

There is a structure to follow when writing a rule of law. You should strive to present your statement of the law in its logical order. This demonstrates your understanding of the subject and makes it clear to the grader. Just as you need a context to make sense of what you hear—just imagine hearing only one side of a telephone conversation—a reader needs a context to understand what you write. You provide it as follows:

- By moving from the general to the specific

There is a "natural" order to writing the rule which is based on a hierarchy of concepts. This means that when you write the rule, you work from the general to the specific. Your analysis should begin with a statement of the general rule and then move to the exception, not vice versa. The general rule provides a context for understanding and appreciating the role of the exception.

For example, suppose your problem requires you to evaluate a challenge to a federal expenditure brought by a taxpayer and the question turns on whether the taxpayer has standing. Since the general rule is that a federal taxpayer lacks standing to raise a constitutional challenge to federal expenditures, then surely you are dealing with one of the exceptions. Consequently, before you identify the exception and evaluate its merits, you must preface the discussion with a statement of the general rule.

- By defining each legal term of art

When your statement of the rule contains a legal term of art, your next sentence should be a definition of that term. This is one of the easiest ways to go about building a complete statement of the rule in a logical and methodical manner. The sentences flow almost effortlessly because one statement leads naturally to the next.

- By using the following building blocks of rule construction

Elements: Even if you've identified a specific element of a rule as the one in controversy in your problem, you still need to include a general statement identifying all of the elements.

For example, suppose your issue is whether a party's possession of property was uninterrupted for the statutory period to satisfy a claim in adverse possession. While the heart of your analysis will be this question of continuous possession, you will preface your analysis with a general statement identifying the basic elements required for a cause of action in adverse possession: actual and exclusive possession, hostile to the true owner, notorious and open, and uninterrupted for the statutory period. Then you will focus on the element or elements in controversy. The point is that even though only one or two of the elements may be in dispute, you need to identify all of them to provide context. (While you will also need to offer a brief statement as to why they are not in dispute, this part will be addressed in the analysis section.)

Exceptions: exceptions to the general rule are the stuff of which bar exam essays are made. In fact, you can pretty much count on the questions to force you to deal with exceptions because that's where the problems typically arise in the real world.

Distinctions: often you will have a question where the state law differs from the federal rule or the common law from the statutory law. Be sure to identify such distinctions to show how application of one rule as opposed to the other would yield a different result. The following are some examples of distinctions between state and federal and common law and statutory law. They show how you can demonstrate your grasp and understanding of critical nuances in the law—and gain points from your grader—with just an additional sentence or two in your answer. As you prepare for the bar, make note of such exceptions and look for them on exam day.

The "Dying Declaration" distinction:

Under the Federal Rules of Evidence, a statement made under the belief of impending death concerning what the declarant believed to be the circumstances of his impending death is admissible in a prosecution for homicide or in a civil action. FRE 804(b)(2). Unlike the federal rule, however, such testimony is admissible in New York only if the declarant dies and the death is the subject of a homicide charge.

The common law's "mirror image rule" and UCC 2–207:

Under the common law, the "mirror image rule" requires that an acceptance conform exactly to the terms of the offer and any variation is deemed a counter-offer and terminates the offeree's power of acceptance. The result under the UCC 2–207 is radically different. Here, a contract for the sale of goods may occur even if the acceptance "states terms additional to or different from those offered." 2–207(1). Consequently, in one case we have a contract whereas in the other we don't.

c. *Writing the application*

How you set up the rule now drives the structure of the analysis. Your statement of the rule provides a blueprint to follow for your discussion of the facts. Work from your articulation of the rule to guide your application of the facts. Match up each element/factor you've identified in the rule with a fact, using the word "because" to make the connection between rule and fact. This ensures that you write facts "plus" the significance of those facts. Think of writing the application portion of your analysis in terms of a formula:

**Application = Rule + Fact,
where "+" is "because"**

(A = F + R)

Consider the following examples:

1. Jess may have committed a "trespass" *(rule)* **because** (+) she "walked onto Farmer Dell's

cornfield to pick corn without his permission" *(facts)*.

2. Ted acted in "bad faith" *(rule)* **because** (+) he "counted on the good price he was paying for the raw materials when he decided to increase operations" *(facts)*.

3. Sam the shareholder has a basis to "pierce the corporate veil" *(rule)* of Carl Corp. **because** (+) Carl was "the sole shareholder and freely intermingled funds, used corporate funds to pay both corporate and personal expenses, maintained only one set of accounting books, and never held any corporate meetings" *(facts)*.

d.   Writing the conclusion

If the call-of-the-question asks for a specific answer, then be definitive. State your conclusion as to that issue. If there are multiple issues, then once you've completed your analysis of one issue, move on to the next. And it's as simple as that—begin a new paragraph and write,

> *"The next question is whether Spencer's offer was accepted when Ben said he'd take two cartons but delivery had to be September 15th, not the 20th."*

5.   Automate the Process

One of the primary purposes of taking practice exams is to make the process of reading and answering the questions so routine that you'll follow it instinctively on exam day. ***Your main focus will be***

on what you write, not how you write it. **Aside from allowing you to focus on substance, having a plan saves time and prevents panic because you know exactly what to do.**

Note: When you first start working with essays, you will not be timing yourself. At this point, your goal is gaining familiarity with the structure and content of the questions and using them to help you learn the law in the context in which it is tested. ***Only in the last few weeks before the bar exam should you time your responses.***

Beginning with your practice sessions and then on the bar exam, follow these steps each and every time you approach a question:

a. Allocate your time for each question and set your timetable

Since you know the precise composition of questions for your exam, figure out how much time you have for each question. Create your own "clock" by writing down the starting and ending times for each question. Follow this clock throughout the exam to stay on track.

Budgeting your time and working within that time is the only way to ensure that you'll complete the exam—or come as close as possible. You begin working toward this goal the minute you start studying for the bar exam. Every practice essay is a dress rehearsal.

b. Scan the exam but answer the questions in order

You want to get a sense of the entire exam but it's usually best to simply follow the order of questions when answering them. If you start to read each question before deciding which one to answer, you'll waste precious minutes and dilute your concentration. Instead, take one at a time as you find them.

On the other hand, you need to be flexible. For example, if you begin a question and find that no matter how hard you try, you can't make any progress. Give yourself a couple of minutes and then move on to the next question. You don't want to waste valuable time when you could be working productively elsewhere. Chances are that when you return to this question later, it will come to you.

c. Start at the end of the question with the call-of-the-question

The interrogatory, or "call-of-the-question," lets you know what is required of you. This informs your subsequent reading of the fact pattern and ensures that you read "actively" for the information you need.

From the interrogatory, determine whether it's a "general" or "specific" style essay. A "general" style essay will leave the question open-ended. The following are particular favorites of bar examiners:

- *"Analyze fully."*

- *"Identify all possible claims and defenses. Explain fully."*

- *"Discuss the cause(s) of action and possible defense(s)."*

On the other hand, a "specific" essay will present a precise question to be answered:

- *"Was the court correct in granting Plaintiff's motion for summary judgment?"*

- *"Did the Surrogate correctly admit Ben's will to probate?"*

- *"Does Wanda have a right to maintenance?"*

- *"Were the numbered rulings correct?"*

Next, identify the subject area from the call-of-the-question, if possible. This helps you focus on the relevant facts and disregard any non-issues as you read the hypothetical. Finally, note any instructions to follow in writing your response. Before you demonstrate your analytical skills with what you write, you'll want to show that you can follow basic directions. If you're asked to write on only one side of the paper or skip every other line, then you must do so. If you're asked to assume a role—law clerk or judge—then be sure to play the part. If you're asked to draft a memo, begin your response with a mock memo heading. If you're asked to reach a conclusion, then by all means answer the question. In addition to your knowledge of the substantive law, your ability to read and follow directions is a vital lawyering skill being tested on the bar exam.

d. Read the entire question for the first time

1. Skim through the problem, spending no more than a couple of minutes to acquaint yourself with the general story and the parties.

2. Re-read the call-of-the-question and set your focus.

e. Read the question for a second time, but this time read "actively"

1. Identify the area of law and the legal relationship between the parties.

2. Circle amounts of money, dates, locations, quantities, and ages.

3. Note the words "oral" and "written."

4. Identify issues as they appear by writing the words which characterize the legal principle, i.e., "merchants," "excited utterance," etc., instead of underlining. If you underline, you might not recall why you did so and you'll have to reread the passage, wasting valuable time.

f. Outline your answer

Resist the impulse to start writing immediately—it doesn't matter what others around you are doing—it's worth a few minutes to think through the problem and plan your response. After you've completed your second read, and before you write your answer, organize your ideas into an outline based on the relevant issues.

If there is more than one interrogatory in the question, read all of them before you begin writing: chances are the bar examiners have "divided" the issues into separate questions and you need to do the same.

Now I can hear you thinking:

- *What do I put in an outline?*

- *How do I outline effectively without wasting precious exam-writing time?*

The answer is to outline **only** the rule of law. Usually, it's all you need as a guide to writing a complete answer. The process of outlining lets you see things you might otherwise miss. By using the "thought triggers" provided by the outline, you proceed through the analytical steps necessary to write a complete answer.

Here are the steps for outlining:

1. If appropriate to your jurisdiction's essay style, use each interrogatory to set up your numbering scheme and organize your answer.

2. For each interrogatory, identify the issue in controversy. The issues come from one of two possible sources, depending on the particular form of the essay:

   In the specific-style essay, use the interrogatory to guide your articulation of the issues.

   In the general-style essay, determine the issues directly from the fact pattern.

3. For each issue, consider the "building blocks of the rule" relevant to addressing your problem:

   (a) procedural elements (i.e., standard for summary judgment)

   (b) the general rule

   (c) elements/factors

   (d) exceptions to the general rule

   (e) distinctions

   (f) defenses/limitations

4. For each rule, match it to the relevant facts. Here, "charting the rule" with respect to the facts is helpful in writing a solid analysis.

OUTLINING THE RULE

Typically, your thought process will not be this organized. It's far more likely you'll jump to the specific rule necessary to answer the issue in dispute—usually the exception—and forget to include the rest in your essay. Here's where an outline can help you build a complete rule paragraph. After formulating the issue, consider the following steps:

Step 1: What is the *specific rule* brought into controversy by the facts?

_____

Are there *legal terms* of art to define?

_____

Step 2: What is the *general rule*?

_____

Build the general rule of law:

A. Are there *legal terms* to define?

B. Are there *exceptions* to the general rule?

C. Are there *elements/factors* to be identified?

Step 3: Is there a *relevant distinction*?

(i.e., between the common law and the UCC or state law/ between federal and state law?)

Step 4: Does the party have a relevant *defense*? or is there a *limit* **to the reach of the rule?**

Step 5: What are the *consequences* of applying this rule to the facts?

For example, should evidence be excluded under the *exclusionary rule*?

Is the party entitled to damages? If so, what kind? Punitive? Economic? Equitable?

Step 6: Is there a ***procedural element*** to consider? A motion? What is the standard? (i.e., summary judgment)

RULE OUTLINE WORKSHEET

Let's see how this works with an actual bar exam question. Suppose you are answering Question 4 of the February, 2007 New York Bar Exam. The first sub-question is:

> *"Assuming the police had probable cause, was the arrest of Archie lawful?"*

After framing your statement of the issue as something like …

> *"The issue is whether Archie's arrest violated his Fourth Amendment rights when the police arrested him in his home without an arrest warrant?"*

… you are ready to consider the relevant rule. Here is where the Rule Outline can help—it provides a sequence of questions to guide your thinking so you will write a complete rule statement and not just the bare bones. Your goal is to internalize the "prompt questions" and use them to outline what you will write. Although you may *think* through a problem in the following order, you may have to reorder the steps before you write so that it flows from the general to the specific.

Writing only words or phrases to guide your writing of the essay, here's what your outline might look like:

Step 1: What is the **specific rule** brought into controversy by the facts?

"Exigent circumstances" exception

Are there **legal terms** of art to define?

Evanescent evidence

Step 2: What is the **general rule**?

4th Amendment to Constitution

Build the general rule of law by:

A.   Are there **legal terms** to define?

Search and seizure, warrant requirement, probable cause, Aguilar–Spinelli test

B.   Are there **exceptions** to the general rule?

Emergency rule

C.   Are there **elements/factors** to be identified?

NOT APPLICABLE

Step 3: Is there a **relevant distinction***?*

(i.e., between the common law and the UCC or state law/ between federal and state law?)

NOT APPLICABLE

Step 4: Does the party have a relevant **defense**? or is there a **limit to the reach of the rule?**

NOT APPLICABLE

Step 5: What are the **consequences** of applying this rule to the facts?

> (i.e., should evidence be excluded under the **exclusionary rule**?)

unlawful arrest because without warrant

> Is the party entitled to damages? If so, what kind? Punitive? Economic? Equitable?

<u>*NOT APPLICABLE*</u>

Step 6: Is there a **procedural element** to consider? A motion? What is the standard? (i.e., summary judgment)

<u>*NOT APPLICABLE*</u>

CHARTING THE FACTS

New York Bar Exam February 2007

Question 4

The police received a tip from an anonymous source that Bernard had been murdered. A day later, Bernard's dead body was found behind the steering wheel of his own parked car. In the back seat of the car, the police found a jacket that had Archie's full name sewn in the collar. Inside one of the jacket pockets was a sealed blank envelope. The police opened the envelope and found a note from Archie to Bernard in which Archie demanded that Bernard tell him the location of some money that the two had stolen together, "or else."

The police took a statement from Carol, who said she knew Archie and Bernard. She saw them leave a neighborhood tavern together and ride off in Bernard's car on the night Bernard was reported to have been murdered. Carol also reported to the police that Archie called her the next day and said that he was getting out of the country.

The police went to Archie's home without an arrest warrant and found the front door slightly ajar. They entered and searched the house. Archie was found inside a closet and was arrested for the murder of Bernard. At that time, he was given his Miranda warnings.

Over his objection and without counsel, Archie was then placed in a line-up, where he was identified by

Darlene. Darlene lives near where Bernard's car was found. She said she saw Archie running from Bernard's car just after she heard a shot fired.

After his arraignment, and outside the presence of his assigned counsel, Archie, after signing a waiver of his right to counsel, was questioned by the police. He gave a statement to them admitting that he shot Bernard.

Archie's attorney moved to suppress (1) the note found in Archie's jacket; (2) the line-up results; and (3) Archie's statement. The court denied the motion in all respects.

(A) Assuming the police had probable cause, was the arrest of Archie lawful?

(B) Assuming the arrest was lawful, were the court's rulings on (1), (2) and (3) correct?

Chart for (A): Was the arrest lawful?

Rule	Fact(s)
Exigent circumstances	Anonymous tip night before they found body—had time
	Archie told Carol he was getting out of the country—no time
Warrant	Police went to house w/o warrant—door ajar—entered
Seizure	Arrested Archie in his home
Probable cause; Aguilar/Spinelli	Bernard's body in car with Archie's jacket in back seat; statement from Carol

g.   Write the essay

Now that you've framed an outline based on the rules which address the issues raised in the question, you're ready to write your analysis. But first take a moment to re-read the interrogatory and make sure that your outline addresses each of the questions asked.

When you write, you'll follow your outline, referring to each point to prompt your thinking. This will lead you through the issues and sub-issues as they naturally unfold and assures that your answer will be well-organized.

1.   Use sub-headings

The purpose for using sub-headings is as much for the writer as it is for the reader. They promote organization—both of thought and expression. Your choice of sub-headings should be simple and direct. Often, you need look no further than the interrogatory for your sub-head: i.e., "Motion for Summary Judgment," "Identification of Damages," "Easement by Prescription." Sub-headings are very useful when answering multi-issue hypotheticals to keep parties and causes of action separate. Consider such possible sub-headings:

Dan v. ABC Company

Buyer's Remedies

Jon's Defenses

2.   Write IRAC

(a) Write the issue using the "whether, when" construction to combine rule with fact. Each issue is the focal point around which you'll write your analysis.

(b) Identify the controlling rule of law with, **"Under the"** [*state the controlling law: common law, federal rule, state-specific statute, etc.*].

(c) Write a complete paragraph of law for each issue by working from the general to the specific and defining each legal term of art.

(d) Introduce your analysis with **"Here"** or **"In this case."**

(e) Match each rule of law with a "fact" using "because" to link the two.

(f) Conclude and continue: offer a conclusion with respect to the issue and repeat the process where each issue and sub-issue forms the basis for a separate IRAC analysis.

h. When time is up, move on to the next question

You must follow your timetable faithfully. You simply cannot "borrow" time from one question for the next. This never works. Instead, you must continue on and keep within your "clock." If you have time remaining when you've finished all the questions, then you can go back. You'll probably only have time enough to jot down a few words but if you use your outline, this should be sufficient to guide you to the key points.

6.   "Be in the Moment"

No matter how much you've studied, how many practice exams you've taken, and how carefully you've outlined and considered what's likely to be tested, once you get to the exam, you must be prepared to let go and "be in the moment." This means that you respond to what the bar examiners ask of you and not what you want to tell them. The questions are carefully crafted to test you on certain material; if you turn the questions around or avoid answering them, you're thwarting their agenda and substituting your own. Trust me—there's no better way to ensure a poor or even failing grade than to ignore what's asked of you. Answering the bar examiners' questions is the only way to show what you know.

E.   PRACTICE MAKES POINTS

1.   Gaining Familiarity with the Questions

The key to success in any endeavor is preparation. Familiarity with the structure of the essay questions and how you respond to them will go a long way in alleviating your anxiety on test day. You job is to practice the approach we've just outlined so that it becomes so automatic by test day that you move from one step to the other without missing a beat.

The difficulty, of course, is finding the time to practice these skills. Finding time will be one of your greatest challenges during the bar review period. You'll be torn in several directions at once—going to bar review lectures, reviewing your notes, memorizing the law, writing essays, answering multiple choice questions, and taking simulated MPT exams. Still, there are ways to ensure that you accomplish all that you must. Once again, it comes down to knowing your own strengths and weaknesses and working with them.

A bit of common sense goes a long way. If you have solid writing skills and law school essays were your strong point, then there may be no need to write out complete essay answers. Instead, what you will do is focus on identifying issues and outlining the rules needed to address those issues. You should aim to outline at least two bar examination essays every day during your two month bar prep period. Pay particular attention to articulating the issues. As you've learned by now, it takes skill to move from the interrogatory or general question to the specific issue in controversy. Only sufficient practice will enable you to articulate issues with ease. Outline all of the essay questions available from your jurisdiction, then move on to the essays from your bar review course.

On the other hand, if writing was not one of your strengths, you must write complete essay answers. It will not be sufficient for you to merely outline the rules according to the issues; you need to practice writing according to the outlined formula until it becomes automatic and the words flow from your pen. There is no short cut. The key to building your confidence, your competence, and your efficiency will come only from practice, practice, and more practice.

2.   Working with Sample Answers

Finally, whether you've written out entire essays or only outlined the issues and rules, be sure to read the sample answers. Read all of them, even when there are several candidate samples for each question. For example, New York provides two candidate answers whenever possible, as does New Jersey. On the other hand, Connecticut gives seven sample answers for each question, providing the applicant with an opportunity to see a range of scores. Connecticut's bar examiners identify the scoring system and you can read for yourself what was considered a "much below average" response as opposed to a "much above average" response, and everything in between.

Reading selected candidate answers is an excellent way to become familiar with the predilections of your jurisdiction. However, be careful to read with a discerning eye toward the rules of law expressed in student papers: the bar examiners are careful to point out that they are only "sample" answers, not "model" answers. Consequently, you may find what you consider errors in statements of the law. Use this to your advantage: if you're reading the answers "actively" as indeed you should be, then you will identify these errors and be sure to articulate the correct rule of law. Further, you should compare each sample answer to the IRAC model and fully analyze the construction. Then you should compare the sample to your own answer, element by element, taking the time to evaluate what you've written. To truly benefit from the sample answers, it's not enough to skim through them: you must deconstruct them using forensic IRAC.

F. OTHER ESSAY WRITING TECHNIQUES

1. Use Sub-headings to Keep Answers Organized

As we discussed earlier, sub-headings keep you focused. Be sure to use them where appropriate.

2. Write on Only One Side of the Paper

If you write on only one side of the paper in the booklet, the left side is available to add explanatory notes. Hopefully, your use of an outline will avoid the need to direct the reader to additional notes but should it become necessary, this is the least disruptive method of doing so.

3. Write in Paragraph Form

You would be surprised how many candidates forget the dictates of basic paragraph formation and write in a "stream of consciousness" style worthy of William Faulkner. When your essay appears as one solid mass to a grader who has but minutes to spend per paper, imagine the result. Instead, make your paper easy on the eyes. Use paragraphs to show your progression of thought and the sequence of your analysis. Indent and skip a line between paragraphs. Whatever you do to make your grader's job easier, makes you the grateful beneficiary.

4.   Do Not Overly Rely on Underlining, Capitalizing, etc.

If you emphasize everything you write, the effect is lost. You can underline "buzz words" but if you are writing in the language of the law, all you write is worthy of note.

G.   EMERGENCY MEASURES OR "WHAT TO DO IF"

1.   You Freeze and Begin to Panic

Aside from the usual exam jitters, the bar exam does present a unique set of circumstances. After all, it's not many tests that we take with thousands of other candidates at the same time and place. The surroundings alone prove problematic for some. Assuming, however, that this is not the cause of your fright but rather, you've just read the question and your mind has gone blank.

If you begin to feel panicky, stop whatever you're doing and breathe deeply. You want to regain your sense of control and composure immediately. Implement the following step-by-step approach:

(a)   Review the question.

(b)   Start with what you know: identify the area of law again and see if it provides insight.

(c) Focus on the basics. See if you can provide definitions. Remember, rules are really just definitions. The next step is to see if you can build on these definitions to write your paragraph of law.

(d) Finally, call on the resources you developed in law school. Lawyers act; they do not react. Think deliberately and respond accordingly.

2. You Don't Know the Rule of Law

This is everyone's greatest fear, law student and lawyer alike. What you must do is learn to rely on your training and instinct. Force yourself to go through the following steps:

First, ask

"What is the issue?" You can formulate this from the question you are directed to answer. Even if you're not sure of the rule, you can figure out what it is that the examiners want you to consider. Focusing on identifying the issue will allow you to regain your composure and lead you back to the structure of thinking like a lawyer.

Write the issue, whether or not you "know" the rule you need to apply. Formulating the issue will get you points from the grader because it shows that you can identify the legal problem from the facts.

Next, ask

"What principle of law is implicated by this issue?" Now you're thinking like a lawyer.

This will either lead you to the rule from the recesses of your memory or you'll have to improvise. When you improvise, rely on your knowledge of general legal principles and standards to guide you. Use what you know about the law in general to build a specific rule for your problem.

In such cases, begin by identifying the general legal concept implicated in the problem. Some possible questions to ask include,

- Has there been a violation of a fiduciary obligation?

- Are the standards of due process /equal protection implicated?

- Has the requirement of good faith been breached?

- Are the "best interests of the child" at stake?

These questions become your starting point. As you study, you'll find more basic questions that you can rely upon to trigger your thought process. Think of them as your mental checklist.

For example, if you're asked about recoverable "damages" in a particular case, rely on what you know about "damages" in particular areas of the law and proceed from there.

(a) If it's a contracts problem, you know every breach of contract entitles the aggrieved party to sue for damages. The general theory of damages in contract actions is that the injured party should be placed in the same position as if the contract had been properly performed, at least so far as money can do this. Compensatory damages are designed to give the plaintiff the "benefit of his bargain."

(b) On the other hand, if it's a torts problem, you know that the overall goal is to compensate plaintiff for unreasonable harm which he or she has sustained.

And finally, even if you can't find the issue or principle of law, you can break down the problem into the elements common to every case and proceed from there:

(a) Identify the parties and the nature of their relationship.

Is it that of employer/employee, landlord/tenant, buyer/seller, parent/child, husband/wife?

(b) Identify the place(s) where the facts arose.

Did the events occur in a public area, a private home, a school, a waterway, a farm?

(c) Identify whether objects or things were involved.

Was there a transaction involving the sale of goods? Is the ownership of land or chattel in dispute?

(d) Identify the acts or omissions which form the basis of the action.

Was there a robbery, an assault, an act of discrimination?

(e) Determine whether there is a defense to the action.

Is there a basis for self-defense, justification, privilege?

(f) Characterize the relief sought.

Are the parties seeking damages? Are they monetary or equitable damages, or both?

These questions allow you to gain access to the problem when your initial read is fruitless. From any one of these topics, it is but a short step to finding the principle of law implicated in the question. It might be a very good idea to memorize these topics and have them readily available to "jump-start" your thought process.

H. HOW FORENSIC IRAC WORKS WITH ESSAYS

As you've just seen, an effective essay follows the IRAC structure. As a result, your essays should be organized around an "issue," a "rule," an "application," and a "conclusion" for each and every issue and sub-issue you identify on an exam question. Once you've written an essay, therefore, you have all the evidence you need to use our forensic principles. By examining what you've written through the legal lens of IRAC, you'll be able to evaluate your own work.

Forensic IRAC works by examining each sentence you've written in terms of its place in the IRAC structure of legal analysis. Now don't laugh or think I've been watching too many television crime dramas (even though I have!), but I've called the process forensic IRAC because the techniques we're going to use are similar to those employed by crime scene investigators, accountants, medical examiners, and any of the forensic experts who go back over the trail of evidence to determine how that evidence led to a particular result. While such experts rely on fingerprints, ledger books, and DNA, we use IRAC.

As I've said, we need to step inside your head to see the way you thought about the exam problem—how you approached it, how you read the facts, and what they meant to you. What you've written leaves an identifiable trail—something like your DNA but instead of identifying your biologic self, it identifies your cognitive self. You should think of forensic IRAC as deciphering a code, where each sentence you've written is a clue to piecing together how you approached a problem. It works because when you write, you take the inherently private and internal process called "thought" and make it public—and provide just the way into your head that we need.

1. Applying the Technique

The first step in the process is to write an essay. Assuming that you've written an essay answer during one of your practice sessions, the next step is to put it away. Move on to something else—review your lecture notes, prepare some flash cards, write another essay. You're not ready to be objective about something you've just completed. You're too close to see what you've *really* written as opposed to what you *think* you've written. The mind's eye is funny that way: you can read something you've written over and over again and never see the errors because your eye will correct them based on what your mind intended. The only way to overcome this tendency is to distance yourself from your work so you can look at what you've written with a fresh eye and a clear mind. I strongly recommend that you write an essay one day and review it the next.

Sometime the next day, or much, much later that same day, take out the bar exam question and your essay. Re-read the question and then your answer. Now you're ready to proceed. The plan is simple: use IRAC analysis to detect any flaws in that analysis.

As you read your essay, consider each IRAC element against the criteria outlined below. This allows you to evaluate what you've written with the critical eye of a grader and identify your individual strengths and weaknesses. More importantly, by showing you exactly what to look for in each step of an IRAC analysis, you'll be able to pinpoint exactly where in the process any weakness occurs. Then, by following the suggested cures for that particular problem, you'll be able to correct it.

What follows is something like a troubleshooting section in a technical manual where system faults are identified and applicable solutions are provided.

2. When You Have Trouble Finding the "Issue"

A failure to properly identify the issue(s) results in a "scattershot" approach in the rest of your answer—a real "hit or miss" situation when it comes to racking up exam points. You may even have written an opening *"The issue is whether"* statement, but it merely restates the interrogatory without articulating the legal question underlying it. As a result, you're misled into thinking you've identified the issue when in fact you've missed it altogether.

Generally, you can tell that you've had difficulty in "spotting the issue" by what you've written in either the rule or the application portion of your essay, or both.

a. *How You Can Tell When it Shows Up in Your Statement of the Rule*

When you fail to identify the legal issue, it's likely to turn up as a problem in your statement of the rule. One of the following may occur:

- You may find that the rule discussion is so *general and open-ended* that it completely overlooks the precise rule implicated by the facts

- Your analysis *glosses* ("sketchy") over the rule so lightly that the grader can't be sure whether you knew the relevant rule or merely happened to mention it

- You've stated the wrong rule altogether

Look for examples of the following in the rule section of your essay:

- Lengthy, treatise-like discussions of general legal topics.

  This is a pretty common situation where you've provided lots of "law" but it's too general to address the particular problem implicated by the facts. Typically, what you've managed to do is dance around the topic without engaging it.

  Here, you've decided to show the bar examiners how much time you've spent studying so you display that knowledge by writing everything you know. What happens is that you provide far more information than is necessary, often miss the relevant point, and take up valuable exam time without adding to your grade.

- A rule "dump."

  This may be hard for you to believe but it's not your job to recite all the law you've managed to memorize. I can understand that if you think this way, there's no such thing as a "wrong rule" and the more you write, the better off you'll be. But sorry, it doesn't work like this. Writing about a rule, even if it's correctly stated, is "wrong" if it's not the rule implicated by the facts.

  For example, suppose your problem concerns whether Ben and Dylan entered into an agreement for Dylan to purchase Ben's house and the problem presented in the facts was whether the acceptance was "timely." If you were to include a lengthy discussion of the Uniform Commercial Code and why it doesn't apply to the sale of a home, you are way off base. There is rarely a need to discuss non-applicable law. I hate to say "never" because there might be a time when you may need to make a comparison or analogy, but a good general rule to follow is not to discuss non-applicable rules. There's hardly enough time to discuss the applicable law.

• A discussion of the "wrong" rule.

There are a couple of reasons why you might have written the wrong rule on an exam answer (see also the next section on *When you have trouble writing the "Rule"*), but one very likely reason is that you didn't begin with a proper identification of the issue. It's relatively simple: if you don't define the legal problem, how do you know which rule to apply?

b. How You Can Tell When it Shows Up in Your Application

In these cases, your discussion may ramble and roam, moving without any logical transition from topic to topic. Or it may simply repeat the facts from the hypothetical. What's interesting, however, is that a knowledge of substantive law may be indicated by the choice of vocabulary, but since what's written doesn't connect with what's asked in the question, the points gained are very few, if any.

Look for examples of the following in the application portion of your essay:

- No connection between the call-of-the-question and the application section of your answer.

  When you're asked a specific question in a problem, then your analysis must be tailored to that question. For example, if your hypothetical asks, *"Was the court correct in admitting testimony of the parties' prior oral agreement?"* then what the grader is probably looking for is an analysis of the parol evidence rule with respect to the facts. If, on the other hand, all you wrote about was the duty of parties to act in good faith in the performance of the contract, then you've completely ignored the question you were asked to consider.

- Facts in the hypothetical are repeated instead of analyzed.

  One very good reason for restating facts instead of analyzing them is failure to work from the legal question. The issue provides focus and direction: it's the "problem" you solve with your "analysis." Without identifying a problem, you have nothing to answer, so you flounder and fall back on narrative.

  - A contradiction or discrepancy between what the rule requires and how the facts are analyzed. This problem is best illustrated by an example. Consider the following:

> *"Sam agrees to supply Murray Inc. at the end of the growing season in August of this calendar year with all the Spud potatoes that Murray Inc. might require at a price of $100 per ton, delivery included."*

You are also told that no specific quantity is stated in the contract but Sam estimates that Murray would need approximately 30 tons based on what other manufacturers in the area and industry require with similar needs. Because Murray is getting such a good price for potatoes from Sam, it decides to expand operations and launch a new product, thereby increasing its demand for potatoes by one-third.

After correctly identifying the issue as one involving a requirements contract and stating the relevant UCC provision, the bar candidate proceeds to discuss a "mutual mistake" in the parties' understanding of how many potatoes would be required. The candidate writes that a mistake was made at to the number of potatoes involved since *"Murray assumed at the time of contract that he would need 40 tons of potatoes but decided after the contract to make a new type of potato chip and would need an additional 20 tons while Sam estimated Murray would need 30 tons."*

This answer is incorrect on several levels:

1. It is incorrect with respect to the rule at issue because the discussion should focus on

whether Murray Inc.'s increased demand was made in "good faith" and whether it was "unreasonably disproportionate" to a stated estimate or comparable requirements;

2. It is incorrect with regard to a claim for mutual mistake since the actual number of potatoes could not be a mistake since no number is defined in a requirements contract; and finally, even if it were a mutual mistake, the mistaken belief would have to be held at the time of the contract's formation, not subsequently. Here the candidate discusses Murray's initial assumption about the quantity and then a subsequent increased need. This is not a legal mistake but an erroneous prediction about the future.

The problem is that the analysis does not follow the requirements of the rule. Instead, there is a serious disconnect between rule and fact, indicating a genuine lack of understanding.

c. Suggested Remedies

The following is a suggested strategy for identifying the legal issue raised by a hypothetical factual situation.

Summary of steps:

1. Begin your analysis by identifying the call-of-the-question.

2. Articulate the issue based on the interrogatory.

3. Develop an outline of what you need to discuss according to the issue.

Learn to think of the issue as your "legal compass" or, if you prefer a sports analogy, think of it as keeping your "eye on the ball." Either way, what happens when you focus on the issue is that you write strong, effective exam answers by discussing the right rule and appropriate facts.

Strive to articulate the issue by formulating the legal question presented by the facts. Ask yourself: *"what is the theory"* or *"what is in controversy"* in these facts. That is the issue. Even in jurisdictions that present such open-ended interrogatories as "analyze fully," you must strive to identify the issues and sub-issues as completely as possible in terms of the relevant rules and which facts bring those rules into controversy. This is the only way to ensure that you'll be on the right path in your analysis.

Now let's see how you might do this:

1. Begin your analysis by identifying the call-of-the-question.

    Does it ask a **specific question** like one of the following

    - Was the court correct in granting the motion for summary judgment?
    - Can the defendant successfully assert the defense of justification?
    - Were the numbered rulings correct?
    - Does the homeowner have a cause of action in trespass?

or does it present a ***general, open-ended question*** like one of these

- Discuss the rights and liabilities of all parties.

- Discuss all causes of action.

- Analyze fully.

2. Articulate the issue based on the interrogatory.

   (a) *When working with a specific question:* identify the legal controversy behind the ruling/ defense/question by asking yourself:

   "What is the theory behind this position?"

   Let's look at some examples. Suppose the call-of-the-question is something like this:

   "Was Ben's decision not to publish John's book exercised in good faith?"

   Do not write as your statement of the issue:

   "The issue is whether Ben's decision was made in good faith."

   This is merely a restatement of the interrogatory.

   Instead, you need to review the facts to determine what is in controversy about Ben's decision, i.e., what he did or didn't do in reaching his decision. After carefully reviewing the facts, you'll probably find that the legal "controversy" is:

> *"The issue is whether Ben exercised good faith in deciding not to publish John's book when he refused to read the revised manuscript and relied only on a preliminary draft."*

Let's look at another example. Suppose you're asked the following:

> *"Did Ben and Dylan have an enforceable agreement?"*

Once again, your task is not restate the question, but to look closely at the facts to see what is in dispute between the parties regarding the agreement and come up with something like this

> *"The issue is whether Dylan's acceptance of Ben's offer to ship the shoes formed a contract when Dylan's acceptance contained a different delivery date."*

By identifying the legal issue as one concerning the formation of a contract when terms in the acceptance varied from terms of the offer, your discussion of the rule and the facts will focus on the UCC's "battle of the forms" and its difference from the common law's "mirror image rule."

(b) *When working with a general-style question:* identify the nature of your task by determining whether you need to identity causes of action, possible defenses, remedies, etc.

3. Develop an outline of what you need to discuss according to the issue.

Once you've identified your issue, stay with it and let it guide you through your analysis. By keeping the issue in sight at all times, you'll avoid getting side-tracked and going off on tangents.

(a) When working with a specific question

- Each issue forms the basis for a separate IRAC analysis. Still, you must remember that there are usually issues within issues. Each main issue is very likely to break down into sub-issues and each sub-issue gets its own IRAC treatment.

- Outline the rule. List any elements or factors. Note only the exceptions or limitations relevant to your facts. The same is true with defenses. Note only the defenses to be raised based on your facts.

- As you write your analysis, work only from your articulation of the rule to guide your application of the facts. Here your statement of the rule provides a blueprint to follow for your discussion of the facts. You simply match up each element/factor you've identified in the rule with a fact, using the word "because" to make the connection between rule and fact.

(b) When working with a general-style question

With this type of interrogatory, you've got more work to do but it's not any more of a challenge if you consider the following:

- Use subheadings to organize your response

  Your choice of sub-headings should be simple and direct. You can organize your discussion around the parties or the causes of action.

- Structure discussions around the issues/sub-issues and defenses.

  If you're working with a fact pattern that's long on issues but short on characters, sometimes it's useful to organize around the causes of action.

  This might come up in a criminal law problem where you're dealing with one actor who's committed a series of possible crimes. Here, you might consider organizing your IRACs around each crime as a way to avoid jumping from one act to another. This will ensure that you focus on one crime and its attendant elements at a time. You'll want to discuss whether each element is satisfied and whether there are any defenses before moving on to consider another crime.

3. When You Have Trouble Writing the "Rule"

There are two separate and distinct problems which can show up in the rule portion of your exam answer. The first, and by far the most troublesome is where there's a genuine ignorance of the law. You may state the wrong rule or refer to the right rule, but state it incorrectly, either in whole or in part. The second problem occurs where there's a demonstration of substantive knowledge, but it's sketchy and incomplete. Here you don't state "enough" rule to provide an adequate context for analyzing the facts.

No doubt these are both very serious problems. However, while the bar exam grader treats both problems alike with respect to the amount of points lost on your exam, we need to figure out which problem is yours. It makes a difference in how we go about fixing it.

a. When You Don't Really Know the Applicable Rule

We've repeated this so many times by now that it should come as no surprise to read once again that if you don't *really* know the rule—by which I mean understand it thoroughly, its elements, its consequences, and how it operates—then you can't answer the question correctly. There's no way to fake your way because the language of the law is precise and your explication of the rule must be clear to allow for a meaningful analysis.

First, let's consider an overview of how this problem "presents" and some general "remedies." Then we'll discuss each one in detail to understand how the problem occurs, what it looks like, and consider some specific remedies.

The Overview:

How you can tell

Look for examples of the following in the "rule" section:

☐ Substituting your words for legally significant language.

☐ Using imprecise language and meaningless phrases.

☐ Relying on buzz-words.

☐ Failing to use legal terminology, thus sounding as if written by a non-lawyer.

☐ Misstating the law.

☐ Writing illogical, disjointed statements of the rule.

Look for examples of the following in the "application" section:

☐ Repeating the facts without stating their legal significance.

☐ Writing logically inconsistent statements.

☐ Failing to distinguish between relevant and irrelevant facts.

How you can remedy

As you well know, there are a number of reasons why you don't know something. The most obvious reason is that you simply didn't spend enough time studying and memorizing the black letter law. On the other hand, a lack of knowledge can result from an inability to integrate and learn legal principles. Sometimes, you may spend adequate time in study but the time spent is ineffective because you're not focused on the right stuff.

In addition to reviewing your notes and memorizing black letter law, you are going to integrate the following tasks into your study plan:

- Re-write the rules of law in your own words while conserving the legal "terms of art."

- Put the parts/elements of rules together in a way that forms a logical whole. Memorize them.

- Having memorized the rules, make sure you understand how to apply them to new fact situations.

- Practice turning rules into issues and questions. Don't stop at memorizing the definition of a "merchant." Learn to ask yourself, "what's the ***consequence*** of finding that the party was a merchant with respect to the transaction in dispute?"

The Specifics:

Now we're ready to get to work. The best way to tell that you really don't know the rule is by checking what you've written for *imprecise or incorrect use of legal language*. When you don't really understand the rule, it "presents" through a failure to use precise legal terminology, incorrect paraphrasing, or the substitution of legal buzz-words for legal analysis. Another way a lack of true understanding "presents" is a failure to use legal vocabulary where it would be appropriate and expected. You want to incorporate the basic vocabulary of each subject into how you think and what you write.

(1). Substituting your words for legally significant language

The language of the law is precise: change the word and you change the meaning. Not only will you change the meaning, but you'll show the bar examiner in a word (sometimes a single word will betray you) that you've totally disregarded the law and failed to appreciate the special meaning of key language. While it's often necessary to paraphrase the rule, it's essential that you maintain the integrity of the rule by preserving the legally significant language.

(2). Absence of legal vocabulary

Like every other profession, the legal profession has its own specialized language and your job upon entering the field is to speak it fluently and precisely. The bar examiners are looking for evidence in your writing that you have learned the language of the law.

(3). Dependence on "buzz-words" without back-up

Now that I've told you to use precise legal language, I'm going to add a *caveat*: don't substitute legal vocabulary for legal analysis—even when it's the right legal vocabulary. While the right word will carry you far, it won't get you there by itself. When used properly, "buzz-words" are an appropriate shorthand for conveying information, but that must be followed with solid analysis where required—which turns out to be most of the time.

b.   When   Your   Statement   of   the   Rule   is Incomplete or Unorganized

First and foremost, the bar examiners expect your exam answer to demonstrate a firm grasp of "black letter law." Quite aside from a sound mastery of legal principles and basic knowledge of core substance, a firm "grasp" of the law means that you know exactly how much detail is necessary to provide for a meaningful factual discussion. It also means that the law is expressed in a logical and coherent manner.

The Overview:

How you can tell

Look for examples of the following in the "rule" section:

☐   "Snippets" of law, buzz-words, and catch phrases in place of complete sentences and full explanations.

☐   Lists of "elements" without definitions.

☐   Identification of the relevant exception but no statement of the general rule to provide context.

☐ Statements of law without a logical connection between them.

How you can remedy

☐ Follow the building block approach to construct your rule of law

    ☐ *Explain* the elements in your rule.

    ☐ *Define* the legal terms.

    ☐ Identify the *general rule* that provides the context for the exception.

    ☐ Include any relevant *federal / state distinctions* or *common law / statutory law distinctions.*

Look for examples of the following in the "application" section:

☐ Solid factual discussion that appears element-based but without any explanation/ identification of the element.

☐ Analysis of the legally-relevant facts but without reference to the supporting legal framework.

☐ Statement of facts but no statement connecting up why that rule is significant in this particular case.

How you can remedy

☐ Build your legal context by working backwards from what you've stated in the facts to determine the scope of the rule necessary to lay a foundation for what you've discussed.

☐ With respect to a fact, ask yourself **why** you found this fact sufficiently relevant to be discussed. This forces you to identify the legal basis for relevancy.

The Specifics:

The challenge for most students is deciding what to include and not writing too much or too little. The other problem is writing the rule in its logical order. We'll break this down into two steps and begin with writing enough of the rule.

(1). Writing enough of the rule

Happily, I can provide a "general rule" when it comes to writing the rule:

Write enough about the rule to provide the context in which you will analyze the facts. The rule and the facts are inextricably linked. Your analysis of the facts will not make sense unless you have first identified the rule which determines the relevance of those facts.

The question we now need to consider is *"how do you know when your statement of the rule is inadequate, incomplete, and insufficient to do the job?"* It's likely to appear as follows:

• You write "snippets" of law, relying on buzzwords and catch phrases.

• You list "elements" without explanation or definition.

- You discuss the "exception" and omit the context of the "general rule."

Look for examples of the following in the rule section of your essay:

- Buzz-words and legal phrases instead of complete fully developed statements of the law.

- "Elements" without explanation

The following is an example where elements or factors are identified but not otherwise defined. Unless you were to develop each further in the course of a factual analysis, this is far too cryptic to serve as the complete recitation of the rule.

> *There are four elements required to form an agency relationship: a. manifestation of assent; b. subject to control of the principal; c. fiduciary relationship and d. act on his behalf.*

Suppose you were given a set of facts and asked to determine whether an agency relationship existed and the *only* information you had to work with was this one sentence. Would you be able to make a determination? As you can see, there are too many gaps in information to allow you to evaluate any facts. After all, you wouldn't know any of the following:

> *Who has to "manifest assent"?*
>
> *Assent to what?*
>
> *What's a principal?*
>
> *What's a fiduciary?*

What does it mean to "act on behalf of an-other"?

The remedy is simple: include more substance by working from the foundation you've created. If you've listed elements, then define them; if you've identified factors, then explain them. You can include this in your essay either in your "rule paragraph" or by weaving the rule into your factual analysis.

• The "exception" without the "general rule"

If you've identified an exception to a general rule as the critical factor in your problem, then you must also include the general rule. A statement of the general rule provides much-needed context for understanding the exception.

A good example of working from the exception to the general rule are questions that test the Fourth Amendment's prohibition against unreasonable searches and seizures and its corollary, the exclusionary rule. Of course such questions are not limited to the Fourth Amendment. Given the nature of the law, the list is practically endless: when is there not an exception to a rule? All this means is that when your task is to analyze whether an exception applies, you want to include a statement of the general rule before you turn your attention to the specific exception brought into controversy by the facts of your problem.

Let's consider the following example: a search incident to a valid arrest.

Example: Fourth Amendment and warrantless searches

Don't just write ...

Pursuant to a lawful arrest, the police officer can make a warrantless search of an automobile if there is reason to believe it contains contraband.

without including the general rule ...

Under the Fourth Amendment, a person has the right to be free from unreasonable searches and seizures by the government. A search will normally be considered unreasonable if it is not conducted pursuant to a validly executed warrant based upon probable cause unless one of the exceptions applies.

(2). Writing the rule in its logical order

There is a structure to follow when writing a rule of law. You should strive to present your statement of the law in its logical order. This demonstrates your understanding of the material and makes it easy for the grader to follow. In the process, it helps insure that you write enough of the law by covering related concepts.

Thoughtful legal analysis requires a logical development and presentation of the applicable law. The bottom line is that you must know how a rule breaks down to write it in an organized manner; you must understand the flow of the rule and how the pieces connect. You must learn and understand not only the individual parts but the links between them.

Writing the rule according to its logical order is really just another way of saying that your writing should be organized. Using these principles will keep you organized without thinking about it— follow them and you're discussion will be naturally organized.

Consider the following hierarchy of concepts when you write the rule:

* Move from the general to the specific.

Your analysis should begin with a statement of the general rule and move to the exception. Moving from the general to the specific is simply the natural order of things.

* Define each legal term of art.

When your statement of the rule contains a legal term of art, your next sentence should be a definition of that term. This is one of the easiest ways to go about building a complete statement of the rule in a logical and methodical manner. The sentences flow almost effortlessly (and seamlessly) because one statement leads naturally to the next.

4. When You Have Trouble Writing the "Application"

This is by far the simplest problem to correct because the essay has the rules in place but fails to analyze the facts. Clearly, the writer implicitly acknowledged the relevance of the facts or he or she would not have recognized the need to discuss that rule.

The Overview:

How you can tell

Look for examples of the following in the "application" section:

☐ Mere repetition of the facts from the hypothetical.

☐ Conclusory statements.

☐ Reliance on such language as "obviously," "clearly," and "evidently."

☐ Avoiding the question to be analyzed by using "if" and "should." For example, leaving the discussion at stating "*if* the breach was material" instead of evaluating whether or not it was. Or turning the question over to the judge—"*should* the court find that the words were constituted a dying declaration"—and then not evaluating whether they were and what consequences would flow from that finding.

☐ There is no mention of any of the individual facts—no use of dates, times, ages, amounts, relationships, locations—nothing that ties the analysis to the specific facts of the problem.

☐ Absence of the word "because."

How you can remedy

☐ Match up each element/sub-element in the rule to a fact.

☐ Use the word "because" to make the connection between rule and fact.

☐ Make sure that every conclusion you reach is supported by an explanation of the "why" behind it.

☐ Make sure you "use" every fact of consequence in your analysis.

The key in writing the "application" and not simply a recitation of the facts from the hypothetical is to understand that application is analysis. It is explaining the legal significance and consequence of each fact. Generally, this is a golden opportunity to rack up exam points because once you've identified the rule, all you have to do is discuss the facts with respect to each of the identified elements. Some refer to this as a "cut and paste" between the law and the facts or a "matching up" of rule with fact. Either way, the end result is the same: a solid legal analysis.

Let's see how this works

We'll begin with the most common form of application error—recitation in place of analysis. Recitation occurs when you've simply rewritten the facts that were given to you in the hypothetical. We can change all that with a word.

a. The importance of "because"

Use the word **"because"** to draw the connection between rule and fact. "Because" is the single most important word to use when writing your application. Using the word "because" forces you to make the connection between rule and fact. You'll find that you can also make use of the words "as," "since," and "when"—they often serve the same function as "because."

b. Conclusory statements

Even if you struggled with "conclusory" statements throughout law school, there is no reason you can't cure the problem for the bar exam—just study the following examples.

What not to write:

The specifications in this agreement are express conditions.

What you should write:

*The specifications in this agreement can be considered express conditions **because** the contract language uses that of express condition **when** it states the hardwood floor "shall be" of a particular type.*

What not to write:

In addition, Newman will say that the oral agreement contradicts the writing of the agreement which is not allowed under the parol evidence rule.

What you should write:

*In addition, the oral agreement contradicts the written the agreement **because** the oral conversa-*

tion between Ben and Newman allowed Ben to wallpaper the kitchen any time while the written agreement specifies that wallpapering must be done after the cabinetry is completed.

What not to write:

In this case, while Pete the police officer was giving Dan a sobriety test, he noticed that Dan fit the description of an eyewitness to the robbery, giving the police officer probable cause to arrest Dan.

What you should write:

*In this case, Pete the police officer realized that Dan fit the description of the suspect, providing probable cause for arrest, **because** Dan had bright red hair, was wearing a green and yellow sweater with purple patches and pointy-toed alligator cowboy boots, fitting the description provided by the eyewitness to the robbery.*

c.   Avoiding analysis with "If"

This is the case where you allude to what needs to be discussed—*if the courts finds bad faith*—and then fail to evaluate the conduct. Either you don't know what it means to evaluate the facts or consider the job done by simply referencing them. In either case, it's a point-buster.

This is an easy fix: show all work. Writing an exam answer is like solving a math problem: if you leave out the evaluation, it's like saying that to solve for X, you need to first multiply and then divide— and then not doing it!

I.   A CHECKLIST FOR LEARNING TO WRITE "BAR–RIGHT" ESSAYS

Have you followed the steps for learning to write "bar-right" essays?

1.   Have you identified your audience?

☐   Are you familiar with the guidelines and information for bar candidates provided by your state's bar examiners?

☐   Do you understand what they expect in an essay answer in terms of tone, specificity of detail, and style?

2.   Do you know what subjects will be tested?

3.   Do you know the composition of the questions on the state portion of your bar exam with respect to the following?

☐   The number of essays?

☐   The number of state-based multiple choice questions, if any?

4.   Based on the composition of the exam, do you know how much time to allocate for each question?

5.   Have you "de-constructed" sample exam questions from your jurisdiction to see:

☐   Whether to expect a *"single issue, outcome specific"* style essay, a more general, *"multi-issue"* style essay, or a combination of both?

☐   How different subject areas are combined within a single essay?

☐ How procedural issues are combined with substantive issues?

☐ How bar examiners use vocabulary to signal issues?

☐ How bar examiners use vocabulary to identify non-issues?

☐ Patterns in questions and how often particular topics are tested?

4. Have you "de-constructed" sample answers from your jurisdiction to learn:

☐ Whether they follow the steps of a basic IRAC analysis?

☐ How to use the "whether, when" construction to state an issue that combines rule with fact?

☐ How to incorporate "distinctions" into statements of the rule?

☐ How to use "signal" language?

☐ How to use "because," "since," "as," and "when" to write a solid analysis that combines law and fact?

J. AUTOMATING THE EXAM WRITING PROCESS

Have you internalized the process of reading and answering essay questions so that it will be automatic on bar day? Do you know to:

1. Allocate your time for each question and set a timetable on scrap paper?

2. Scan the entire exam but return to the beginning to answer the questions in order, while remaining flexible to answer out of sequence if you need to?

3. When you start to read, do you:

☐ Begin with the interrogatory at the end of the question?

☐ Check to see whether it's a *"single issue, outcome specific"* style essay or a more general, *"multi-issue"* style essay?

☐ Note any instructions to follow in writing your response?

4. On reading the entire question for the first time, do you:

☐ Read through the fact pattern to get a sense of the problem and the parties?

☐ Return to the end to re-read the interrogatory and set your focus?

5. On reading the question for a second time, do you read "actively" to:

☐ Identify the area of law and the legal relationship between the parties?

☐ Circle amounts of money, dates, locations, quantities, and ages?

☐ Note such key words as "oral" and "written"?

☐ Characterize legal issues in words rather than underlining?

6. Do you outline your answer before writing and:

☐ Articulate an issue for each interrogatory?

☐ Build a rule of law for each issue by following the Rule Outline?

☐ If necessary, "chart" each rule with the relevant fact(s) for your essay's application section?

7. When writing an essay, do you follow an IRAC-based analysis and:

☐ Use the "whether, when" construction to combine rule with fact when writing the issue?

☐ If appropriate, begin with a conclusion that explicitly answers the question asked?

☐ Consider the rule in terms of context and consequences?

☐ Identify the controlling rule of law with, "***Under the*** *[state the controlling law: common law, federal rule, state-specific statute, etc.]?*"

☐ Write a complete paragraph of law by compiling the building blocks for the rule of law by considering:

- ☐ procedural elements?
- ☐ the general rule?
- ☐ exceptions to the general rule?
- ☐ distinctions in the law?
- ☐ limitations?
- ☐ defenses?

☐ Follow a hierarchy of concepts by:

- ☐ moving from the general to the specific?
- ☐ defining each legal term of art?

☐ Introduce your analysis with *"**Here**"* or *"**In this case**"*?

☐ Match each "element" in your rule of law with a "fact" using "because" to link the two?

☐ Conclude and continue to the next issue?

K.   RELEASED BAR EXAM ESSAY QUESTIONS

The practice materials which follow are released bar exam questions and answers and were downloaded from the websites of their respective jurisdictions. The questions and answers were selected to show a range in approach, substance, and format. For additional practice questions, consult the website for your jurisdiction or the NCBE website.

New York State

    February 2008, Question 1

    Sample Candidate Answers

    Answer De-construction

New Jersey

    July 2005, Question 3

    Sample Candidate Answers

    Answer De-construction

Multistate Essay Exams

    July 2001, Question

    Model Analyses

RELEASED BAR EXAM ESSAY QUESTIONS

NEW YORK STATE

February 2008 Bar Examination

Question Number 1[37]

Ana, Bob and Cal were the sole directors and sole shareholders of Feet, Inc., a closely held New York corporation which owned and operated retail shoe stores. Ana, Bob, and Cal each owned 75 shares in the company. On January 2, 2002, Ana, Bob and Cal signed a written shareholders' agreement which provided in pertinent part:

Upon the death of any shareholder, Feet, Inc. shall, within sixty (60) days of receipt of a written demand from a duly appointed estate representative, purchase the shares of the deceased shareholder for $1,000 per share.

When the agreement was signed, the three directors orally agreed that the buy back provision would apply only if the corporation was making a profit.

In addition to being a director of Feet, Inc., Ana was also a licensed real estate broker and the sole director and shareholder of Ana's Realty, Ltd., a New York corporation. In June 2007, the directors of Feet, Inc., with Ana participating, voted to enter into a contract with Ana's Realty, Ltd. Prior to the vote, Ana disclosed to Bob and Cal that she was the sole

37. This is a released New York State bar exam essay available at www.nybarexam.org/Q & A208.htm.

shareholder and director of Ana's Realty, Ltd. The vote was two to one with Cal voting against the contract. The written contract provided that if Ana's Realty, Ltd. located a store for Feet Inc. to purchase, Ana's Realty, Ltd. would receive the customary commission of six per cent (6%) of the sales price when title closed. Ana soon found a desirable store at a favorable price, and in October 2007, Feet, Inc. purchased it.

In November 2007, Ana sent a written purchase order to Sal, the president of Shoe Co., and ordered 2,000 pairs of boots, to be delivered to the new store on or about December 1, 2007. The terms of the purchase order called for payment in full upon delivery.

On December 1, 2007, Shoe Co. delivered 2,000 pairs of running shoes to Feet, Inc.'s new store. Ana immediately had the shoes placed in an unlocked storage shed on Feet, Inc.'s property and notified Sal that she was rejecting the shoes. Sal told Ana that the shoes would be picked up within the week. However, three days later the shoes were stolen, and Sal told Ana that he was holding Feet, Inc. responsible for the loss of the shoes.

Cal died in December 2007. On February 1, 2008, Executor was duly appointed as the executor of Cal's estate. Executor gave Ana and Bob a written demand that Feet, Inc. purchase Cal's shares of stock pursuant to the written shareholders' agreement. Bob then informed Executor that Feet Inc. had not made a profit for the past three years, and therefore, the corporation would not buy back Cal's shares. Executor has confirmed that Feet, Inc. has not made a profit for the past three years.

(a) Is Feet, Inc. liable to Shoe Co. for the loss of the running shoes?

(b) Was the contract between Feet, Inc. and Ana's Realty, Ltd. voidable?

(c) Is evidence of the oral agreement admissible in an action by Executor to enforce Feet Inc.'s obligation to purchase Cal's shares of stock under the written shareholders' agreement?

February 2008 Bar Examination—New York

As stated by the Board of Law Examiners in its release of questions and answers to bar candidates, "[t]he sample candidate answers ... received scores superior to the average scale score awarded for the relevant essay [and] have been reprinted without change, except for minor editing. These essays should not be viewed as "model" answers, and they do not, in all aspects, accurately reflect New York State law and/or its application to the facts. These answers are intended to demonstrate the general length and quality of responses that earned above average scores on the indicated administration of the bar examination. There answers are not intended to be used as a means of learning the law tested on the examination, and their use for such a purpose is strongly discouraged."[38]

Question Number 1

Sample Candidate Answer 1

A.   The issue is when a seller sends nonconforming goods and the buyer rejects for nonconformance, who bears the risk of loss on the goods.

When a contract is entered into for the sale of goods between merchants, the buyer bears the risk of loss once the goods leave the control of the seller, unless the contract provides otherwise. Where the contract provides that goods are to be delivered to a specific

38.   *See* New York Board of Law Examiners at www.nybarexam.org/pastexam.htm (last visited August 23, 2008).

place, then the seller bears the risk of loss until the goods are delivered to such place. As the contract in this case was between merchants, then ordinarily Ana would be liable once the goods left Sal's control. Because the contract provided that the goods were to be delivered at the new store, Sal bears the risk of loss until Ana receives the goods.

Another issue is when the goods shipped to the seller are nonconforming, what are the obligations of the parties and who bears the risk of loss.

Once the goods are received by the buyer, the buyer has a reasonable opportunity to inspect the goods to ensure they are conforming to the contract before accepting delivery. If the goods are not conforming, the buyer must reject the goods within a reasonable period of time and notify the seller of the rejection. The seller is then responsible for the risk of loss on the nonconforming goods because there has been no acceptance. However, if the buyer does not take reasonable steps to prevent the destruction or loss of the nonconforming goods when the seller has indicated they will retrieve them within a reasonable period of time, the risk of loss transfers to the buyer.

In the present situation, Ana immediately rejected the shipment of nonconforming shoes upon delivery and immediately notified Sal that she was rejecting the shoes. Because of this rejection, Sal still bears the risk of loss on the shoes. Where the seller has indicated they will retrieve the nonconforming goods within a specified period of time, the buyer has a duty to protect the goods from loss for that time period. Here, Ana is under a duty to exercise reasonable care to prevent the loss or damage of the shoes until Sal can retrieve them. By placing the shoes in an unlocked storage shed, Ana has breached her duty to reasonably protect the shoes until Sal can retrieve them within the week. Sal has not abandoned the shoes, because he indicated he would pick them up within a week, and therefore Ana cannot reasonably rely on any defenses that Sal intended to abandon the shoes. In this case, because Ana breached her duty to protect the conforming goods until Sal was able to pick them up within a week, Feet Co. is liable for the loss of the shoes and Sam can recover the value of the shoes as damages. Sam will not be able to recover the shipping costs because they were nonconforming goods. Furthermore, if the shoes had not been damaged because of Ana's negligence, Ana would be entitled to recover from Sam her reasonable damages for storing the nonconforming shoes until Sam had retrieved them. As the shoes no longer exist, Ana is not entitled to recover anything for their storage and she must pay Sam damages for his loss. Sam still has the opportunity to cure his breach of the contract by sending conforming goods because the contract provides that the boots be delivered on or about December 1. Therefore, Sam is not in present breach of the contract if he ships conforming goods (boots) and they arrive within a reasonable time after Dec. 1.

B.   The issue is whether in a closely held corporation, an interested director transaction is voidable because it was not approved by enough disinterested directors.

Interested director transactions are not invalid provided that a number of mechanisms are complied with to ensure the fairness of the transaction. The transaction must be disclosed to the Board of Directors and either all of the disinterested directors must approve the transaction, or the transaction is approved by a majority director when quorum requirements are met. Failure to disclose the transaction before it is voted on renders the contract voidable, however if after the approval the Board of Directors determines the transaction was fair and reasonable and not an improper attempt by the director to abuse their position, then the Board may ratify the transaction.

In this case, the contract is voidable because it was not approved by a majority of the disinterested directors. There are only three directors in Feet Inc. To have quorum would require a majority of the directors present, which is satisfied in this case because all are present, and a majority of disinterested directors must approve the interested transaction. Ana and Bob approved the transaction but because Ana was an interested director, her vote does not count. Therefore, the transaction was not properly approved by the majority of disinterested directors and is void unless the directors determine that the transaction was fair and reasonable. Because of the few directors in this corporation, it is unlikely that the Board will determine that the transaction was fair. Therefore, the transaction is voidable and likely will be voided.

C.   The issue is whether an oral modification to a contract is admissible to determine the meaning of the contract.

The Parol Evidence Rule allows the admission of evidence of the terms of an agreement that the parties intended to be included in the agreement, but were not reduced to the writing where on its face the obligations of the parties are not clear or the terms are ambiguous. Evidence or writings created after the agreement was signed are not admissible under the Parol Evidence Rule.

In this case, the oral modification was entered into concurrently with the execution of the shareholders agreement. The Parol Evidence Rule will allow such evidence to be admissible to clarify the terms of the agreement. This agreement is clear on its face, and does not contain any ambiguous terms and therefore it is unlikely that the parties have any argument to admit the evidence of the oral agreement as parol evidence.

D.   The issue is whether oral evidence of an agreement is admissible when interpreting a contract.

Where the parties have reduced their agreement to writing, it is presumed that the writing contains the entire intention of the parties. Any oral modification after the execution of the agreement is therefore not admissible unless the parties can provide evidence that the oral modification was binding in equity.

This may be achieved if the parties can show detrimental reliance on the oral modification, past performance, custom or business practice.

The present agreement has not previously been judged between the parties, however, if it can be shown that execution of the agreement was induced by the oral agreement, then evidence of the agreement will be admissible to provide an equitable remedy.

E.   The issue is whether the written agreement constitutes the Best Evidence.

The Best Evidence Rules requires that when there is written evidence, such written evidence is the best evidence and therefore the only evidence that must be admitted. The Best Evidence rule applies only to legally operative documents such as contracts.

The written agreement in this case is the best evidence. It therefore will not be contradicted by any oral evidence to the contrary absent an ambiguity in the contract. Because the evidence of the provision to buy back shares only if the corporation is making a profit is oral evidence, such evidence does not satisfy the Best Evidence Rule and is not admissible.

February 2008 Bar Examination—New York

Question Number 1

Sample Candidate Answer 2

A.   Is Feet, Inc. liable to Shoe Co. for the loss of the running shoes?

First, there are no agency issues with respect to the purported agreement between Feet, Inc. and Shoe Co. Ana is a shareholder and director of Feet Inc., and there is no evidence that Anna did not have actual express authority to bind Feet, Inc. to a contract for the purchase of 2,000 pairs of boots from Shoe Co. nor is there any evidence that Sal did not have authority to bind Shoe Co.

Second, there is no evidence that there was not an offer and proper acceptance with respect to the purported agreement. There is no evidence that Ana and Sal intended to form a unilateral contract that could only be accepted by Shoe Co. via delivery of conforming shoes or by Feet, Inc. via payment in full upon tender.

Third, there is no evidence that consideration was lacking for the purported contract between Feet Inc. and Shoe Co.

Finally, there is no evidence of any defense to formation or Statute of Frauds issue with respect to the contract. The contract is for a sale of goods, and thus Article 2 of the Uniform Commercial Code applies; under Article 2, a written purchase order may satisfy the Statute of Frauds with respect to a contract for the sale of goods even if it is not signed by the party subject to enforcement so long as both parties are merchants and the party to whom the confirmation is sent does not timely object.

Thus, it appears that there was a binding agreement between Feet, Inc. and Shoe Co. for the sale of 2,000 pairs of boots by Shoe Co. to Feet, Inc. whereby Shoe Co. promised to deliver 2,000 pairs of boots to Feet, Inc. on or about December 1, 2007 in exchange for payment in full upon delivery.

Generally, under Article 2 of the Uniform Commercial Code, a seller of goods must provide goods that perfectly comply with the buyer's expectations—the "perfect tender rule." Obviously, Shoe Co. did not comply with the perfect tender rule—Shoe Co. delivered 2,000 pairs of running shoes instead of 2,000 pairs of boots. Thus, Shoe Co. breached the contract between Feet, Inc. and Shoe Co. Upon delivery of the nonconforming goods, Feet, Inc. had three options: 1) to reject the entire shipment and seek damages for breach of contract equal to Feet, Inc.'s anticipated benefit from the sale of the boots, 2) to accept the entire shipment and seek damages for the difference between the value of the boots and the value of the running shoes to Feet, Inc., or 3) to reject the shipment outright and seek damages. Ana chose the third option, and rejected the goods.

Under Article 2, a buyer may reject nonconforming goods by providing notice to the seller of the intention to reject within a reasonable time after delivery.

Failure to promptly reject within a reasonable time for inspection after delivery may give rise to an implied acceptance. That does not, however, appear to apply in the instant Case, where Ana "immediately" had the shoes placed in an unlocked storage shed and notified Sale that she was rejecting. It appears Feet, Inc. validly rejected the goods, and Sal acknowledged this rejection by indicating that the shoes would be picked up.

Article 2 requires that a buyer that rejects a shipment of goods must take reasonable steps to protect the goods. Further, it appears that Feet, Inc. bore the risk of loss with respect to the shipment of running shoes. The contract between Feet Inc. and Shoe Co. was a "delivery contract"—it required Shoe Co. to deliver the goods directly to Feet, Inc.'s business location. Under Article 2, the risk of loss in a sale of goods under a delivery contract passes from seller to buyer upon delivery to the buyer's location.

Thus, Feet, Inc. should be liable for the stolen shoes both because Feet, Inc. failed to take reasonable steps to safeguard the rejected shoes (by placing the shoes in an unlocked storage shed) and because Feet, Inc. bore the risk of loss for the goods after delivery by Shoe Co. in compliance with the contract.

B. Was the contract between Feet, Inc. and Ana's Realty, Ltd. voidable?

Ana is both a large shareholder and a director of Feet, Inc. Ana also appears to be acting as an officer

of Feet, Inc.—she was placing purchase orders for
shoes. As a director, an officer, and perhaps as a
controlling shareholder participating in management of Feet, Inc., Ana owes two duties to Feet,
Inc.—the duty of care and the duty of loyalty.

Under the duty of care, Ana must discharge her
duties to Feet, Inc. in good faith and with the care,
skill and prudence of a reasonably prudent person
under the circumstances. A director or officer of a
corporation may be shielded from personal liability
for violations of the duty of care by the Business
Judgment Rule (under which courts generally de-
cline to second guess the acts of corporate
management), through reliance on professionals or,
in her capacity as a director, by an exculpatory
clause in Feet, Inc.'s certificate of incorporation.

However, none of these defenses are available for a
director or officer that has violated the duty of
loyalty. As a director, an officer, and perhaps as a
controlling shareholder of Feet, Inc., Ana must discharge her duties to Feet, Inc. in good faith and with
the conscientiousness and honesty of a fiduciary.
Generally, the duty of loyalty forbids a corporate
director, officer or, perhaps, a controlling shareholder from engaging in self-dealing, usurping corporate opportunities, and making secret profits.

The instant case obviously implicates the duty of
loyalty. The contract between Feet, Inc. and Ana's
Realty is a classic "interested director transaction."
Generally, interested director transactions violate

the duty of loyalty owed by a director to the corporation.

Such transactions do not always violate the duty of loyalty, however. An interested transaction may not violate the duty of loyalty if the directors of the corporation approve the interested transaction by a majority vote of disinterested directors or, if such directors cannot form a majority vote, by a unanimous vote of disinterested directors.

In the instant case, the disinterested directors of Feet, Inc. did not sufficiently vote to approve the real estate brokerage contract. Since there are three directors, two must vote in order to act on behalf of the corporation (there is no evidence that the certificate of incorporation provides for unanimous voting). However, since Ana is interested in the proposed transaction, her vote cannot count toward a majority, although it may count toward a quorum. Thus, both of the disinterested directors—Bob and Cal—had to vote in favor of the brokerage contract in order for it to be an approved interested director transaction. By voting against, Cal denied approval. The contract was voidable by Feet, Inc.

C. Is evidence of the oral agreement admissible in an action by Executor?

Generally, a party may not introduce an earlier or contemporaneous oral "side agreement" for the purpose of contradicting the terms of an unambiguous written agreement. This is known as the parol evidence rule. The instant "side agreement" appears to violate the Parol Evidence Rule. It is an oral side agreement meant to be introduced to add a new term to the shareholder agreement.

There are exceptions to the Parol Evidence Rule. Parol evidence may be admitted to clarify ambiguous terms within the "four corners" of the written agreement. Parol evidence may be admitted if the oral understanding at issue arose after the execution of the written contract. However, in the instant case Feet, Inc. does not seek to clarify the terms of the shareholder agreement but to add a new term—a condition precedent to the unambiguous redemption obligation. The introduction of such evidence is forbidden by the Parol Evidence Rule.

Of course, Feet Inc. may have other defenses to the redemption claim. A corporation generally may not redeem its own stock while insolvent—failing to pay its debts as they come due because a redemption or repurchase constitutes a distribution to shareholders.

ANSWER DE–CONSTRUCTION

NEW YORK STATE

February 2008 Bar Examination

Question Number 1

Candidate Sample Answer 1

As you review this sample answer, note the following:

☐ Adherence to IRAC construction

As we discussed earlier in this chapter, New York essays follow the "single issue, outcome specific" format. Note the candidate's use of a formal issue statement in addressing each of questions. In each case, the statement of the issue leads directly to articulation of the rule, followed by analysis of the relevant facts. This construction is followed for answering each subpart of the question.

☐ Development of the rule section using the "building block" approach

Note how the candidate's answer works from the general rule regarding the buyer's duty to inspect the goods upon delivery and the specific rules regarding rejecting non-conforming goods :

"Once the goods are received by the buyer, the buyer has a reasonable opportunity to inspect the goods to ensure they are conforming to the contract before accepting delivery. If the goods are not conforming, the buyer must reject the goods within a reasonable period of time and notify the seller of the rejection. The seller is then responsible for the risk of loss on the nonconforming goods because there has been no acceptance. However, if the buyer does not take reasonable steps to prevent the destruction or loss of the nonconforming goods when the seller has indicated they will retrieve them within a reasonable period of time, the risk of loss transfers to the buyer."

☐ One-to-one application of rule to fact for a solid analysis section

The candidate's analysis regarding the parties' obligations when the seller ships non-conforming goods is strong because it weaves together rule and facts. Further, it relies on the signal language of analysis to guide the reader and reinforce the message. [italics added]

"In the present situation, Ana immediately rejected the shipment of nonconforming shoes upon delivery and immediately notified Sal that she was rejecting the shoes. ***Because of this rejection***, Sal still bears the risk of loss on the shoes. Where the seller has indicated they will retrieve the nonconforming goods within a specified period of time, the buyer has a duty to protect the goods from loss for that times period. Here, Ana is under a duty to exercise reasonable care to prevent the loss or damage of the shoes until Sal can retrieve them. By placing the shoes in an unlocked storage shed, Ana has breached here duty to reasonably protect the shoes until Sal can retrieve them within the week. Sal has not abandoned the shoes, ***because*** he indicated he would pick them up within a week, and therefore Ana cannot reasonably rely on any defenses that Sal intended to abandon the shoes. In this case, ***because*** Ana breached her duty to protect the conforming goods until Sal was able to pick them up within a week, Feet Co. is liable for the loss of the shoes and Sam can recover the value of the shoes as damages. Sam will not be able to recover the shipping costs ***because*** they were nonconforming goods. Furthermore, if the shoes had not been damaged ***because*** of Ana's negligence, Ana would be entitled to recover from Sam her reasonable damages for storing the nonconforming shoes until Sam had retrieved them. As the shoes no longer exist, Ana is not entitled to recover anything for their storage and she must pay Sam damages for his loss. Sam still has the opportunity to cure his breach of the contract by sending conforming goods ***because*** the contract provides that the boots be delivered on or about December 1. Therefore, Sam is not in present breach of the contract if he ships conforming goods (boots) and they arrive within a reasonable time after Dec. 1."

ANSWER DE–CONSTRUCTION

NEW YORK STATE

February 2008 Bar Examination

Question Number 1

Candidate Sample Answer 2

As you review this sample answer, note the following:

☐ Adherence to IRAC construction

Both Candidates follow the basic IRAC structure, beginning with statements of the issue, followed by articulation of the rule, and then a solid analysis of the facts.

☐ The difference between Candidate 1 and Candidate 2 in response to sub-question (c) regarding the admissibility of the oral agreement in an action to enforce the buy-back provision.

While I cannot know for sure, it would seem that the New York Board of Law Examiners chose these two very different responses to the same question to show a range of acceptable answers—acceptable because each identifies a rule of law and analyzes it with respect to the facts. Candidate 1 takes a rather circuitous route through oral modification, the Parol Evidence Rule, ambiguity, and comes to rest on the Best Evidence Rule. Candidate 2 relies solely on the Parol Evidence Rule and whether the side oral agreement is admissible when it adds a term to the written agreement.

Candidate 1 states the issue as one involving the admissibility of an oral modification to explain the meaning of a contract. Strangely, however, the next sentence does not begin with a definition of a contract modification but with the Parol Evidence Rule. Maybe Candidate 1 was not sure how to characterize the facts that indicated the directors made the oral agreement regarding the buy-back provision "when the agreement was signed." If the oral agreement was made after signing the written agreement, then it would be a modification but if it were made prior to or contemporaneous with the writing, then it is a matter of the parol evidence rule.

It seems that the Candidate might have been confused between the inadmissibility of oral agreements to vary or contradict the terms of an integrated writing and when such agreements are admissible to explain ambiguous terms under the contract principle of Interpretation. Nonetheless, the Candidate proceeded to undo the mischief concerning the misplaced emphasis on an oral modification and ambiguity and relied on the Best Evidence Rule. By redefining the issue as "whether the written agreement constitutes the Best Evidence," the Candidate proceeded to define the rule and apply it to the facts and make a convincing argument. Consider this for yourself:

"The Best Evidence Rules requires that when there is written evidence, such written evidence is the best evidence and therefore the only evidence that must be admitted. The Best Evidence rule applies only to legally operative documents such as contracts.

The written agreement in this case is the best evidence. It therefore will not be contradicted by any oral evidence to the contrary absent an ambiguity in the contract. Because the evidence of the provision to buy back shares only if the corporation is making a profit is oral evidence, such evidence does not satisfy the Best Evidence Rule and is not admissible."

RELEASED BAR EXAM ESSAY QUESTIONS

NEW JERSEY

July 2005 Bar Examination

Question Number 3[39]

Paul, a smuggler, has a cargo van filled to capacity with illegal aliens. While leaving the highway, he realizes he does not have enough change for the toll. Paul decides to go through the EZ–Pass lane even though he does not have an account.

Tollbooth Operator ("Operator") notices Paul go through the EZ–Pass lane without paying, but does not see his license number. The very next driver, however, tells Operator, "I just wrote down the license number of that cargo van! He was driving like he had something illegal in there!" The driver then hands the note to Operator. Operator writes the license number down as well as the driver's statement.

Operator notifies the State Police, who later stop Paul. As the officer approaches the van, he hears hushed voices saying, "Paul's a great smuggler, but he drives way too fast." The officer then arrests Paul and takes the illegal aliens into custody. The federal government charges Paul with smuggling.

At a hearing held at the Department of Homeland Security, the illegal aliens state they are unwitting

---

39.   This is a released New Jersey bar exam essay available at www.njbarexams.org/exam/oldexamsjuly2005.htm. Copyright © 2005, all rights reserved.

victims of Paul. Homeland Security, however, determines the entire group consists of enemy-combatants to be held at the United States Naval Base in Guantanamo Bay.

Unable to post bail and awaiting trial in jail, Paul has an epiphany and calls Guru—a mysticist he saw on TV. During their telephone conversation, Paul tells Guru he wants to talk about his situation. Guru tells Paul, "The spirit always listens to calls for forgiveness." Paul then confesses to smuggling the aliens. Unfortunately, the government was listening and recording the entire conversation.

At Paul's trial, Operator testifies as to the contents of his note, explaining he is unable to remember the license number or the witness' comments he wrote, but he would have written the information correctly at the time. The State Police officer testifies about the vehicle stop, including what statements he heard coming from the van. The prosecution seeks to read to the jury the transcripts of the aliens' statements against Paul made at the Homeland Security hearing, claiming it is too dangerous to transport them to the trial. Finally, the prosecution plays Paul and Guru's telephone conversation in which Paul confessed to the crime.

The defense objects to all the evidence proffered by the prosecution and admitted by the judge. The defense seeks to introduce the testimony of Paul's former army commander, who would have stated Paul was a decorated soldier and would never commit any crime. The judge denies the request. The defense then calls a seasoned ex-FBI agent as an expert to testify that Paul's actions did not fit the profile of a smuggler according to the "FBI's Guide to Profiling Smugglers" and to enter the book in evidence. The judge also denies this request.

The jury convicts Paul, who timely files an appeal. You are the appellate judge's law clerk assigned to write a memorandum analyzing all of the trial court's evidentiary rulings, citing the factual bases and all applicable rules of law.

Prepare the MEMORANDUM

July 2005 Bar Examination—New Jersey

Question Number 3

Candidate Sample Answer 1[40]

OPERATOR'S TESTIMONY

The court's ruling admitting the operator's testimony was correct. The operator's note could be used to refresh the recollection of the operator on the witness stand, as long as it is shown to opposing counsel. The information the operator recounted came from a driver, and the driver's statements are both admissible as hearsay exceptions. The license plate number is a present sense impression, and the statement about Paul's driving is an excited utterance.

POLICE OFFICER'S TESTIMONY

The court's ruling admitting the police officer's testimony was correct. He had probable cause to stop the van, after hearing the operator's information. The statements he heard coming form the van is an exception to hearsay as a statement against penal interest by an unavailable witness. The aliens are legally unavailable because they are in military custody as "enemy combatants." The statement is against penal interest because it identified them as either accomplices in smuggling or the objects of smuggling.

40. New Jersey provides two sample candidate answers for each question. *See* www.njbarexams.org/exam/oldexamsjuly2005. htm (last visited August 31, 2008).

TRANSCRIPTS OF ALIENS' TESTIMONY

The court's ruling admitting the transcripts of aliens' hearing testimony was erroneous. As noted, the aliens were legally unavailable to testify at trial. However, their statements at the hearing were not against penal interest, nor do they fit within another hearsay exception. To admit the transcripts would also violate Paul's 6th Amendment right to confront the witnesses against him, because Paul's counsel had not opportunity to cross-examine them when their original testimony was given.

RECORDED TELEPHONE CONVERSATION

The court's ruling admitting the recorded telephone conversation between Paul and Guru was correct, assuming the police obtained a warrant before tapping the line. Tapping a phone line and listening in or recording constitutes a search for 4th Amendment purposes, so a valid search warrant based on probable cause is required. Since Paul had already been arrested, the police most likely had not trouble presenting probable cause and obtaining a warrant. Paul's statement in the recording, confessing to smuggling the aliens, is admissible as an admission of a party.

FORMER COMMANDER'S TESTIMONY

The court's ruling excluding the testimony of Paul's former commander was erroneous. A criminal defendant may present evidence of his good character in the form of witnesses who have personal knowledge of it. The offer of proof is sparse, but presumably defense counsel would have phrased questions to the commander in the proper way, asking him about his opinion of Paul's character for honesty and respect for the law, and about Paul's reputation in the community for these traits. Such testimony opens the door for the prosecution to offer evidence of the defendant's bad character for the same traits, using the same form of question.

EX–FBI AGENT'S TESTIMONY

The court's ruling excluding the testimony of the ex-FBI agent was erroneous. An expert may testify as to the expert's opinion, as long as the expert is first declared an expert witness by the court. Any publication or other source relied on by the expert in forming this opinion must be one that is considered authoritative in the relevant field, i.e. it is commonly relied on by experts. The ex-agent's testimony about the profile of a smuggler would have been relevant, since it would have some tendency to make the proposition that Paul smuggled the aliens somewhat less probable.

FBI GUIDE

The court's ruling excluding the FBI guide was correct. If an expert witness relied on a particular source in forming his or her opinion, relevant portions of that source may be read to the jury. However, the entire source may not be offered into evidence.

July 2005 Bar Examination—New Jersey

Question Number 3

Candidate Sample Answer 2

MEMORANDUM

TO: Judge

FROM: Law Clerk

RE: State v. Paul–Appeal

This memorandum discusses the trial court's evidentiary rulings in the above captioned case.

I.   OPERATOR'S NOTE—NO ERROR

The operator's note is hearsay. Hearsay is an out of court statement offered for the purpose of proving the truth of the matter asserted. This note that purportedly had Paul's license plate number on it is hearsay, because it was made out of court, and is being offered to prove the truth of its contents (i.e. that Paul drove through the EZ Pass lane). Hearsay is inadvisable unless an exception applies. Technically, this situation presents a double-level hearsay problem because there are two statements involved: the motorist's comments and note, plus the operator's note derived from this hearsay. Accordingly, both statements must fall within the independent hearsay exceptions to be admissible.

First, the driver's statement describing Paul's license plate number qualifies as a present sense impression. As present sense impression is a statement made during or immediately after perceiving an event. The motorists' notation of Paul's plate was a present sense impression since she had just observed him run the EZ Pass lane. Thus it is admissible.

Second, the operator's notation of the motorist's note qualifies as a recorded recollection. A recorded recollection exception applies where the witness once made a writing that was truthful and accurate when made, and attempt to refresh the witness's memory has failed, and it otherwise appears trustworthy.

Operator's statement was made by him/her immediately after being told by an eyewitness what the license plate number was. Operator's present memory has failed. There is nothing to suggest that this in untruthful (in real life, this will be confirmed by the picture of your license plate that they take when you don't pay a toll)(operator said he would have recorded this info correctly). Accordingly, it was not error to permit the pros. to read this to the jury.

II. STATEMENTS OF ILLEGAL ALIENS—ADMISSIBLE

The statements of the aliens are hearsay. They were made out of court and are offered to prove the truth of the matter asserted (i.e. that Paul is a smuggler). Thus, an exception must apply or it is inadmissible.

The statements by the aliens qualify as a co-conspirator exception to hearsay. A co-conspirator statement made during and in furtherance of the conspiracy is admissible.

Here, the aliens turned out to not be "unwitting victims", but rather, enemy combatants. Thus, the trial judge could have determined that a conspiracy existed. The prosecution will likely successfully argue that, at the time it was made the conspiracy still existed, and that the statement "Paul drives to fast" is in furtherance of it; i.e. he shouldn't drive so fast or he'll risk us being caught. Thus, it is admissible.

III.   ALIEN'S STATEMENT AGAINST PAUL

This would violate Paul's 6th Amendment Confrontation clause. The Supreme Court recently held in Cranford v. Washington, that in order for testimonial hearsay to be admissible, in a criminal case, the declarant must be unavailable and there must have been a prior opportunity to cross. In that case, Justice Scalia defined testimonial to include, at minimum, statements in response to police interrogatories, and prior hearings under oath.

In this case, the statements by the aliens to the Homeland Security Dept. at the hearing would very likely qualify as "testimonial" for purposes of the 6th Amendment, because they were made (likely) under oath at a prior proceeding. Accordingly, they must be both unavailable and Paul must have had a prior opportunity to cross-examine them or it is inadmissible under Crawford. Since the facts clearly indicate that the aliens are presently unavailable, and Paul never had the opportunity to cross, it should not have been admitted. Note that this will not constitute reversible error if it was a harmless error beyond a reasonable doubt.

IV.   PAUL'S TELEPHONE CONVERSATION

The 4th Amendment applies when (1) there is a Gov't actor and (2) there is a reasonable expectation of privacy. (see US v. Kate). The 4th Amendment requires either a warrant issued upon probable cause or exception if it applies.

Paul's telephone conversation to Guru from the jail cell in not entitled to 4th Amendment protection because one does not have a reasonable expectation of privacy in phone calls placed from a jail. Thus, this recording is admissible on 4th Amendment grounds. Note also that it is not hearsay because Paul is the defendant and thus it is a party-opponent admission.

V.   FORMER ARMY COMMANDER

This testimony should have been admissible. In a criminal trial, the defendant has the opportunity to "open the door" to presenting character evidence for a pertinent trait. He need not wait for the prosecution to attack it first.

Here, the testimony of the Army Commander the Paul would never commit any crimes should have been admitted because it is pertinent to rebut the inference that he was guilty of smuggling. Thus, provided the defense made an offer of proof, (to preserve this objection) this should have been admitted.

VI.   FBI GUIDEBOOK

The judge erred by not admitting this book into evidence. Although it is hearsay, it qualifies under

FRE 803 (18) as a learned treatise, assuming that one of the experts (or the judge by judicial notice) has recognized it as "authoritative." Assuming that it is indeed authoritative, it should have been admitted (by being read to the jury only) undo [sic] this hearsay exception.

ANSWER DE–CONSTRUCTION

NEW JERSEY

2005 Bar Examination

Question Number 3

Candidate Sample Answer 1

As you review this sample answer, note the following:

☐ The organizational scheme

New Jersey essays tend to require its candidates to "issue-spot" and this question is no exception. Since it asks for a memorandum *"analyzing all of the trial court's evidentiary rulings,"* the answer uses sub-headings based on the testimony to organize the response:

Operator's Testimony

Police Officer's Testimony

Transcripts of Aliens' Testimony

Recorded Telephone Conversation

Former Commander's Testimony

Ex–FBI Agent's Testimony

FBI Guide

☐ Responsiveness to the question asked

The call-of-the-question requires the candidate to analyze the court's evidentiary rulings, providing the relevant rule support and factual basis. Each paragraph in the answer conforms to this model.

Consider the following response regarding the admissibility of the police officer's testimony:

[Conclusion] "The court's ruling admitting the police officer's testimony was correct. *[General rule]* He had probable cause to stop the van, after hearing the operator's information. *[Exception]* The statements he heard coming form the van is an exception to hearsay as a statement against penal interest by an unavailable witness. *[Application]* The aliens are legally unavailable because they are in military custody as 'enemy combatants.' The statement is against penal interest because it identified them as either accomplices in smuggling or the objects of smuggling."

ANSWER DE–CONSTRUCTION

NEW JERSEY

2005 Bar Examination

Question Number 3

Candidate Sample Answer 2

As you review this sample answer, note the following:

☐ Strict compliance with directions by adopting a memo format for the answer

This answer begins with a memorandum heading addressed to the Judge from the Law Clerk as required by the call-of-the-question:

"You are the appellate judge's law clerk assigned to write a memorandum analyzing all of the trial court's evidentiary rulings, citing the factual bases and all applicable rules of law. Prepare the MEMORANDUM"

Interestingly, Sample Answer 1 did not follow this format although it was still selected as a sample answer. While "format" is not a substitute for "substance," it is essential to follow all directions. The inclusion of Candidate Sample Answer 2 illustrates the need to be responsive to the question asked.

☐ A similar organizational structure to Answer 1

☐ Substantive differences between Answer 1 and Answer 2

These sample answers have an important message for bar candidates: there is more than one "right" way to answer the question and that an answer need not be "perfect" to be "point-worthy."

After reviewing numerous candidate answers, it seems that jurisdictions often select sample answers based on the differences between them. The message to candidates would be that there is more than one "right" way to answer the question and that an answer need not be "perfect" to be "point-worthy." This supports the bar examiners' claim that what counts is a well-reasoned analysis of the relevant facts and law, and not necessarily the conclusion reached.

This principle seems operative here because there are several points on which the answers differ:

- ☐ Answer 1 discusses the admissibility of the ex-FBI agent's testimony as expert testimony whereas Answer 2 fails to mention it at all.

- ☐ Both Answer 1 and Answer 2 reach the same result with respect to the admissibility of the Operator's note into evidence, but do so by following very different reasoning. Compare them:

Answer 1:

The court's ruling admitting the operator's testimony was correct. The operator's note could be used to refresh the recollection of the operator on the witness stand, as long as it is shown to opposing counsel. The information the operator recounted came from a driver, and the driver's statements are both admissible as hearsay exceptions. The license plate number is a present sense impression, and the statement about Paul's driving is an excited utterance.

Answer 2:

OPERATOR'S NOTE—NO ERROR The operator's note is hearsay. Hearsay is an out of court statement offered for the purpose of proving the truth of the matter asserted. This note that purportedly had Paul's license plate number on it is hearsay, because it was made out of court, and is being offered to prove the truth of its contents (i.e. that Paul drove through the EZ Pass lane). Hearsay is inadvisable unless an exception applies. Technically, this situation presents a double-level hearsay problem because there are two statements involved: the motorist's comments and note, plus the operator's note derived from this hearsay. Accordingly, both statements must fall within the independent hearsay exceptions to be admissible.

First, the driver's statement describing Paul's license plate number qualifies as a present sense impression. As present sense impression is a statement made during or immediately after perceiving an event. The motorists' notation of Paul's plate was a present sense impression since she had just observed him run the EZ Pass lane. Thus it is admissible.

Second, the operator's notation of the motorist's note qualifies as a recorded recollection. A recorded recollection exception applies where the witness once made a writing that was truthful and accurate when made, and attempt to refresh the witness's memory has failed, and it otherwise appears trustworthy.

Operator's statement was made by him/her immediately after being told by an eyewitness what the license plate number was. Operator's present memory has failed. There is nothing to suggest that this in untruthful (in real life, this will be confirmed by the picture of your license plate that they take when you don't pay a toll)(operator said he would have recorded this info correctly). Accordingly, it was not error to permit the pros. to read this to the jury.

Answer 2 recognizes the operator's note as a double-level hearsay problem whereas Answer 1 identifies the hearsay issue by discussing the admissibility of a present sense impression— without ever defining hearsay. Further, Answer 1 discusses the present sense impression and excited utterance exceptions to hearsay while Answer 2 identifies the qualifying exceptions as the present sense impression and the recorded recollection.

☐ Answers 1 and 2 differ as well regarding the admissibility of the statements of the illegal aliens and the FBI Guide.

RELEASED BAR EXAM ESSAY QUESTIONS

MULTISTATE ESSAY EXAMINATION

February 2001, Question Number 2[41]

Three siblings, Andrew, Brenda, and Charles, are equal partners in ABC Partnership, a general partnership, which owns and operates a 2,000–acre farm. ABC does not have a written partnership agreement. The three partners meet periodically to discuss ABC's business but do not hold formal partnership meetings.

Andrew lives on the farm and manages its day-to-day operations. Neither Brenda nor Charles lives on the farm. Brenda owns an accounting business in town and helps keep ABC's books and records. Charles has an irrigation business in town and helps maintain ABC's irrigation system.

Andrew spent $10,000 to purchase a disease-resistant hybrid seed for the farm. Ordinary seed would have cost $6,000. Andrews purchased the seed in ABC's name, but the $7,000 down payment for the seed was made using his own funds. Charles believes Andrew wasted money on this expensive seed because disease has never been a problem for ABC's farm. Charles is particularly concerned because the balance of the purchase price ($3,000) is due in a

41. The MEE has been "Reprinted by Permission" from the February 2001 MEE. Copyright © 2001 National Conference of Bar Examiners. All rights reserved.

month, and ABC does not have sufficient funds to pay the bill. Brenda and Charles never authorized Andrew to buy the more expensive seed and did not ask him to advance his own money for the down payment.

Andrew spends about twice as much time as his siblings conducting ABC business. Andrew has demanded that ABC pay him for the value of his services, although there is no express agreement that any of the partners should be compensated for their services.

Andrew entered into a written agreement with XYZ Farms to swap 500 acres of ABC cropland for 1,000 acres of woodland owned by XYZ that Andrew thinks ABC could divide and develop for a residential subdivision. Charles disagrees with Andrew's plan and is upset that any land would be sold since, in the 50 years that the farm has been operated by the partners' family, no land has ever been transferred. Andrew defends the swap saying, truthfully, that he and Brenda had agreed to the transaction after all three partners had discussed it.

1. Is Charles liable for any part of the unpaid balance on the seed? Explain.

2. Is Andrew entitled to reimbursement from the partnership or the partners for the down payment he made on the seed? Explain.

3. Is Andrew entitled to be paid for the value of all or part of his services to ABC? Explain.

4. Is the land swap agreement with XYZ Farms binding on ABC? Explain.

February 2001 Multistate Essay Examination

Question 2 Analysis

According to the NCBE, "the model analyses to the MEE are illustrative of the discussions that might appear in excellent answers to the questions. They are provided to the user jurisdictions for the sole purpose of assisting graders in grading the examination. These models are not an official grading guide. Some jurisdictions grade the MEE on the basis of state law, and jurisdictions are free to modify the analyses as they wish, including the suggested weights given to particular points, as they wish. Grading of the MEE is the exclusive responsibility of the jurisdiction using the MEE as part of its admission process."[42]

Legal Problems: (1)   Is a general partner responsible for the debts of a general partnership if the partnership has insufficient funds to meet the debt, when the partners did not expressly authorize the debt?

42.   *See* NCBE, Preface to 2001 MEE Questions and Analyses, at www.ncbex.org/uploads/user_docrepos/MEE2001_MEE2001.pdf (last visited November 8, 2008).

(2) Is a general partner who advances his own funds to purchase goods for the partnership entitled to reimbursement from the partnership?

(3) Is a general partner who contributes more services to the general partnership than the other partners entitled to remuneration from the partnership?

(4) May a majority, but less than all, of the partners bind the general partnership to a transaction outside the ordinary course of business without approval of all of the partners?

DISCUSSION

Point One: (20–30%) <u>Partners are agents of a general partnership for the purpose of binding the partnership and are responsible for the obligations of the partnership.</u>

Andrew purchased the special hybrid seed without obtaining the consent of the other partners. As a general rule, partners are agents of the partnership, and, as such, their acts (including entering into contracts) bind the partnership. Uniform Partnership Act (1969) (UPA) § 9(1). "An act of a partner, including the execution of an instrument in the partnership name, for apparently carrying on in the ordinary course the partnership business or business of the kind carried on by the partnership, binds the partnership, unless the partner had no authority to act for the partnership in the particular matter and the person with whom the partner was dealing knew or had received a notification that the partner lacked authority." *Id*. *See also* Revised Uniform Partnership Act (1994) (RUPA) § 301(1).

In this case, the special hybrid seed was purchased in the name of ABC Partnership. Purchasing seed for a farm, including expensive disease-resistant seed, constitutes carrying on in the ordinary course of ABC's partnership business. Because Andrew has operated the farm on a day-to-day basis, the seed vendor could properly assume that the purchase of the seed was for the carrying on the ordinary business of the partnership and that Andrew had authority to make the purchase. As a result, ABC is liable for payment of the seed.

Partners are jointly responsible for the debts of a general partnership. UPA § 15(b). Under RUPA, partners are jointly and severally liable for general partnership obligations. RUPA § 306(a). Because the contract to purchase seed is an enforceable obligation of ABC, Charles is jointly (and, under RUPA, severally) liable with Andrew and Brenda for the obligation.

Point Two: (20–30%) <u>A partner who uses his own</u>
<u>funds to purchase goods for</u>
<u>the partnership is entitled</u>
<u>to reimbursement</u>.

A partner is entitled to be repaid by the partnership
for contributions to partnership property made by
the partner individually. UPA § 18(a). Since Andrew
made the $7,000 down payment from his own funds
as an advance to the partnership, ABC is obligated
to repay him that amount. *See also* RUPA § 401(d)
("A partnership shall reimburse a partner for an
advance to the partnership beyond the amount of
capital the partner agreed to contribute.") Although
the facts imply that ABC does not have sufficient
funds, Andrew still has the *right* to be reimbursed by
the partnership. Since, as previously stated, each
partner is liable for the debts of the partnership,
Charles and Brenda will also be personally liable for
a portion of the down payment if the partnership is
unable to reimburse Andrew.

Point Three: (15–25%) <u>Partners are not entitled to</u>
<u>be paid for their services to</u>
<u>a general partnership, un-</u>
<u>less the partners have an</u>
<u>express agreement to pro-</u>
<u>vide such payments, but</u>
<u>some courts will allow re-</u>
<u>muneration based on an im-</u>
<u>plied agreement</u>.

Andrew claims that he is entitled to be paid by ABC
for his services to the partnership because he con-

tributed many more services than Brenda and Charles. As a general rule, a partner is not entitled to separate remuneration for services on the theory that a partner's compensation for his or her services is his or her share of profits. UPA § 18(f), RUPA § 401(h).

There are two exceptions to this rule. First, in the case of a winding up of the partnership, a surviving partner is entitled to reasonable compensation for services rendered in connection with winding up the business of the partnership. Since ABC is not winding up operations, this would not apply to Andrew's request.

The second exception is where the partners expressly agree to pay a partner for his or her efforts. The UPA is explicit that the rights of a partner as stated in the Act, including the right to receive remuneration, may be changed by an agreement among the partners. UPA § 18. If partners want to pay salaries, they must agree to do so. Harold Gill Reushlein William A. Gregory, THE LAW OF AGENCY AND PARTNERSHIP § 186, at 275–76 (1990). Here the partners had no express agreement to pay any remuneration to Andrew. On that basis many courts would find that Andrew is not entitled to any compensation for his services to ABC. *Yoder v. Hooper*, 695 P.2d 1182 (Colo. Ct. App. 1984). However, other courts have permitted remuneration based on an implied agreement to compensate a partner but there are no facts here to suggest an implied agreement. *Knutson v. Laner*, 627 P.2d 66 (Utah

1981).

Point Four: (25–35%)   <u>All partners must consent to the land swap by ABC Part nership in order for it to be binding on ABC since the action is outside the ordinary course of ABC's business.</u>

As a general rule, matters outside the ordinary course of a partnership's business must be unanimously approved by the partners. UPA § 18(h); RUPA § 401 (j). Although the UPA and the RUPA do not define the type of acts that are sufficiently outside the ordinary course of business to require the consent of all partners, the facts make clear that ABC's sale of 500 acres of farmland and purchase of land to be developed for a subdivision are not within the scope of the ordinary course of business of its farm operations. While a conveyance of land might be in the ordinary course of business when one partner has been given authority in the past to convey pieces of land, this was not the case here. *See Smith v. Dixon*, 238 Ark. 1018, 386 S.W.2d 244 (1965).

Because the transaction was not in the ordinary course of ABC's business and because it was not unanimously approved by the partners, Andrew's actions did not bind ABC. UPA § 9(2); RUPA § 301(2). Should XYZ claim Andrew had apparent authority to sell the land, that claim would fail because the transaction was not in the ordinary course of ABC's business. The nature of the transaction (i.e., not in the ordinary course of the partnership's business) put XYZ constructively on notice that Andrew alone might not have the authority to engage in the transaction.

CHAPTER 8

THE MULTISTATE QUESTIONS

A. ABOUT THE MBE

Multiple choice questions: You either love 'em or hate 'em. No one is ever neutral about them. And with good reason. Your answer is either right or wrong. There's no middle ground or opportunity for partial credit. On an essay, you can score some points even when you've taken a wrong turn if you provide a thoughtful and well-reasoned analysis of the issues and legal principles involved. No such luck with a multiple choice question.

Regardless of how you feel about multiple choice questions, however, you have to deal with 200 of them on the Multistate portion of the bar exam. And unless you're planning to move to Louisiana or Washington, you can't escape them: as of September, 2008, the MBE is administered in 48 states and the District of Columbia.

The MBE poses a challenge for even the best students. It's a challenge because there are so many questions and so little time. It's a challenge because it tests your knowledge of the substantive law, your reading comprehension and reasoning skills, your ability to work quickly and efficiently, and your capacity to remain focused and functioning over a long period of time.

So what's a candidate to do? You need to prepare properly by recognizing the specific skills that are tested on the MBE and then fine-tuning those skills. The MBE tests two abilities: mastery of the substantive law and the ability to analyze a question. Your bar review course provides you with all the substantive law you need to know; your law school education has taught you how "to think like a lawyer." MBE questions require that you put the two together in a very special way.

B. PRACTICING QUESTIONS

Learning the black letter law is one activity; practicing with it in preparation for the bar exam is quite another. It's not enough to memorize and understand elements and rules of law without some idea of how the issues present and will be tested. Unless you know what to expect and practice applying what you've learned in the format in which it will be presented, you will not be able to perform as well as you should on exam day.

Preparation for the MBE requires that you combine your knowledge of the theoretical with the practical. Your goal is twofold: to acquire a detailed understanding of the substantive law and to master the specific manner in which it is tested. This chapter will show you how to practice questions for the multistate portion of the bar exam, a major component of nearly every jurisdiction's bar exam. Although the examples and explanations use MBE questions, the suggested approaches are applicable as well to preparing for multiple choice questions that may be part of the state-portion of your exam.

1.   Primary Sources for Multistate Questions

a.   Your bar review course

In addition to study materials on the substantive law, bar review courses include hundreds of practice questions. You'll want to use them as you complete sections of the course to help you assess your progress in learning the material.

b.   The National Conference of Bar Examiners

The bar examiners are an important source of questions. Periodically, as old MBE questions are retired, the bar examiners release them and make them available. The experience in working with actual MBE questions is invaluable in helping you gain familiarity with the bar examiner's specific use of language and framing of issues.

If you're like most candidates, however, you're probably thinking that the last thing you need are more "study aids." On the contrary: these are not study aids but insights into the minds of the bar examiners. Besides, after spending upwards of $90,000 on a legal education, now is not the time to be frugal about an additional $50 or so. Since the bar examiners write and evaluate and score the questions, doesn't it just make sense to spend your time getting to know how they frame the questions and what they consider the best answer?

2.   Learning the Details and Nuances

As you can see from the subject outlines, the scope of subject coverage on the MBE is very broad. This means that the questions are spread out over a variety of topics and are not "lumped" in any particular area. Even though it may seem that the topic you dread most is showing up on every other question, this is simply not the case.

The breadth of subject coverage is only one consideration when you study for the MBE: you must also consider that the MBE is a national exam. In answering questions, you're responsible for knowing and applying the *majority rule* and not that of your local jurisdiction. All too many bar candidates forget that the MBE tests the current prevailing view and instead apply the local rule of the jurisdiction to answer the MBE question. To avoid this problem and not be distracted by your knowledge of minority views and local rules, you must wear "blinders" on MBE day.

Practicing the questions is no substitute for knowing the black letter law. And know it you must to answer the questions. A superficial understanding of broad concepts won't be enough to allow you to distinguish between the answer choices. You need a detailed understanding of the rules. As you'll see from the following example, the MBE tests details, not generalities:

On December 15, Lawyer received from Stationer, Inc., a retailer of office supplies, an offer consisting of its catalog and a signed letter stating, "We will supply you with as many of the items in the enclosed catalog as you order during the next calendar year. We assure you that this offer and the prices in the catalog will remain firm throughout the coming year."

For this question only, assume that no other correspondence passed between Stationer and Lawyer until the following April 15 (four months later), when Stationer received from Lawyer a faxed order for "100 reams of your paper, catalog item #101."

Did Lawyer's April 15 fax constitute an effective acceptance of Stationer's offer at the prices specified in the catalog?

(A) Yes, because Stationer had not revoked its offer before April 15.

(B) Yes, because a one-year option contract had been created by Stationer's offer.

(C) No, because under applicable law the irrevocability of Stationer's offer was limited to a period of three months.

(D) No, because Lawyer did not accept Stationer's offer within a reasonable time.

Here the bar examiners are looking to trap those candidates with only a superficial knowledge of the contract rules regarding acceptance and the Uniform Commercial Code's rule regarding "firm offers."

Answer Choice (A) is the best answer because it correctly applies the rules regarding the revocability of an offer to the facts of this problem. A candidate can be easily misled in this question by confusing the UCC's "firm offer," the common law's "option contract," and the general principles regarding the revocability of offers.

Analysis begins with articulation of the issue in the fact pattern. The question is whether and on what basis Stationer's offer was still capable of acceptance on April 15. Because this is a transaction involving the sale of goods from a merchant (Stationer is a "retailer of office supplies" so he is "merchant" within the meaning of Article 2), the offer made in the signed writing of December 15 constituted a "firm offer."

Now you need to summon the rule of law: a firm offer is "an offer by a merchant to buy or sell goods in a signed writing which by its terms gives assurance that it will be held open [and] is not revocable, for lack of consideration, during the time stated or if no time is stated for a reasonable time, but in no event may such period of irrevocability exceed three months." UCC 2–205.

Answer Choice (C) is clearly the bar examiner's choice to catch the unwary candidate who reacts to familiar language and misreads the significance of words in the fact pattern. Here the answer choice states that the applicable rule would limit the irrevocability of the offer to a period of three months and the fact pattern makes it a specific point to observe that four months had passed. While Answer Choice (C) states the rule of law correctly, and it is true that four months have passed since the making of the offer, this does not mean that the offer is automatically revoked. The rule serves only to prohibit the merchant from revoking during this time: it need not be revoked. After the three months, the merchant may choose to revoke the offer or not. Since the offer was not revoked after the three month period when the merchant could have revoked the "firm offer," then Lawyer was capable of acceptance, as the rationale in Choice (A) provides.

3.   You Must Be Prepared

As this one example demonstrates quite nicely, you must prepare for the MBE by mastering the black letter law with a level of detailed sophistication. The bar exam is meant to weed out those with anything less. This is not to say, however, that you must walk into the bar exam expecting to know every single rule of law and its fine distinctions. Even if you had all the time in the world to prepare and the memory of an elephant, this wouldn't be possible or necessary to pass the exam. And that's all you need to do—pass. You're not aiming for an "A" or to be at the top of your class. You get the same license to practice law whether you pass by 50 points or just a few.

4.   How to Prepare

Your preparation for the MBE therefore requires that you combine your knowledge of the theoretical with the practical. Your goal is twofold: to acquire a detailed understanding of the substantive law and master the specific manner in which it is tested. In order to acquire this type of knowledge, you need to prepare by practicing the rules in the context in which they are tested. For example, after you've completed a bar review class on an area of the law and reviewed your notes, you're ready to go to work on answering multiple choice questions.

It's important for you to answer as many practice questions as possible during your preparation period. Issues tend to repeat on the MBE and there are only so many ways a particular topic can be tested. Consequently, the more questions you answer, the more likely you are to encounter all the possible issues and the more prepared you will be for them on bar day. Ideally, you should answer thousands of questions. But just "doing questions" is not enough. There is a right way and a wrong way to "do" questions and you need to know the difference.

5. What Does It Mean to "Do" Multistate Questions?

Suppose you were to sit at your desk and answer as many multistate questions as you could in 60 minutes. At the end of the hour, you check your answers and tally your score. Then you proceed to do another set of questions, once again tallying the number of correct responses at the end of the session. Assuming you have put in a couple of hours and have "done" about 65 questions or so, you call it a day. You pack up your books and commend yourself for studying for the MBE. But did you?

Let's say you answered half of the questions correctly.

1. Does this mean that you "know" 50% of the material?

2. Can you be sure your correct responses were "correct" for the right reasons?

3. Do you know why your incorrect responses were wrong?

4. Did you select an incorrect answer choice because you didn't know or failed to identify the controlling rule of law?

5. Did you identify the correct rule but apply it incorrectly to the facts?

6. Did you misread the call-of-the-question?

7. Did you misread the facts?

Unless you can answer these questions, the hours you've just spent "doing" questions was pretty much a waste of time. This approach doesn't work because while you may have "answered" questions, you've not learned to "analyze" questions. And you must know how to reason through a question to arrive at the correct answer choice. This means that you must follow a process in answering questions, one that enables you to remain focused, in control, and conscious of your thought process.

This is necessary for still another reason when you are studying: if you answer a question incorrectly, you must go back to that question and reread it, recreating your thought process, retracing your steps, and comparing your reasoning in the two instances to find the flaw in your analysis.

C. A TWO–PART PROCESS FOR "DOING IT" RIGHT

It is important to recognize that there is a major difference between taking the MBE on bar day and preparing for that day. On the actual exam, you'll work at optimum speed and efficiency because you're in the "exam zone." This is uniquely true for MBE questions because there is a rhythm to working with them which can be cultivated through practice.

But this isn't what happens during practice sessions. Does an athlete set world records during practice or during the competition? Clearly, then, how quickly you can "race" through the questions during your practice sessions is of little value. What matters is what you learn when you practice and how you ultimately perform on bar day.

Now that I've told you what not to do, it's time to explain what you should do. The "right way" to work with multiple-choice questions during the preparation period is a two-part process. It's about:

- Learning how to read and analyze questions
- Learning how to study from them

1. Part One: How to Read and Analyze Multistate Questions

a. *Reading a question*

Because of time constraints, you'll have time for only one reading of the fact pattern. However, don't make the mistake of sacrificing a careful reading for a quick one. You must read carefully and actively to spot signal words and legally significant facts. Pay attention to the bar examiners' particular use of language and look for the following as you read:

- Relationships between parties that signal the area of law and legal duties: landlord/tenant, employer/employee, principal/agent, buyer/seller.

- Amounts of money, dates, quantities, and ages.

- Words such as "oral" and "written," "reasonable" and "unreasonable," among others.

- Words that indicate the actor's state of mind. These are critical in Criminal Law and Torts questions.

  Look for such language as:

  intended

  decided

  mistakenly thought

  deliberately

  reasonably believed

Since you may write in the test booklet, circle or highlight these words and others which "legally" characterize the behavior of the actors.

Never "assume" facts

The bar examiners carefully construct MBE questions to contain all the facts you need to answer the question. You must rely solely on these facts, and no others, to answer the question. Of course you may draw reasonable inferences from the facts but you cannot fabricate your own or create "what if" scenarios.

In addition to keeping to the facts, don't let yourself go off on tangents based on possible theories you see raised in the facts. Sometimes when you read a fact pattern, you'll see the potential for a number of possible causes of action. In such instances, you must refrain from anticipating what the bar examiners will ask by moving forward on your own and formulating responses based on what you "think" might be asked. This is one of the very reasons you'll read the question stem before you read the fact pattern—to keep from going astray. Potentially, this is just as dangerous as misreading or adding facts. Not only does it lead to possible incorrect answer choices but it needlessly saps your time and mental energy.

Avoid temptation and stick to the law

Just as you must remain focused on the facts as presented in the question, you must apply the rule of law to the facts without hesitation or equivocation. You cannot get emotionally involved with the parties or substitute your instincts for what you know is legally correct. It's not your place to find a criminal defendant not guilty when in fact his actions satisfied every element of the crime according to the statute. Or vice versa: if an act does not violate the provisions of a given statute, then whatever you happen to think about the nature of the act (or actor) doesn't matter. It's not a crime if the jurisdiction doesn't make it one. I cannot say it often enough: your job is to follow the law and apply it to the facts mechanically.

Similarly, the bar exam is not the time or place to become "practical" and consider what you think would happen in actual practice. Many candidates have defended their incorrect answer choices by explaining "I know it couldn't happen like that in practice. That's why I didn't choose that answer." This isn't "real" life. It's the bar exam! This is not to say, however, that bar exam questions have nothing to do with the practice of law or the "real rules." It's just that on the bar exam, as in law school, we are studying and working with the theoretical rule of law and what should be, not necessarily what is. The bar exam is no time to worry about the great divide between theory and practice—simply apply the rule of law as you've learned it to answer the questions and you'll be fine.

b. *Analyzing a question*

MBE questions adhere to a particular structure. There is a story or fact pattern followed by the interrogatory or "call-of-the question." While most questions follow this format, in some cases you'll have one fact setting and a series of questions based on those facts. Here, each of the questions will provide additional facts or change the facts in some way so you must be sure to read each question as if it were a new question entirely.

Perhaps because of the stringent time constraints on the MBE, the tendency to panic is greatest on this section of the bar exam. But when you panic, you're no longer in control. When you give up control, you're at the mercy of the answer choices. Then they pick you, instead of the other way around. I'm not going to let you fall into this trap. Instead, each time you answer an MBE question, you're going to "act" in response to the question presented and not "react" to the answer choices. How do you act and not react to the answer choices? *Simple: you have an answer in mind before you even look at the answer choices.*

There are four basic steps for answering an MBE question. You will follow this sequence for every question you practice and on bar day. After a bit of practice, the process will become second nature to you, although initially it will seem artificial, almost contrived, to approach a question this way. But you'll soon see that it yields results.

For each question, you will:

1. Read the *call-of-the-question* or stem and then read the fact pattern

2. Find the *issue* in the facts

3. Identify the *rule* that addresses the issue

4. Reach a *conclusion* without looking at the answer choices

5. Fill the gap from your answer to the best

answer choice by translating your answer to match one of the options

Let's look at each step in detail:

(1) Read from the "bottom up"

Begin each MBE question by reading the question stem. Reading the interrogatory first serves two important functions:

- It helps to identify the area of law. Often, but not always, you can determine the subject area of the problem from the call-of-the-question. Then you can use this information to inform your subsequent reading of the fact pattern.

- It often identifies the point of view you must adopt to answer the question. For example, if you're asked to determine a party's most likely claim or best defense, then you'll want to read the fact pattern with an emphasis on that party's point of view.

(2) Find the issue in the facts

Note: While MBE questions are issue-based, ana-
lytical questions, not every multiple choice
question is structured this way. Sometimes
the question is straightforward and you
either know the answer or you don't. If you
have one of these questions, you'll eliminate
the issue-formation steps.

After reading the interrogatory, you're ready to read the fact pattern and find the issue. Your ability to identify the main issue in each question is crucial to selecting the correct answer choice. For most candidates, it's not intuitive to engage in an IRAC analysis to answer an objective multiple choice question. However, MBE questions are organized around a central issue in the fact pattern and individual issues in each of the responses. The only way to distinguish between the answer choices is to identify the legal question raised in the fact pattern.

The process is the same you use to spot issues in essay questions. After you read the call-of-the-question ask, *"What is the legal theory behind this question?"* As soon as you've identified the legal theory, you're in a position to articulate the rule of law that addresses that issue.

(3) Move from the issue to the rule to articulation of the answer

After you've identified the issue raised in the facts, determine the appropriate rule of law, apply the rule to the facts, and reach a conclusion—all without so much as a peek at the answer choices. By determining the appropriate outcome before looking at the answer choices, you're in control and not at the mercy of the bar examiners' distractors.

However, this approach is not practical when you have the type of question where the answer choices provide additional information which must be individually evaluated. This happens where you're asked a question such as

"Which of the following questions will NOT present a substantial issue in Plaintiff's claim for damages"

as opposed to

"Will Dan prevail?"

In the first example, you must consider the merits of each individual answer choice before you can make a decision whereas in the second you can form your own answer based solely on the fact pattern.

(4) Fill the gap from "answer" to "answer choice"

After you've decided what the answer should be, you're ready to look at the answer choices. Don't expect the bar examiners to phrase the answer in precisely the words you're looking for—these words won't be there. Instead, you'll have to "fill the gap" between your words and the words the bar examiners have chosen to express the answer. And they do such a good job of camouflage that candidates often don't recognize the correct response even though it "says" exactly what they want! ***Sometimes it's a matter of determining which of the answer choices leads to the same result.***

Consider the following MBE question, where the array of answer choices nicely illustrates the dangers that await the unwary candidate:

Hydro–King, Inc. a high-volume, pleasure-boat retailer, entered into a written contract with

Boater, signed by both parties, to sell Boater a power boat for $12,000. The manufacturer's price of the boat delivered to Hydro–King was $9,500. As the contract provided, Boater paid Hydro–King $4,000 in advance and promised to pay the full balance upon delivery of the boat. The contract contained no provision for liquidated damages. Prior to the agreed delivery date, Boater notified Hydro–King that he would be financially unable to conclude the purchase; and Hydro–King thereupon resold the same boat that Boater had ordered to a third person for $12,000 cash.

If Boater sues Hydro–King for restitution of the $4,000 advance payment, which of the following should the court decide?

(A) Boater's claim should be denied, because, as the party in default, he is deemed to have lost any right to restitution of a benefit conferred on Hydro–King.

(B) Boater's claim should be denied, because, but for his repudiation, Hydro–King would have made a profit on two boat sales instead of one.

(C) Boater's claim should be upheld in the amount of $4,000 minus the amount of Hydro–King's lost profit under its contract with Boater.

(D) Boater's claims should be upheld in the amount of $3,500 ($4,000 minus $500 as statutory damages under the UCC).

In this question, the issue is what, if anything, is a buyer entitled to when the buyer repudiates a sale and the seller re-sells the item but would have sold it to the second buyer anyway? It's the classic case of the lost volume seller. Application of the rule tells us that the seller is entitled to receive his lost profit on the first deal—the one he made with the repudiating seller. Under these facts, that would be $2,500 (the sales price of $12,000 minus the manufacturer's cost of $9,500). So Hydro–King would have made a $2,500 profit from Boater and is entitled to keep $2,500 of the $4,000 advance payment and Boater gets back $1,500.

Now I'm ready to find this answer among the answer choices. Of course, it's not going to appear in precisely these words. Instead, I'll have to determine which of the answer choices leads to the same result. Answer Choice (C), the correct answer, effectively states the result I've reached. Boater's claim is $4,000—less Hydro–King's lost profit. Answer Choice (B) is not completely correct because while it acknowledges Hydro–King's entitlement to its profit on both sales, it requires that Boater's claim be denied in its entirety. As we know, this need not be the case where, as here, the advance payment was in excess of the lost profit.

c.   *Analyzing the answer choices*

It is important to recognize that analysis of the answer choices deserves as much of your time and attention as the fact pattern or story. Maybe more.

(1) Identify the issue in each answer choice

Not only is there an "issue" in the fact pattern, but there is an "issue" in each answer choice. Actually, it's more of a legal theory that's operating in each of the answer choices and unless you figure out the individual theories, you won't be able to distinguish between the answer choices. Only the issue that addresses and answers the one presented in the fact pattern can be the correct answer choice.

(2) If necessary, use "the process of elimination"

Sometimes, despite all your best efforts to work through a question according to the process outlined here, you may find that the only way to arrive at an answer choice is through the process of elimination. As we discussed, the bar examiners are particularly adept at "hiding the ball" by expressing the correct answer in a way that's less than obvious.

In these cases, you'll have to examine each of the answer choices and eliminate those that can't possibly be correct. You've already learned how to eliminate an incorrect answer choice based on whether its legal theory addresses the issue in the fact pattern. Now you'll learn some other common devices for eliminating incorrect answer choices. Even though you may be using techniques to answer the questions, you're still "acting" and not merely "reacting" to whatever sounds reasonable.

When can't an answer choice be correct?

(a) When it's not completely correct

The first rule for eliminating incorrect answer choices is that an answer choice must be entirely correct or it is wrong. For example, suppose an answer choice recites a correct statement of the rule of law but its application to the facts in the problem is flawed. Or vice versa: perhaps the answer choice is factually correct but cites an inapplicable rule. In each case, the answer choice is incorrect and can be eliminated. Don't be misled simply because the statement is partially correct.

(b) When it misstates or misapplies a rule of law

Here's where solid preparation on learning the black letter law is essential. You need to know the law to distinguish between answer choices that misstate or misapply the law.

Some common examples include the following:

- Answer choices that improperly identify the requisite elements of a crime or tort by either overstating or understating the necessary elements.

- Answer choices that rely on inapplicable principles of law.

  For example, since the MBE has adopted Article 2 of the Uniform Commercial Code, you must be sure to apply its principles to questions involving transactions in goods. If you apply a common law rule to resolve the issue, you'll reach the wrong result and you can be sure it's one of the answer choices purposely included to distract you. For instance, where the common law and the UCC diverge on such points as the requirements for modifications, option contracts, and acceptances, the bar examiners find fertile grounds for test questions.

This is by no means limited to contracts. Look for similar situations to arise in other areas of law. Evidence questions are another good example. Here the potential conflict is between the Federal Rules of Evidence, the common law, and the rules of your particular jurisdiction. The MBE requires that Evidence questions be answered according to the Federal Rules.

• Answer choices that rely on the minority rule instead of the majority rule.

The rule to be applied on the MBE is the majority rule, not the minority. It no longer matters what your Contracts or Torts professor argued "should" be the prevailing view; what counts on the MBE is the modern, prevailing view. Learn it and apply it unless directed otherwise.

(c) When the answer choice mischaracterizes the facts

Once again, active reading skills will go far in detecting this type of error. Look for contradictions between the facts in the story and the facts as characterized in the answer choice. Such an answer choice cannot be correct. Nor can an answer choice that requires you to make assumptions that go beyond the facts in the fact pattern. While it's often necessary to make reasonable inferences, you should never have to add facts to arrive at the correct answer choice. If the bar examiners want you to consider additional or different facts, they will provide them.

(3) Watch out for "because," "if," and "unless"

Just when you thought it safe to answer a question, leave it to the bar examiners to muddy the waters with a single word. You'd think it would be enough to have four answer choices to test a candidate's ability to work through the details without resorting to further modification of the text of each alternative. But the bar examiners are experts at getting the most out of a question. With a single, well-placed word such as "because," "if," or "unless," they're able to transform the entire meaning of a sentence—and unless you're careful, your score!

While doable, dealing with "because," "if," and "unless" takes a bit of practice. It also takes active and careful reading. A "modifier"—whether it's "because," "if," "unless," or some equivalent—is used in the answer choice to connect the "conclusion" (the outcome to the interrogatory) with the "reasoning" in support of that conclusion. For example, an answer choice might state,

> "Yes, because Dan was a third-party beneficiary of the original Smith–Jones agreement."

Here, "yes" is the "conclusion" or direct answer to the question asked; "Dan was a third-party beneficiary" is the reason that supports the conclusion; and "because" is the link between the two.

(a) Working with "because"

On the MBE, "because" is the predominant modifier and the simplest to master. The following is a typical "because" answer choice:

> "Succeed, because Ben had promised her that the offer would remain open until May 15."

Such "because" statements are relatively straightforward. Simply ensure that the reasoning supports the conclusion both on a factual and legal basis. If either is incorrect, then the entire answer choice is incorrect and can be eliminated.

> In addition to "because," remember to look for words that act like "because" in answer choices such as "since" and "as." These words are synonyms and serve the same function as "because." Your analysis will be the same.

(b) Working with "if"

Unlike "because," when "if" is the answer choice modifier, you need determine only whether the reasoning could support the conclusion. It need not always be true, but only possible under the facts in the hypothetical. Be alert to possible "if" synonyms: "as long as" and "so long as." Remember, "if" is a conditional word and words of condition will be the trigger in such instances.

Consider the following example from a past MBE:

Dora, who was eight years old, went to the grocery store with her mother. Dora pushed the grocery cart while her mother put items into it. Dora's mother remained near Dora at all times. Peterson, another customer in the store, noticed Dora pushing the cart in a manner that caused Peterson no concern. A short time later, the cart Dora was pushing struck Peterson in the knee, inflicting serious injury.

If Peterson brings an action, based on negligence, against Dora's mother, will Peterson prevail?

(A) Yes, if Dora was negligent.

(B) Yes, because Dora's mother is responsible for any harm caused by Dora.

(C) Yes, because Dora's mother assumed the risk of her child's actions.

(D) Yes, if Dora's mother did not adequately supervise Dora's actions.

Let's examine the "if" answer choices employing our understanding that an "if" answer need only be plausible, based on the facts, to be correct. Remember, before you get to the answer choices, you've already formulated your own possible answer based on the interrogatory. Here, since the problem is based on an action brought in negligence, your mind should be ticking off the elements of a negligence claim: duty, breach, causation, harm.

Answer Choice (A) states that Peterson will prevail in a negligence action *if* Dora was negligent. The question stem states, however, that Peterson brought the negligence action against Dora's mother, not Dora. Thus, since Answer Choice (A) doesn't directly address the question, it can't be the best answer.

On the other hand, Answer Choice (D) addresses the issue of Dora's mother's actions. It poses the situation where Dora's mother did not adequately supervise Dora. You need to ask yourself whether in this instance a finding of negligence is possible: does Dora's mother have a duty to supervise her child and would she have breached that duty if she failed to do so? In this case, she would be negligent so (D) is the correct answer choice.

(c) Working with "unless"

In its own way, "unless" is as restrictive as "because." For an "unless" answer choice to be correct, it must present the *only* circumstance under which the conclusion cannot happen. If you can conceive of even one other way the result could occur, then the answer choice cannot be correct.

Consider the following example from a past MBE.

David built in his backyard a garage that encroached two feet across the property line onto property owned by his neighbor, Prudence. Thereafter, David sold his property to Drake. Prudence was unaware, prior to David's sale to Drake, of the encroachment of the garage onto her property. When she thereafter learned of the encroachment, she sued David for damages in trespass.

In this action, will Prudence prevail?

(A) No, unless David was aware of the encroachment when the garage was built.

(B) No, because David no longer owns or possesses the garage.

(C) Yes, because David knew where the garage was located, whether or not he knew where the property line was.

(D) Yes, unless Drake was aware of the encroachment when he purchased the property.

Let's look at Choice A, the first of our two "unless" answer choices. Applying the "unless" strategy, you would ask yourself: "Is there any way Prudence could prevail if David was unaware of the encroachment when the garage was built?" Remember, as soon as you read the call-of-the-question, you considered the definition of trespass: one who intentionally enters the land of another. All David had to do was intend to build the garage and then build it. It doesn't matter whether he was aware or unaware of the encroachment in order to commit a trespass. Consequently, Prudence could prevail and Choice A cannot be correct.

Now let's look at Choice D. This answer choice brings Drake, the subsequent purchaser of the property, into the picture. Here's a good example of eliminating an answer choice because it doesn't address the issue in the problem. Prudence has brought the trespass action against David, not Drake. Assuming, however, that you didn't see this and instead was transfixed by the "unless" modifier, you'd come to the same result but it would take longer. You'd ask, "Is there any way Prudence could prevail if Drake was unaware of the encroachment when he purchased the property?" Now you'd see that Prudence could prevail in an action against David if Drake was unaware of the encroachment. Whether Prudence has an action in trespass against Drake is simply not the issue in this question and should not be a factor in your analysis.

Choice C is the correct answer choice. The reasoning addresses the central issue in the problem which is whether David committed a trespass. What Choice C states is right on point—both legally and factually. Legally, David would have committed a trespass if he intentionally entered the land of another. The facts tell us that David built a garage that encroached on his neighbor's property. Choice C fits all the criteria and must be correct.

(4) If you must guess, do so with a strategy

While it sounds like an oxymoron to "guess with a strategy," it's true nonetheless. You've absolutely nothing to lose by guessing since there are no penalties for incorrect answers on the MBE. Even if you can narrow the odds only slightly, you've got a decent shot at making a correct selection.

(a) Eliminate all the obviously incorrect answer choices

Usually you can safely eliminate one or even two responses as incorrect. Now that you've narrowed the field a bit, even if it's a little bit, you're ready to make the most of some informed guesses.

(b) Dismiss answer choices that address other principles or unrelated rules of law.

Of course the bar examiners won't be so obvious as to include Evidence principles in answer choices for Contracts questions, but they will include common law rules in Article 2 Sales problems and cite standards for negligence when strict liability is at issue.

Similarly, be alert to answer choices that seem to be from the applicable body of law but really are not. Such distractors are common in "cross-over" areas where the distinctions between subjects are blurred and somewhat artificial. For example, problems in Criminal Procedure may contain answer choices that draw on rules from Constitutional Law and Evidence. Remember, it's the law school that imposes boundaries around the law for pedagogical purposes. The law itself does not impose such rigid demarcations.

On the other hand, do not be quick to dismiss all such cross-overs. Remember, contracts for the sale of land, while topically in Property Law, still require application of contract principles. And breach of warranty, while a traditional contract claim, is often asserted in products liability actions.

(c) Find your compass—the issue

When in doubt anywhere on the bar exam—the essays, the MPT, or the MBE—remember that the legal issue is your guide. It allows you to distinguish between relevant and irrelevant rules and facts, thus providing the single most effective answer choice eliminator.

Reread the question and focus solely on finding the issue in the fact pattern. Then identify the issue in each of the answer choices. One answer should be responsive to the issue in the fact pattern.

(d) Be wary of words which speak in absolutes

Assuming that the issue is disguised, then you still need to distinguish between answer choices. In this case, carefully consider statements that include such words as "always," "never," and "must." No doubt you learned as a first year law student that there are few if any certainties in the law. For practically every rule, there is an exception—if not two or three. Use this knowledge wisely and be wary of answer choices which include words of certainty. *If you can think of just one instance where it wouldn't be true, then the statement can't possibly be your best choice and you can safely eliminate it.*

(e) Finally, after you've given it your best shot, move on

With only 1.8 minutes per question, there's only so much time to allow for doubt. No matter how well you've prepared, there are bound to be questions that present difficulty. Just don't dwell on them or you'll squander precious time that could be spent on questions you can answer.

2. Part Two: How to Practice Multiple-choice Questions

This part of your work is about how to study from the questions to learn the law. It focuses on developing your knowledge of the substantive law by working through targeted, subject-specific questions.

a.   The difference between studying and taking the exam

There is a huge difference between studying for the exam and taking it. Yet the more I work with students, the more I realize that they don't know the difference.

When studying, your primary goal is to learn the black letter law and how the bar examiners test that law. It is to use the questions to learn the material and find out what you don't know and why. At this point, it is not to test and grade yourself. However, our instinct when working with multiple-choice questions is to choose an answer, check it, and move on to the next question. Or we "do" blocks of questions and tally up the score, taking comfort if the number of correct answers choices are greater than 50%. In either case, no real knowledge is gained and genuine learning opportunities are lost.

b.   Here's what you should be doing

Suppose you are trying to answer a question and find you're not quite sure of the rule. You can't identify all the elements or you can't recall the specific language of the exception. Now is the time to look it up. It is not "cheating" to look up the rule to help you work through an analysis of the question. This is learning through repetition and reinforcement. The process of going back to your subject outlines and study notes to help you work through a specific problem is learning in context and an essential part of the study process.

Consider the following approaches when using multiple-choice questions to study the black letter law. They ensure a maximum return on your investment of time and effort.

(1) The "numbers" factor and de-constructing MBE questions

As mentioned earlier, you should be prepared to answer hundreds, if not thousands, of multiple-choice questions. Having said that, it is not so much the quantity of questions that you answer as the quality of the process involved in answering each question.

If you answer a question according to the process outlined here for analyzing a question and its answer choices, you will be reviewing four to five related rules of law each time you work your way through a single question. Not only are you working with multiple rules per question, but the rules are related by issue and presented in a factual context which aids in memory retention. You will remember the rules of law you learn in association with these multiple-choice questions because they are rooted in a factual context.

Let's see how this works. Consider the following MBE question:

Frank owned two adjacent parcels, Blackacre and Whiteacre. Blackacre fronts on a poor unpaved public road, while Whiteacre fronts on Route 20, a paved major highway. Fifteen years ago, Frank conveyed to his son, Sam, Blackacre "together with a right-of-way 25 feet wide over the east side of Whiteacre to Route 20." At that time, Blackacre was improved with a ten-unit motel.

Ten years ago, Frank died. His will devised Whiteacre "to my son, Sam, for life, remainder to my daughter, Doris." Five years ago, Sam executed an instrument in the proper form of a deed, purporting to convey Blackacre and Whiteacre to Joe in fee simple. Joe then enlarged the motel to 12 units. Six months ago, Sam died and Doris took possession of Whiteacre. She brought an appropriate action to enjoin Joe from using the right-of-way.

In this action, who should prevail?

(A) Doris, because merger extinguished the easement.

(B) Doris, because Joe has overburdened the easement.

(C) Joe, because he has an easement by necessity.

(D) Joe, because he has the easement granted by Frank to Sam.

It is easy enough to see that to answer this question, you must know the rule regarding easements. But clearly you need to know more than just the basic definition to answer this question. If used properly, this question and its four answer choices provide an opportunity for you to review the general rule of easements and four inter-related issues:

- creating easements
- terminating easements
- nature and types of easements
- transferring easements

Here's where most bar candidates fail to make use of a critical learning opportunity: instead of taking the time to analyze each of the answer choices and review the substantive law implicated in each, the candidate selects an answer and moves on. Of course this is the proper way to proceed on the exam or when practicing under simulated test conditions but not when you're studying. It's incorrect because even if you've selected the correct answer, you need to make sure you know *why* each of the other answer choices is incorrect. It's not enough to have a vague understanding of why they are wrong: you must be able to fully articulate the reason based on the applicable rule of law.

I can practically hear you thinking that there's not enough time in the world to study this way and certainly not when preparing for the bar exam. Once again, you're wrong. To borrow a very old, but appropriate expression, you're being "penny wise and pound foolish."

That's because of the way MBE questions are constructed. Answer choices are carefully crafted to represent the range of issues associated with the main issue in the question. Consequently, while it might be the incorrect answer choice for this question, it might be the right answer next time, given a different emphasis in the fact pattern. As I mentioned earlier, issues tend to repeat on the MBE and there are only so many ways a particular topic can be tested. You need to know the main issues and the related bundle of sub-issues and there is no better way to see how they come together than by de-constructing each MBE question during your study time.

Since I know you cannot read a multiple-choice question without answering it, the correct answer to this question is (D). Can you explain why? Can you explain why each of the other answer choices is incorrect?

(2) How long this takes

It should take approximately 1½ to 2 hours to answer about 15 to 20 questions if you work through them the way I've just outlined. This may seem like a very long time to do so few questions but if you consider that you've reviewed approximately 30 to 40 points of law in the process, then you'll realize just how much you've learned.

(3) The timing factor

Although we discussed the importance of incorporating timed practice exams into your study schedule in an earlier chapter, it's important to review it again with respect to practicing MBE questions.

If your goal when practicing Multistate questions (or any part of the exam) is to learn from the questions, then how long it takes to read and answer a question is not the primary concern. Rather, it's whether you absorbed anything meaningful from the exercise. It doesn't matter how long it takes to answer a question, but whether you answered the question correctly and did so for the correct reason. Even without focusing on the clock, your speed will increase naturally with practice as you become comfortable with the process of analyzing questions and more competent with the law.

Still, I strongly recommend that you include a minimum of two or three "timed" sessions when preparing for the MBE. The first session should occur about three weeks into your review period and be devoted to determining whether you can meet the general guideline of answering 17 questions in a 30–minute period. You must average 33–34 questions per hour to complete the 100 questions in the three-hour MBE sessions.

Also, you should plan to include at least one practice session to be a simulation of a complete three-hour test period covering 100 questions. This should occur about two weeks before the actual bar exam. You need to know whether you can sustain your concentration for such a long period of time. It's a very different experience to answer 100 questions than it is to answer 25 questions. It's also a different experience when the questions come at you in a completely random manner as opposed to the topical approach you've been following during your practice sessions where you know the general subject matter of the questions. Unless you've had an opportunity to perform under these conditions, you won't be able to assess your performance accurately.

Assuming your test session begins at 9:15 and ends at 12:15, the following is a timetable with appropriate milestones:

Time	Question Number
9:45	17
10:15	33
10:45	50
11:15	67
11:45	84
12:15	100

c. *When to practice questions*

You are not ready to work with questions until you've studied the black letter law. There is limited value, if any, in trying to answer questions before you've studied the rules. But working through questions *after* you've studied will give you a pretty good indication of what you know and what you still have to learn.

Still, this doesn't mean that you can afford to wait too long before you move from studying your notes to answering questions. Working with rules as you learn them by applying them in the context of new factual situations is the most effective way to find out what you really know. You should incorporate questions as part of your study plan as soon as you've covered a topic in your bar review course.

You are ready to begin practicing questions when you have:

- Completed the sessions of your bar review class in an area of the law, and

- Reviewed your notes with a focus on the black letter law

Note: *Do not wait until you feel you have memorized the black letter law before you begin practicing questions. You will learn the law as you work through the questions.*

d.   Target a topic

Let's assume you've attended the bar review lectures on contract formation under both the common law and the UCC. You've reviewed your notes and otherwise "studied" contract formation. You're convinced that you pretty much know what you need to know about offer and acceptance.

Now, and only now, are you ready to apply what you've learned to answering the questions.

Begin by selecting a group of questions from the specific area of law you've just reviewed. In this case, you're going to answer only questions dealing with contract formation issues.

Note: *When you order sample MBE questions from the bar examiners, you're sent an actual 200–item exam. Therefore, you'll have to peruse the answer key which identifies questions by topic. Select a topic and make a list of those question numbers on* *your answer sheet. Follow the list when answering the questions.*

By practicing groups of questions in a particular area of the law, you can:

*   Identify your strengths and weaknesses

If you consistently answer questions dealing with a particular rule of law incorrectly, this means that you need to return to your notes and review that topic more thoroughly before attempting more MBE questions. You simply don't know the law well enough.

*   Begin to see patterns in the facts

When you practice questions of a particular type together, you can see their common characteristics and realize that there are only so many variations of a fact pattern with respect to a single legal issue. This allows you to become familiar with the way particular topics are tested. As a result, your comfort level increases.

*   Become familiar with the bar examiners' specific use of language

In addition to becoming familiar with the types of facts that invoke certain rules, by working with groups of questions in a particular area, you also become accustomed to the bar examiners' very specific use of vocabulary. Frequently, the difference between a correct and incorrect answer choice turns on the meaning and significance attached to particular language in the fact pattern. Your ability to identify such words is critical and only practice with actual MBE questions will provide the opportunity to gain this familiarity.

The following example shows that you must be attuned to the signals in the language as well as the rules:

Structo contracted with Bailey to construct for $500,000 a warehouse and an access driveway at a highway level. Shortly after commencing work on the driveway, which required for the specified level some excavation and removal of surface material, Structo unexpectedly encountered a large mass of solid rock.

For this question only, assume the following facts. Structo informed Bailey (accurately) that because of the rock the driveway as specified would cost at least $20,000 more than figured, and demanded for that reason a total contract price of $520,000. Since Bailey was expecting warehousing customers immediately after the agreed completion date, he signed a writing promising to pay the additional $20,000. Following timely completion of the warehouse and driveway, which conformed to the contract in all respects, Bailey refused to pay Structo more than $500,000.

What is the maximum amount to which Structo is entitled?

(A) $500,000, because there was no consideration for Bailey's promise to pay the additional $20,000.

(B) $500,000, because Bailey's promise to pay the additional $20,000 was exacted under duress.

(C) $520,000, because the modification was fair and was made in the light of circumstances not anticipated by the parties when the original contract was made.

(D) $520,000, provided that the reasonable value of Structo's total performance was that much or more.

Here, your ability to select the correct answer choice depends on whether you attach the appropriate legal significance to two words that appear in the fact pattern: "unexpectedly" and "accurately." If you read quickly, instead of actively, it's very easy to miss the signal language:

First, that finding a solid mass of rock was *unanticipated* ("unexpected"), and

Second, that Structo was acting in *good faith* ("accurately") when he told Bailey that the cost of putting in the driveway would cost more than originally contemplated.

Unless you draw the appropriate inferences from these words, you won't conclude that the parties entered into a valid modification when Structo asked for more money to complete the job which required more work than originally bargained for by the parties and Bailey signed a writing promising to pay the additional $20,000.

Instead, you'll find a lack of consideration (Answer Choice A), be led down the path of coercion (Answer Choice B), or possibly allow a recovery in restitution (Answer Choice D). Sadly, each incorrect answer choice would be for "want of a word."

While time is indeed a pressing factor, you can see that it's more important to read actively than it is to read quickly. Fortunately, it's far easier to become an active reader than it is to become a faster reader. It just takes practice.

D. HOW FORENSIC IRAC WORKS WITH MBE QUESTIONS

Our use of the forensic IRAC method operates somewhat differently when we apply it to objective, multiple choice questions. That's because in some way, short answer questions have already narrowed the field of possible errors. There are two basic skills at work in answering multiple choice questions: your knowledge of the law and your ability to analyze the questions, which in turn relies heavily on your reading comprehension skills. An incorrect answer choice, therefore, is the result of a flaw in one of these areas.

The key to working with multiple choice questions, therefore, is learning to identify the flaw in the reasoning behind an incorrect answer choice. Just like we needed to figure out what you were thinking when you wrote an essay, we need to get inside your head and figure out what you were thinking when you selected a multiple choice answer.

1. Applying the Technique

When practicing multiple choice questions, if you answer a question incorrectly, you must go back to that question and reread it to reflect on what you were thinking the first time you read the question. Specifically, your task is to recreate your thought process, retrace your steps, and compare your reasoning in the two instances to find the flaw in your analysis. This may be the only way to figure out how you made a mistake. And until you know why you select wrong answer choices, you can't make the necessary corrections. That's why it's essential—*absolutely essential*—that you answer only one question at a time when working with multiple choice questions. If you try to answer more than one at a time, you won't remember what you were thinking when you selected an answer choice with respect to a particular question. Self-awareness is essential to the analytical process—you need to know how you reasoned through a question.

How to proceed:

a. Answer a question following the approach outlined above:

- Read actively from the stem (or call-of-the-question) and then to the fact pattern

- Find the issue

- Move from the issue to articulation of your own answer

- Translate your "answer" to fit an available "answer choice"

b.   Check your answer.

2.   If You Answered the Question Correctly

Read the explanation for the correct answer choice if explanations are available. Even if you answered correctly, you want to make sure that you did so for the right reason. If you got the "right" answer for the "wrong" reason, proceed as if you answered incorrectly.

3.   If You Answered the Question Incorrectly

If you made an incorrect answer choice, you must go back to the question and read it again, beginning with the stem. As you read, pay close attention to what you are thinking and compare what you are thinking now to the first time you read the question.

What's most important in this exercise is the real-time feedback. If I were sitting with you while you were reading, I would stop you every 30 seconds or so and ask you to tell me what you were thinking. This forces you to put into words exactly what's going on in your head at the moment, something you're probably not doing—at least not consciously—and you must do it. That's because the only way to identify if you've gone down a wrong path is while your thoughts are still fresh in your mind.

You can learn to see why a thought is the wrong one to be having at the time by answering the questions I've posed for you below. Even though I'm not with you to lead you through the steps, you can do it for yourself by asking the questions I would ask:

(1) Look at the question stem: was my first answer choice one that answered the precise question that was asked?

(2) As I re-read the fact pattern, am I noticing facts that I overlooked the first time?

(3) Did I confuse the parties and that's why I evaluated the problem incorrectly?

(4) Did I overlook such legally significant words as "reasonable," "unexpectedly," or "accurately"?

(5) Do I find my mind wandering as I read?

(6) Am I rereading the same sentence because I have trouble remembering what I've just read?

(7) Am I reading into the problem words and facts that are not there?

The problem addressed in question #7 is difficult to detect, but it is a primary reason for incorrect answer choices. You therefore must find out if this is something you do. This is how:

• Start by examining your incorrect answer choice. Re-read it and ask yourself what led you to choose that answer.

- This requires that you go back to the fact pattern and see if you can find which words or facts led you to select that particular answer choice.

- Identify the basis for your answer. There had to be a reason—some basis you relied on for selecting that particular answer. We know it was the wrong reason, but we still need to know what your reasoning was at the time in order to step in and correct it at that point.

- Determine whether you "read into the facts" or added your own. This alters the nature of the problem. *You must never "assume" facts.* The bar examiners have carefully constructed the question to contain all the facts you need to answer the question. You must rely solely on these facts and no others. Of course you may draw reasonable inferences but you cannot fabricate your own facts or create "what if" scenarios.

- Don't let yourself go off on tangents based on possible theories you see raised in the facts. Sometimes when you read a fact pattern, you'll see the potential for a number of possible causes of action. Let the stem for the question guide your analysis.

- Sometimes you don't "add" facts but see implications which have no basis in the facts. This leads you astray in your analysis as well. Let the facts dictate your direction.

(8) Am I disregarding an important exception and jumping immediately to the general rule?

(9) Am I not connecting with the significance of the facts and that's why I can't identify the legal problem?

(10) Does this question require application of statutory law and not the common law? Did I disregard this before?

(11) Am I applying the minority view instead of the majority rule?

(12) Am I misapplying the rule to the facts?

(13) Am I "reacting" to answer choices instead of "acting" in response with an analysis of the issue presented?

(14) Did I get emotionally involved with the problem and substitute my instincts for what I know is legally correct?

(15) Did I become "practical" and replace the black letter law for what I thought would occur in actual practice?

4. Figure Out What Your Answer Means

If you answered "yes" to questions 1 through 7, then you most likely have a reading problem.

You therefore choose the incorrect answer choices because you've misread a fact either in the fact pattern or the answer choice. This is usually the result of sloppy reading because you're intent on reading quickly rather than carefully. A hasty reader is likely to overlook the specific use of vocabulary and the significance of modifiers in the answer choices. These types of errors and omissions go directly to your reading of the problem, not necessarily to your knowledge of the substantive law or to your analysis of the legal question. In fact, your difficulties with reading may prevent you from getting to the actual problem in controversy.

If you've been able to identify your problem as one of reading, now you have a direction in which to work. You can and must learn to read questions "actively." Because of time constraints on an exam, you may have time for only one reading of the fact pattern. However, you can't sacrifice a careful reading for a quick one. You must read carefully to spot signal words and legally significant facts. *Slow down and watch what happens.* Train yourself to look for the following as you read and if you may write in your test booklet, do not hesitate to circle the relevant language:

- Relationships between parties that signal the area of law and legal duties: landlord/tenant, employer/employee, principal/agent, buyer/seller.
- Amounts of money, dates, quantities, and ages.
- Words such as "oral" and "written," "reasonable" and "unreasonable," among others; and
- Words that indicate the actor's state of mind such as "intended," "decided," "mistakenly thought," and "deliberately," among others.

If you answered "yes" to questions 8 through 15, then you may have a problem with either application or the rule.

It's often difficult to distinguish between the two problems because they are closely related in the dynamic of answering multiple choice questions. Problems with analysis are process-oriented while problems with the rule are substance-based. But they can and do overlap as evidenced in these questions.

Analysis Problems

Conquering a problem with analytical skills not only involves close, accurate reading of the text, but it also requires exactness in following the structure of legal analysis in the context of multiple choice questions. This requires that as you re-read the question, you focus on answering the following:

- Did you properly analyze the question?

    1. Did you begin by reading the call-of-the-question?

    2. Did you identify the issue in the fact pattern?

    3. Did you move from finding the issue to forming your answer?

    4. Did you fill the gap from "your answer" to find one of the answer choices?

- Did you properly analyze the answer choices?

1. Did you identify the issue in each answer choice?

2. Did you use the process of elimination by determining when an answer choice can't be correct?

   (a) Was the answer choice completely correct?

   (b) Did the answer choice misstate or misapply a rule of law?

   (c) Did the answer choice mischaracterize the facts?

What you should do

The basic remedy for reading and application-based problems is practice—lots and lots of it. ***There's no real secret: the more questions you work your way through, the more careful and conscious a reader you become.*** In some ways, answering a multiple choice question is more a science than an art but rigor in application of the method will yield favorable results.

Rule Problems

Let's face it: if you don't know the black letter law, you can't distinguish between the answer choices. The key in analyzing the question after you've identified the issue is to articulate the rule of law that addresses that issue. If you don't know the rule, you can't get to this step. Remember, it's not enough to know bits and pieces of rules or simply be familiar with the terminology. Buzz-words will not help you here. The only thing that works is complete and thorough understanding of the rule—in its entirety.

If you answered "yes" to questions 8 through 12, consider the following:

If you cannot summon to mind the relevant rule as soon as you've articulated the issue, then you must return to your notes and review the substantive law in detail. Your problem is with knowledge of the rules and you must be comfortable with answering the following questions as soon as you read a fact pattern:

- What is the legal problem presented by the facts?

- What area of law is implicated?

- What is the specific rule of law that governs under these facts?

On the other hand, if you answered "yes" to questions 13 through 15, then something slightly different may be happening and requires a different approach. Let's look at each one individually.

If you "react" instead of "act":

When you find yourself "reacting" to answer choices instead of "acting" in response to them with a careful analysis of the issue presented, then some changes in procedure are required. This type of problem is basically one of control: Because you've lost control of your thought process in analyzing the problem, you've placed yourself at the mercy of the answer choices. Then they pick you, instead of the other way around. How do you act and not react to the answer choices? *The answer is simple: formulate your own answer to the interrogatory before you even look at the answer choices.* Practice questions this way until it becomes habit and you'll see what a difference it makes.

If you ignore the rule:

If you find yourself substituting your instincts for what you know is legally correct, you're headed for trouble. You must apply the rule of law to the facts without equivocation. You can't get afford to get emotionally involved with the parties and let your sympathies interfere with what you know is legally correct. It's not your place to find a criminal defendant not guilty when in fact her actions satisfy every element of the crime. And conversely: if an act doesn't violate the provisions of a given statute, then whatever you happen to think about the nature of the act (or actor) doesn't matter. It's not a crime if the jurisdiction doesn't make it one. Your job is to follow the law and apply it to the facts mechanically.

If you substitute "practice" for "theory":

If you find that you become practical on exams and replace the black letter law for what you think would occur in the real world, then you're going to end up with some incorrect answers. The bar exam is not the time or place to become "practical" and consider what you think would happen in actual practice. When answering an MBE question, apply the rule of law as you've learned it and you'll be fine.

CHAPTER 9

THE MULTISTATE PERFORMANCE TEST

A. THE PURPOSE OF THE MPT

In a perfect world, there would be no tests and a test like the bar exam would be "outlawed" instead of required for the practice of law. Short of some kind of a miracle, however, tests and the bar exam are going to be around for a while. But what would you think of an exam where the issue is identified and you're given all the law that's relevant to addressing that issue?

The good news, and you're due for some good news by now, is that the MPT can be the easiest part of your bar exam. Unlike the other portions of the exam where you're called upon to work solely from your memory, here you're given the legal issue and all the law you need to resolve the issue. You're given the law because this portion of the bar exam is designed to test your proficiency in the basic skills you've developed in the course of your legal education and not just your ability to memorize. According to the National Conference of Bar Examiners, the goal of the MPT is to test "an applicant's ability to use fundamental lawyering skills in a realistic situation." Each test, therefore, seeks to evaluate your ability to complete a task which a beginning lawyer should be able to accomplish.

The sum total of your law school experience has prepared you for this part of the bar exam. It just does so in a way that looks different because the MPT puts all the elements together in a manner that is new to students who have not yet had the opportunity to work with case files and clients. However, having worked with case files and clients, I can assure you there no mystery to it nor any substitute for proficiency in the most basic of skills.

But now that I've told you about the positive part about the exam, I must be fair and tell you about the negative. And just like there's always an opposing argument, there's always a downside. Here it's the time pressure. In most jurisdictions, you have but 90 minutes to read through anywhere from 15 to 25 pages, analyze the problem, outline your answer, and write your response. In California, where the Performance Test is a three-hour exam, you can just imagine the length of the file and the number of issues to which you must respond. As a result, the MPT is basically a test of your ability to work within time constraints and remain organized and focused.

Still, the MPT remains the most "doable" portion of the bar exam. It's not difficult "legally." The challenge is to get through the pile of information you are given and address only that which is required of you as set forth in the task memo. What we're going to do is develop the strategy you'll use when taking this exam. Your goal is to make your approach to the material so mechanical that come test day, it's pure routine.

B. THE SKILLS TESTED ON THE MPT

On the MPT, the bar examiners are interested in testing your fundamental lawyering skills. The focus is on your ability to comprehend what you read, organize information, think logically, extricate the relevant from the irrelevant, write clearly, and above all, follow directions.

1. Reading Comprehension

First, you'll be called upon to read. But there's a very real difference between the type of reading you've engaged in for your law school classes and what you'll do for the MPT. Here you must read pro-actively, with a critical eye toward solving a specific problem rather than answering a professor's questions in class. You must read carefully and quickly, all the while searching for useful information and answers to the particular issue you've been asked to resolve.

2. Organizational Skills

Second, you must organize your time and the materials effectively to complete the required task in the time allowed. The MPT is extremely time-sensitive, perhaps even more so than the essay or multiple choice components of the bar exam in that you'll have but 90 minutes in which to read and analyze an assortment of unfamiliar materials and compose any one of the following written assignments—a memorandum of law, a letter to a client, a persuasive brief (including subject headings), a contract provision, a will, a proposal for settlement, a discovery plan, or a closing argument, to list but a few of the possibilities.

3.   Communication Skills

Third, you must be able to write concisely, coherently, and in a tone and manner consistent with the nature of the assignment. In short, you must demonstrate your mastery of the language of the law and convince the bar examiners that you "sound" like an attorney ready to begin the practice of law.

4.   Ability to Follow Directions

Finally, you must be able to follow directions. It sounds so simple and basic but it's often ignored in the haste to begin writing. The MPT is task-specific: you must perform the task identified to receive credit. If you're instructed to write a letter to a client and instead write a persuasive brief, you'll have done nothing but demonstrate to the bar examiners your inability to read and follow simple directions.

The directions on the MPT are important for yet another reason: they may ask you to identify *additional* facts that would strengthen or, alternatively, weaken a party's position. Since adding facts to a professor's hypothetical is a basic law school "no-no," you'd never think to do such a thing—not unless you had read the directions. The ability to follow directions closely will save you time and energy, both on the bar exam and in practice.

C.   HOW THESE SKILLS ARE TESTED

The bar examiners test these skills by simulating the experiences of a new attorney. You'll be given a "client file" and asked to complete what would be considered a typical assignment for a first year associate. Each assignment is designed to test a discrete set of legal skills in the context of one of the following settings:

- Fact analysis tasks
- Fact gathering tasks
- Legal analysis and reasoning problems
- Problem solving tasks
- Ethical issue problems

1.   "Analyzing the Facts"

In a fact analysis problem, you'll be called upon to analyze a set of facts where the primary focus will be to separate the relevant from the irrelevant. Here the rules of law will serve to help you organize the facts.

Such tasks might include:

- Drafting an opening statement
- Drafting a closing argument
- Preparing a set of jury instructions
- Writing an affidavit

I can practically hear you thinking—"I've never done that. I'd have no idea what to do. And you said that this was the most doable part of the exam!" Not to worry. The bar examiners do not expect you to have performed all or even any of these tasks during your law school career. What they do expect, however, is that you'll be able to follow their instruction memo and rely on your basic legal training to complete the assignment.

If you think about it, performing these kinds of tasks can be something of a welcome change from the rest of the exam. After all, you get to "perform" like a lawyer, albeit on paper. Can't you just imagine yourself delivering an opening statement like: "Ladies and Gentlemen of the Jury. The prosecution must prove all four of the following elements beyond a reasonable doubt before you can find my client guilty of this crime. Reasonable doubt requires that...."

What comes next? A statement to the jury that the testimony they're about to hear won't support the elements of the crime so that they'll have to find your client "not guilty." Your opening statement will discuss the facts of the case but you'll organize that discussion around the elements of the crime.

2.   "Gathering the Facts"

Fact gathering is a basic lawyering task. It requires that you be able to identify the theory of your case and what facts you need to prove to make that case. Consequently, in a typical fact gathering problem, you'll be required to gather evidence. The focus will be on sifting through information to determine what's relevant to your problem and then using that evidence to defend or support your case.

Typical fact gathering tasks include:

- Drafting a discovery plan

- Preparing a set of interrogatories
- Drafting questions to ask a witness on cross examination

"Fact gathering" tasks, like "fact analysis" tasks, test your ability to use the rule to discriminate between relevant and irrelevant facts. For example, while the focus in drafting a set of interrogatories is on questions to elicit facts, you must understand and use the controlling rule to determine what facts you need to gather.

3. "Legal Analysis and Reasoning"

Happily, in a legal analysis problem, you'll feel right at home. Here, the focus will be on analyzing the rules of law from the cases and applying them to the facts in your File to resolve the legal issue. Sound familiar? These problems are most like law school exams but with a major difference: the MPT will articulate the precise legal issue(s) for you. You just need to follow directions carefully and answer the precise question that is asked of you.

Typical legal reasoning tasks include:

- Writing an objective memorandum
- Writing a persuasive memorandum of law or trial brief
- Writing a client letter
- Writing a letter to opposing counsel

4. "Solving a Problem"

In a problem solving assignment, you'll be called upon to evaluate courses of action and outline viable options. The focus is on your ability to develop strategies for solving a problem and meeting your client's needs. You may even be called upon to suggest such non-legal solutions as mediation or counseling.

Examples of problem solving tasks include:

- Drafting a will or contract provision
- Drafting a settlement proposal or separation agreement

5. "Ethical Issues"

As a bar candidate, you're expected to comport with the applicable ethical standards in your representation of a client. Consequently, you may find ethical issues raised in your problem. You're expected to recognize such issues and resolve them according to the ethical standards of the profession. Conceivably, the bar examiners could raise an ethical issue without providing specific rules in the Library; in such cases, you must rely on your general knowledge of the rules of professional conduct. Be alert in your reading of the facts to potential conflict of interest issues, violations of fiduciary obligations, and breaches of attorney/client privilege.

D. COMPONENTS OF THE MPT

The MPT consists of the following parts:

1. The File

The File contains all the factual information about your case. It may consist of such documents as excerpts from deposition testimony, client correspondence, police reports, medical records, invoices, purchase orders, witness interviews, contract provisions, a lease, or a will. While the File contains all the facts you need to know about your problem, it also contains "irrelevant information." Just as in "real life" where your client will volunteer much more information than you actually need or is relevant to the legal problem, and witnesses may be unreliable or have faulty memories, the File may include irrelevant or ambiguous information, unreliable and conflicting witness testimony, and inconsistent statements.

2. The "Task" or "Instruction" Memorandum

This is the single most important document in the File because it contains your directions. It is the first memorandum in the File and introduces your problem. After reading this memo, you'll know whether you are to write an objective memorandum, a persuasive brief, a client letter, or any one of a number of other tasks. Your goal will be to answer the questions posed in this memo and perform the assigned task as precisely as possible.

3. The Library

The Library contains all the legal authorities you'll need to complete the assigned task. And it contains the *only* legal authorities you may use to solve the problem. While outside knowledge is useful to guide your understanding of the law, you must rely solely on the law presented in the Library.

The Library may consist of statutes, codes and commentaries, constitutional provisions, regulations, rules of professional conduct, cases, and secondary sources such as Restatement provisions. The cases may be actual cases, modified cases, or cases written specifically for the exam. So too with the "rules"—they may be actual rules or rules written specifically for the MPT. This means that even if you think you are familiar with a rule or a case from your law school classes, you must still read all the material in the Library. You cannot assume that the material has not been modified. Certainly, there may be rules that the bar examiners have not altered, such as the UCC, provisions of the United States Constitution, the Bill of Rights, or the Federal Rules of Evidence. In these instances, the directions will so advise.

If no Library is provided, then any law necessary to resolving the problem will be provided in the File.

E. STRATEGIES FOR SUCCESS ON THE MPT

1. Having a Plan

In working with students to prepare for the MPT, I've put together a set of guidelines that students found helpful and subsequently used as a blueprint to guide them through the problems during practice sessions and on test day. Following this plan saves time and prevents panic: if you know what you are going to do, and practice the routine sufficiently, it becomes second nature to you by test day.

2. Practicing from Actual MPTs

Like the other parts of the bar exam, preparing for the MPT requires practice. Still, preparation for the MPT is unlike preparation for the other parts of the bar exam. Here you're not tested so much on your knowledge of black letter law as you are on your ability to extract legal principles from cases and statutes and apply these principles to solve a specific client problem. The commercial bar preparation courses provide a comprehensive review of the substantive law. Unfortunately, such courses are not designed to cultivate the analytical and writing skills you need on the MPT. These are the skills you should have developed in law school and these are the skills you must fine tune on your own.

Reprints of the MPT questions and a discussion of the issues and suggested resolutions of the problems as contemplated by the drafters of the MPT are available from the National Conference of Bar Examiners. They have prepared grading sheets which describe the issues the candidate should discuss and the grading guidelines. While the point sheets are very helpful in identifying the issues you need to address in your answer and their corresponding point allocation, the point sheets do not provide the words themselves. Individual jurisdictions may release candidate answers just as they do for essays. If your jurisdiction releases sample MPT answers, be sure to review them as carefully as you do sample essay answers. For many students, the overriding concern is just how to get started: how to write the opening sentence, the point headings, and the case summaries. Your first task is to acquire a good number of available MPTs and only then are you ready to begin. I would suggest a minimum of six.

3.   Following the Blueprint

The strategy for success is simple: you practice the following approach until it becomes automatic. Follow each step of the sequence for each MPT—first as you practice, and then on test day. The goal is for this process to become so mechanical that you do not waste any time but get to work immediately. You remain calm because you always know what your next step will be.

Let's get to work.

a.   *Read the instructions*

There is an instruction sheet on the back of every MPT. Read it in its entirety *now*. You don't want to waste time on exam day performing a routine task you can do beforehand. However, on bar day, you'll scan the instruction sheet just to make sure it's the same one you've read during practice—you don't want any surprises. You'll pay particular attention to paragraph 2 and read it carefully to verify the jurisdiction.

The instructions are straightforward but pay careful attention to the following:

(1) **Paragraph 2:** defines the jurisdiction of the MPT

The MPT is set in the fictitious Fifteenth Circuit of the United States, in the fictitious State of Franklin. In Franklin, the trial court is the District Court, the intermediate appellate court is the Court of Appeal, and the highest court is the Supreme Court.

On the MPT, as in practice, you must know the court structure before you read the cases so you can determine what is mandatory and what is merely persuasive authority.

(2) **Paragraph 4:** describes the Library

Occasionally, cases may seem familiar to you. The examiners may have patterned the case after a famous case. You are instructed not to assume any knowledge but to read thoroughly as if all were new to you. You are also told to assume that the cases were decided in the jurisdictions and on the dates shown. What are the bar examiners really telling you? They are telling you that jurisdiction and case dates are significant because:

    (i)   "Jurisdiction" tells you what is *mandatory* as opposed to what is merely *persuasive* authority.

    (ii) "Case dates" may be a way of determining whether the more recent case overruled the earlier case.

(3) **Paragraph 5:** some advice

You are advised to work ***only*** from the facts in the File and the law in Library.

(4) **Paragraph 6:** suggested time allocation

The bar examiners suggest that you spend half your time on reading and outlining and half your time on writing. You could go five (5) or so minutes either way but you should not spend less than 40 minutes on either task. It's simply insufficient to get the job done.

(5) **Paragraph 7:** What the examiners are looking for

   (i) Responsiveness to the instructions in the task

   (ii) Content

   (iii) Thoroughness

   (iv) Organization of response

Note that fully one-half the available points are not so much about the substance of what you've written but whether you've answered the question that is asked of you and organized your response in a meaningful manner. This reinforces the importance the bar examiners place on your ability to remain focused and structured in your response.

b. Review the Table of Contents

Use the Table of Contents to begin your *"active reading"* of the MPT.

From this page, you can identify:

(1) **Whether it's a statutory or a common law problem.**

If you have a common law problem, which will
be obvious when all you have are cases in your
Library, then it's likely that you'll have a bit
more work to do; typically, you'll have to synthesize the applicable rule from the cases.

(2) **The area of law.**

From the listings in the Library, you can determine the general subject area, sometimes more.
For example, if you see provisions of the Franklin Commercial Code listed in the Table of
Contents, it's a sure bet you have a problem
involving a sales of goods.

(3) **Don't let the area of law cause needless
worry or anxiety.**

Examiners may choose an unfamiliar area of
law or one that you don't particularly like. In
such cases, the key is not to let the subject
matter distract you. You'll be given all the
relevant law you need to solve the problem so
even if it happens to be an area of law in which
you think you're weak, it doesn't matter. And if
it's an unfamiliar area of law, the bar examiners
know that too and the problem will be relatively
basic and solvable by using the provided
materials.

c. *Read the Task Memo*

This is the *single most important document* in the
File for the following reasons:

(1) **It introduces your problem**

The task memo provides the relevant background facts, introduces the parties, and sets forth the nature of your task.

(2) **It states your issue**

The task memo reveals the precise issue you're asked to resolve. It may appear in the form of the questions you're asked to address in a client letter, in the argument you need to make in a brief, or even in the supervising attorney's theory of the case.

Read this portion of the memo two or three times to be certain you have identified the issue. Write the issue on your scratch paper so that you remain focused as you proceed. Be careful not to change or vary the language of the question.

Most jurisdictions will provide scratch paper. If not, carefully follow the directions on the instruction sheet as to where you're allowed to write your notes.

(3) **It contains your directions**

Read the directions very carefully. The bar examiners may request that you do more than simply analyze the facts in light of the relevant law and write an objective evaluation; they may request that you identify additional facts that would strengthen a party's position, state the most persuasive arguments that can be made to support a given position, or identify likely outcomes.

Look for exclusions.

Sometimes you are told **not** to consider a specific issue. In these cases, the issue would most likely jump out at you when you read the problem and your first response would be to discuss it. **Your job is not to discuss it.** Fight the desire to do so because the graders are lying in wait to take off points for those who fail to follow basic instructions.

(4) **It identifies your task**

You will be told whether to write an objective memorandum, a persuasive brief, a client letter, or any one of a number of other possibilities.

From your task, you should:

(i) *Identify your point of view: is it objective or persuasive?*

You want to know whether you will be advising or advocating. This informs the nature of your reading because you'll read the materials with a critical eye. For example, if you know you must write a persuasive brief with subject headings, you'll read the cases with an eye toward formulating them.

(ii) *Identify your audience: lay or legal?*

You want to know your audience because it allows you to adopt the proper tone in your writing. There is a difference in how you would write to your client, a layperson, as opposed to your adversary, another attorney.

d. Review the Instruction Memo (if applicable)

If the examiners think you need guidance in completing your task, they'll include a second memo in the File. There are guidelines for opinion letters, persuasive briefs, memorandums, etc. Each memo will tell you exactly what to include (and sometimes what *not* to include) in your paper. Be sure to follow these guidelines to the letter.

For example, the instruction memo will advise you whether your persuasive brief requires a statement of facts or not. A "persuasive brief" might require a factual statement while a "trial brief" might not. Sometimes you might be asked to include a "jurisdictional statement" as well as a statement of facts. Only a careful reading of the instruction memo will ensure that you know what to include in your assignment. Even if the instruction memo specifies a task you think you know well, **do not** skip the instruction sheet. Sometimes the examiners have modified the task or require a particular format.

In addition to providing general guidelines, sometimes the instruction sheet will include specific examples for you to follow in drafting your document. Such examples might be sample interrogatories, will and contract provisions, jury instructions, and questions for cross-examination, to name a few. The examples are included for a very good reason: they are your "models." Follow them!

An important part of your preparation for the MPT is to read these memos now and be completely familiar with them so that on test day you need spend only a few precious moments reviewing them before proceeding. You must check the instruction memo even if it seems familiar because it's never safe to assume that it's identical to one you've seen in practice.

e. Read the Library

Although the first part of the exam booklet is the File, this is not where you'll begin. Instead, you're going to begin with the Library.

Reading the law first informs your subsequent reading of the File. If you read the File first, with its various excerpts from depositions, client communications, and attorney notes, it would be more difficult, if not impossible, to sift relevant from irrelevant information. You simply could not know which facts were "relevant" until you knew the law and how the cases in your jurisdiction have interpreted that law. While reading the Library first does not guarantee you won't have to review it again, it will make your subsequent reading of the File meaningful and immediately productive.

Caution: Irrelevant rules

There may be some authorities in the Library that are irrelevant to your analysis. Clearly, you won't know what is or is not relevant at this point. You must wait to make that judgment until after you've read the facts in the File. What's important to remember is that there might be "law" in the Library that won't be applicable to your analysis. Let your issue and the facts be your guide.

Follow this sequence:

(1) **Read the cases**

Read the earliest case first and proceed in chronological order.

Sometimes, just as in the real world, the later case will modify the holding in the earlier case or it will build on the ruling in the earlier case. Often, the cases are not related but you won't know until you've read them. Then it doesn't matter which you've read first. It's just easier to get in the habit of always beginning with the earliest case.

Reading the cases in the Library tends to be the most time-consuming part of the MPT. Even if you're a fast reader, it will still consume too much of your time if you read these cases like you did in law school. Instead, you're going to read like a practitioner. Practicing attorneys read cases to find what they need from them: the rule of law in their jurisdiction and the basic facts.

Therefore, when you read a case, you will:

(i) **Verify the jurisdiction.**

Immediately check the jurisdiction of the decision to determine the authority of the case. Assess whether it's mandatory or merely persuasive. Pay attention to the jurisdiction of cases cited by courts in their decisions: sometimes they will discuss other cases. Once again, you need to know whether or not you must follow that ruling.

(ii) **Identify the rule of law.**

The cases are the means by which the examiners feed you the law. Sometimes, they'll be so blunt as to have the court state something like,

"During the past 30 years, we have developed a two-pronged analysis for evaluating the validity of a premarital agreement."

Such a statement is a "gift"—it gives you the rule and its two elements. Sometimes, your gift will not appear in the form of a rule with "prongs." In such cases, the elements will be listed as the requirements of a crime or they'll appear in a statute. Simply break the statute into its component elements and proceed accordingly.

(iii) **Skim the facts to get a sense of the story.**

On the MPT, the cases are constructed in a very particular order: facts, rule, and application of facts to rule. MPT cases closely resemble actual cases. Therefore, you can read the first few words of each paragraph and you'll know exactly where you are. Consider skipping the first few paragraphs and jump right to the rule. If you're insecure about skipping around, then read the entire case but merely skim the facts quickly. You can pick up the relevant facts from the court's application.

(iv) **Read the footnotes.**

Footnotes hold a special place in the hearts of bar examiners because they know that students tend to ignore them. That's why bar examiners like to put them in cases. Don't ignore them. They are there for a reason. More than half the time, they contain critical information.

(2) **Use the rule of law to form your outline**

Adapt the rule to form your "mini working outline." Use the elements, the "prongs" of a rule, or the components of a statute to form the roman numerals of your outline. A general outline is then in place as you read the rest of the Library. You can add to and refine your understanding of the rule as well as add any exceptions or limitations to the rule as you read the other materials in the Library.

When you read your File, you can do either of the following:

1. Simply add your "facts" in the space beneath the appropriate rule.

Or

2. Create a *parallel set of point headings* where you'll note the facts from your case that correspond to each of the elements of the rule.

If you create this outline when you first find the rule, you'll have prepared the foundation for writing your assigned task.

(3) **Read the statutes, codes, commentaries**

Pay close attention to any "official comments" in a statute or code provision. Such comments are a means for the bar examiners to highlight an issue, draw your attention to a counter-argument, or signal a legal distinction.

Outlining the Rule from Cases

Let's see how it's done. Look at Test 2 of the February 1997, MPT, *In re Hayworth and Wexler*. Here the Library contains a case, *In the Matter of Watson*, and several provisions of the Franklin Professional Code. The court in *Watson* tells you when a premarital agreement will be found valid and binding in the State of Franklin:

> During the past 30 years, we have developed a two-pronged analysis for evaluating the validity of a premarital agreement. *Under the first prong, the court must decide whether the agreement provides a fair and reasonable provision for the party not seeking enforcement of the agreement.* If the court makes this finding, then the analysis ends and the agreement may be validated. *If the agreement is not fair, the court must invoke the second prong and decide: (A) whether full disclosure has been made by the parties of the amount, character, and value of the property involved, and (B) whether the agreement was entered into intelligently and voluntarily on independent advice and with full knowledge by both spouses of their rights.* (Emphasis added to indicate rule)

Use this statement to create your outline. The court lays it out for you: it tells you there's a two-part rule and then it further divides the second prong into two parts, A and B. Your outline should look something like this:

I. Agreement must be **fair and reasonable** for the party not seeking enforcement

What is "fair and reasonable"?

    a. Not when "grossly disproportionate" in favor of petitioner

  b. Not when it denies party common law and statutory rights

  c. Not when it prevents party from making any claim against or seeking any rights in husband's separate property

  Note: When a court uses such terms as "fair and reasonable," rely on the factors it considers in its evaluation and use them as your criteria. In this case, sub-points a, b, and c were the specific factors the Watson court considered in evaluating whether the pre-nup was fair and reasonable.

If fair, then enforceable.

II. If not fair, ask

  A. Was there full disclosure of

   (1) **amount,**

   (2) **character,** and

   (3) **value** of the property

and

  B. Was the agreement entered into

   (1) **intelligently**

   (2) **voluntarily**

   (3) on **independent advice** and

   (4) with **full knowledge by both spouses of their rights**

Your outline shouldn't be any longer or wordier than this. Underline or highlight the key words to help you remember them as you read the File. As you can see, the factors in the second part of the test are so clear as to not require additional explanation. You can simply "match" up the facts in your case with the requirements of the test.

If you've left space under each part of the rule, you can simply write in your facts or you can create a parallel set of point headings. It really doesn't matter so long as it is perfectly clear to you.

This outline is invaluable to you. It ensures that you won't leave out any elements when you begin your analysis, an oversight that's quite easy to make under the extreme pressure of exam writing.

I devised this technique when one of the students I was working with failed to include the first prong of the rule in his analysis of this problem. It seems that in his eagerness to write his answer, he overlooked the first part of the rule and referred only to sub-parts A and B in his analysis. He told me that he had trouble making sense of the problem but when he reviewed the case, he saw that it was supposed to be a two-part rule and thought that parts A and B were the two parts. That is when he realized the value of preparing an outline. And, so will you.

f. Read the File

After you've read the Library and outlined the rule, you're ready to return to the File and add the relevant facts to the appropriate places in your outline.

Don't be surprised if you find yourself reading a fair amount of material that you believe is irrelevant. As you may recall from writing your Statement of Facts in legal memos and briefs, you need to include more than the "bare bones" in your factual statement to provide the reader with the necessary background information. Consequently, you'll be faced with what seems like an avalanche of information as you proceed. It will be more manageable if you follow this advice:

(1) **Write the issue above your outline.** By reading the File with the issue clearly in place, you can more easily identify the legally relevant facts from the sea of material in front of you. As you proceed, add the critical facts to the appropriate part of your outline. By now you should have a clear picture of the problem and how you can resolve it.

(2) **Characterize the legal relationship of the parties and your client.** Are they buyer and seller, teacher and student, husband and wife, employer and employee? By thinking of the parties in terms of their legal relationship to each other, you'll be alert to the legal significance of the facts contained in the depositions, transcripts, and correspondence.

g.   *Reread the Task Memo*

After you've written the outline, review the task memo. Ask the following questions:

- Has my outline incorporated or accounted for each required element?

- Are the relevant facts noted?

- Is the applicable legal authority cited?

- Do I account for how the law and the facts support my theory?

- If appropriate, has contrary authority been cited and distinguished?

If necessary, add to the outline.

h.   Review the Instruction Memo

Quickly check the memo once again to verify your task and the required components.

i.   Write your response

After completing your reading of the Library and File, you're ready to begin the task of writing. Remember, your job is to discuss the issues and the controlling rule of law. Here is where you get your points. Don't waste time "warming up" by reciting the facts or providing needless background information.

(1) **Adopt the tone and format required for your task.**

For example, if you're asked to write a client letter, you must adapt your writing style accordingly. This means that you recognize your reader is a layperson and if you use any legal terms in your letter, you'll explain such terms in a manner that an ordinary citizen would comprehend. Also, you'll want your assignment to resemble a letter so you'll include a mock letterhead and an introductory statement. Even though it's a letter, you'll want to guide your reader (and the grader) through your analysis so use sub-headings to separate the issues.

Your letter might begin something like the following example which is based on the July 1997, MPT, *In re Kiddie–Gym Systems, Inc.*:

Jerome A. Martin, President

Kiddie–Gym Systems, Inc.

4722 Industrial Way

Bradley Center, FN 33087

RE: Loss by Fire of Installed Playground Equipment at Bradley Center Shopping Mall

Dear Mr. Martin,

I am writing to respond to your inquiries concerning the liability of your company, KGS, for the loss of the playground equipment. I've reviewed the applicable law and the following is our opinion with respect to the issues we've discussed.

<u>Risk of Loss</u>

The first issue is whether your company bears the risk of loss for the playground equipment destroyed in the fire at Cornet's Bradley Center Shopping Mall.

Similarly, if you're asked to write an objective memorandum of law, you'll assume a neutral tone and objectively evaluate the facts in light of the applicable law. Alternatively, if you're asked to write a legal brief or any form of argument, you'll adopt the tone of an advocate and use forceful and persuasive language.

(2) **Write Persuasive Subject Headings**

Perhaps the most challenging task for candidates is when they're asked to include subject headings in their argument. Most students have not had the opportunity or the need to write subject headings since their first year of law school. And if you're like most students, you struggled through it and promptly forget about it. Unfortunately, commercial bar prep courses are not going to teach you how to do this because there isn't time and quite simply, it's not their job. Still, you have the opportunity to rack up considerable points with just a few sentences.

Let's be honest: a grader is inclined to look favorably upon a paper that immediately sets forth the proper tone and has apparently followed directions. For the bar examiners don't leave it to chance that you'll write effective subject headings: they give specific directions on what they want and what they don't want. The instruction memo for the July 1997, MPT, *State v. Devine*, provides the following example:

Improper: THE WITNESS IS COMPETENT TO TESTIFY.

Proper: A FIVE–YEAR–OLD WHO ADMITTED HER MOTHER WOULD NOT PUNISH HER FOR LYING, BUT STILL TESTIFIED SHE KNEW THAT LYING WAS WRONG, IS COMPETENT TO TESTIFY.

The key to writing an effective subject heading is simple:

> *State the legal conclusion you want the court to reach and the factual basis on which it can do so.*

I drafted the following sample point headings. They address the two issues for the trial brief on evidentiary proffers you're asked to prepare for *State v. Devine*.

I.   TESTIMONY OF A HIGHLY TRAINED DETECTIVE THAT HE OBSERVED DEFENDANT SELLING WHAT APPEARED TO BE COCAINE TWO DAYS BEFORE DEFENDANT'S ARREST FOR COCAINE POSSESSION WITH INTENT TO DISTRIBUTE IS ADMISSIBLE BECAUSE IT SHOWS DEFENDANT'S STATE OF MIND.

II. OFFICER FUSCO'S TESTIMONY AS TO DEFENDANT'S ARREST AND CONVICTION FOR POSSESSION WITH INTENT TO DISTRIBUTE BUT EIGHTEEN MONTHS PRIOR TO HIS CURRENT ARREST FOR POSSESSION WITH INTENT IS DISTRIBUTE, IS ADMISSIBLE TO SHOW INTENT.

The following are some guidelines to writing subject headings:

- The purpose of point headings is to provide the reader with an outline of your argument.

- Each point heading is written as a conclusory

statement that combines the law with the relevant facts.

- It should be a coherent, logical, and persuasive thesis sentence.

- Do not state abstract principles of law.

- Do not write objective, neutral statements.

- If your adversary would agree with your statement, then you haven't written it right.

The good news is that if you practice writing point headings now as you prepare from the practice MPTs, they will flow from your pen on test day.

(3) Write Effective Case Summaries

Another important skill to review and practice before test day is writing case summaries. A common error is to write summaries of what the cases are about instead of simply reducing a case to its core facts, holding, and reasoning. Typically, you've not written case analyses on law school exams and unless you've written legal papers or worked on one of your school's journals, chances are that your only exposure to writing such summaries was in your first year legal writing class.

Your goal on the MPT is not to write a case brief or even a lengthy analysis but to concisely state the holding and facts of the Library case and then compare that case to the facts of your case.

When working with the Library, the most common error is to include long passages and quotations from the cases in your text. *Do not do this!* It adds nothing to your legal argument (and no points) but adds tremendously to your writing time. Instead, focus on the facts, holding, and reasoning of the opinion and write something like this:

> "In *Lopez*, the court held that the school board acted constitutionally when it required profanity be deleted from a student-produced film before it could be shown. The court reasoned that the school board had not censored the students' expression of ideas but prohibited the use of profanity in expressing those ideas and thus the board's requirement was content neutral and served a valid pedagogical purpose." *Lopez v. Union High School District*.

Here, you've provided the holding in the case, its factual basis, and the reasoning the court relied upon in reaching that decision—and all in two sentences!

(4) **Use Effective Case Analysis**

Equally important is to give adequate treatment to the cases in the Library. The bar examiners expect you to apply the rule from these cases to the specific facts in your case. For example, in the July 1999, MPT, *Kantor v. Bellows*, you're asked to write a letter to your adversary explaining why your client is entitled to the equitable distribution of her husband's law degree and license to practice law. One requirement is that you include a specific dollar demand and justify that amount. In responding to this request, you might consider the following

to show how you've used the materials in the
Library to support your argument:

> "Linda is entitled to a distributive award of
> $335,000 as compensation for her contributions to
> Bill's degree and enhanced earning capacity."

After explaining how you arrived at this figure,
you'd explain its legal justification:

> "In determining the disposition of property in di-
> vorce actions, the court considers several factors
> such as the income and property of each party at
> the time of marriage and at the time of the com-
> mencement of the action, and the direct and indi-
> rect contributions made to the acquisition of mari-
> tal property, including the career of the other party.
> Section 5, Franklin Domestic Relations Law. While
> the Franklin Court of Appeal in *Sooke v. Sooke*
> made a distributive award to the wife of only 40% of
> the value of the husband's medical degree, the facts
> in that case are not as compelling as the ones in our
> case. Here, Linda is entitled to one-half of the value
> of Bill's enhanced earning capacity because the
> parties agreed that both would have the opportu-
> nity to pursue legal careers and that Linda would
> work while Bill attended law school first."

You can see how easily it would be to continue
with the relevant facts from the File and compare and contrast with the facts from *Sooke*.
Clearly, this is more than a superficial analysis
and you've developed your argument by synthe-
sizing the applicable law and the facts from
your case.

(5) Citation

On the MPT, as in practice, you must "cite" to
the relevant authority. However, "official" cita-

tion form is not required for the MPT. Simply use abbreviations and omit page references. With cases, a reference to the plaintiff's or defendant's name is sufficient. Your goal is to attribute an authority for your statement, thus demonstrating to the grader that you've used the Library effectively and that you're familiar with the need for proper legal documentation.

F. TIME IS OF THE ESSENCE

1. Allocating your Time

While I've left the matter of timing to the end, it may well be the most important point to consider. Clearly, you must complete the assignment to maximize your points. The bar examiners suggest that you allot 45 minutes to reading the materials and 45 minutes to organizing and writing your response. This is sound advice. Moreover, if you follow the strategies I've outlined, you'll be organizing your response while you're reading the materials, thereby maximizing your productivity.

2. Finding Your Baseline

Of course, you can have no real idea of how long any of this will take unless and until you've done it. Therefore, after you've read one or two of the MPTs to get a sense of what they're about, select another one and just read and outline the materials, practicing the techniques you've just learned. Note how long it takes you to do this. This is your baseline *reading and outlining* time. Then, proceed to write the response. Once again, time yourself. This is your baseline *writing* time. Do not be surprised or disheartened if it seems to take several hours to get through the materials. This is normal the first time you approach new material. Still, the experience will be somewhat different for everyone. Some read faster than others; others have difficulty writing. You need to learn how long it takes you to perform each of these tasks.

Once you've established your reading and writing baselines, you can concentrate on improving your time. Learning to allocate your time is a challenging but not insurmountable task. You can do it with practice. You must practice the strategy until it becomes automatic and your approach is consistent. Don't wait until test day to see how long it takes you to dissect a case for the rule and prepare a response. *You'd never wait until the day of your road test to practice parallel parking, would you?*

G.   BAR EXAMINATION MPT CHECKLIST

Follow the Blueprint:

I.   Reviewing the Instructions

    1.   Did you scan the paragraphs to check the requirements?

    2.   Did you verify the jurisdiction paragraph to know what is *mandatory* as opposed to what is merely *persuasive* authority?

II.   Reviewing the Table of Contents

    1.   Did you identify the general area of law?

    2.   Did you determine whether it's a statutory or common law problem?

III.   Reading the Task Memo

    1.   Did you identify the issue you're asked to resolve? Are there sub-issues?

    2.   Did you identify your specific assignment by

        a)   Noting the precise nature of the task: memo, brief, letter, contract provision, will provision, cross examination questions, etc.?

        b)   Identifying your point of view: is it objective or persuasive?

        c)   Identifying your audience: is it a lawyer or layperson?

    3.   Did you note any exclusions?

IV. <u>Reading the Instruction Memo</u>

   1. Did you note whether a particular format or structure is required?

   2. If a brief was requested, do you need to include

     a) A statement of facts?

     b) A jurisdictional statement?

     c) Persuasive subject headings?

   3. Are there specific examples/models to follow?

V. <u>Reading the Library</u>

   1. Did you read the cases first?

   2. For each case, did you

     a) Read the earliest case first and proceed chronologically?

     b) Verify the jurisdiction to determine whether its mandatory or persuasive authority for your problem?

     c) Skim the facts to get a sense of the story?

     d) Identify the statement of the rule?

       • Is it element-based?

       • Do you need to synthesize from the cases?

       • Is it a "multi-part test" formulated by the court?

     e) Note any footnotes?

2. Did you adapt the rule in the cases to form your outline?

3. Did you review the statutes, codes, commentaries?

VI. <u>Reading the File</u>

1. Did you begin by

   a) Writing your issue above your rule outline?

   b) Characterizing the legal relationship of the parties: Are they buyer and seller, teacher and student, husband and wife, employer and employee, attorney and client?

2. Did you identify the relevant facts based on your knowledge of the law from the Library?

3. Did you add these facts to the appropriate sections of your rule outline?

VII. <u>Preparing to Write</u>

1. Did you review the task and instruction memos to verify the issue and the task?

2. Has your outline incorporated each required element?

   (a) the applicable legal authority?

   (b) the relevant facts?

VIII. <u>Writing the Response</u>

1. Did you answer the question that was asked of you?

2. Did you adopt the tone and format required for the task?

3. Did you write persuasive subject headings?

    - Did you state the legal conclusion you want the court to reach and the factual basis on which it can do so?

    - Is each point heading written as a conclusory statement that combines the law with the relevant facts?

    - Is it a coherent, logical, and persuasive thesis sentence?

    - Have you avoided abstract principles of law?

    - Would your adversary agree with your statement?

4. Did you give adequate treatment to the cases in the Library?

5. Did you avoid copying passages from cases or statutes?

6. Did you make relevant arguments on how the law and the facts support your theory?

7. Has contrary authority been cited and distinguished?

8. Did you cite to the appropriate authorities for statements of the rule?

CHAPTER 10

TAKING THE BAR EXAM

A. BEING IN THE MOMENT

No matter how hard you've studied and how many practice exams you've taken, once you get to the bar exam, you must let go and "be in the moment." This means that you respond to what the bar examiners ask of you and not want you what to tell the bar examiners you know. Trust me—there's no better way to ensure a poor grade than to ignore what is asked of you. By answering the question, you'll be showing what you know.

Everything you've been doing during bar review has prepared you for this moment. And, if you've prepared properly and you're willing to surrender to the questions, you'll find the "exam zone." Like a "runner's high," it's a feeling that there is only "the now." It's where you're on auto-pilot and your training takes over. You've connected with whatever it was you were working to achieve: for the athlete, it's that connection of mind and body that allows for peak performance; for the law student, it's that command of the material that lets you see the issues in the facts and allows you to write with clarity and cogency. Your thinking and writing come together—it flows because you flow.

B. IMPLEMENTING THE METHOD

It's finally arrived. Your test booklet is on the desk in front of you. What follows is a step-by-step approach for taking the exam. It's a blueprint you can follow to guide you through practice sessions and then implement on test day. Following this plan saves time and prevents anxiety: if you know exactly what you're going to do, and practice sufficiently, the process becomes second nature. On exam day, you can count on the routine to take over and prevent you from freezing up. You'll soon be in the "exam zone."

1.   What Should I Do in the Moments Before the Exam?

- Sit calmly and do not think about anything or anyone else while the proctors are handing out the exam materials.

- Be alert and listen carefully: you must follow all instructions.

- Do not worry about any other part of the exam. Focus solely on what is right in front of you. It requires and demands your full and undivided attention.

2.   What Should I Do When Told to Begin?

These are critical minutes for setting the pace and tenor of your exam experience. You want to start smoothly, work efficiently, and above all, remain focused and calm. Here's how to do it:

- Make sure you've followed the proctor's directions for identifying your exam papers.

- Write down what you're afraid you'll forget on scrap paper.

If you're worried that there's something you're likely to forget during the course of the exam, write it down on scrap paper. It only takes a few minutes and buys peace of mind.

• Scan the exam

Since you know the composition of the exam from your preparation, there's no need to scan any part of the bar exam except for the essays. Here you may want to get a sense of the general topics before you begin. More than that is not necessary.

3.   How Should I Allocate My Time?

Just as you "set your clock" during practice sessions, do so now:

• Using the exact time you were told to begin the exam, set your timetable as you did during practice sessions.

• Write down the starting and ending times for each question.

• Follow this clock throughout the exam to stay on track.

4.   How Do I Keep a Handle on my Timing With the MBE?

As you know from practicing MBE questions, they are presented in a completely random manner so that both the subject matter and the complexity of the question varies from one question to the next. As you work through the exam, keep an eye on your clock to gauge your progress. This should keep you in line.

You have to complete between 16 and 17 questions in a 30–minute period, averaging 33–34 questions every hour to complete the 100 questions in a three hour period; set your "clock" on the half hour with appropriate milestones.

Assuming your exam begins at 9:15 and ends at 12:15:

Time	Question Number
9:45	17
10:15	33
10:45	50
11:15	67
11:45	84
12:15	100

5.   What If I Get Stuck on an MBE Question?

Here you have two options:

- You can circle the question in your test booklet and return after you've completed the entire exam.

- You can make your best choice and move on.

  With only 1.8 minutes per question, there's only so much time to allow for doubt. No matter how well you've prepared, there are bound to be questions that present difficulty. Don't squander precious time that could be spent on questions you can answer.

6.   What If I Get Stuck on an Essay Question?

While we've covered this topic in a previous chapter, we'll review some relevant points again here:

- Have I forgotten the rule of law? What should I do if my mind goes blank when I read the question and nothing comes to mind?

  ☐ Ask: *"What is the issue?"*

      You can formulate the issue from the question you are asked to answer. Focusing on identifying the issue will allow you to regain your composure and lead you back to the process of thinking like a lawyer.

  ☐ Write the issue, whether or not you "know" the rule at this point. Formulating the issue will get you points from the grader because it shows that you can identify the legal problem from the facts.

  ☐ Next ask: *"What principle of law is implicated by this issue?"*

      Now you're thinking like a lawyer. This will either lead you to the rule from the recesses of your memory or you'll have to improvise. When you improvise, rely on your knowledge of general legal principles and standards to guide you.

- How do I use what I know about a topic to build on it?

  If you're asked about recoverable damages, rely on what you know about "damages" in particular areas of the law and proceed from there.

☐ For example, if it's a contracts problem, you know every breach of contract entitles the aggrieved party to sue for damages. The general theory of damages is that the injured party should be placed in the same position as if the contract had been properly performed, at least so far as money damages can do this.

Ask,

- Is plaintiff entitled to his "expectation interest" or "the benefit of his bargain"?

- If not, can plaintiff seek reliance damages?

- Was defendant "unjustly enriched" so plaintiff may recover in restitution?

- Does an action lie in specific performance? Was the contract for a sale for real property or a unique piece of personal property?

☐ On the other hand, if it's a torts problem, very different policy considerations are involved. The tort system compensates for both economic and non-economic loss since its goal is to provide redress of a civil wrong.

- What if I can't find the issue or principle of law?

If you really hit a roadblock, you can break down the problem into the elements common to every case and proceed from there. The following prompts allow you to gain access to the problem when your initial read is fruitless. From any one of these topics, it is but a short step to finding the principle of law implicated in the question:

☐ Identify the parties and the nature of their relationship.

Is it that of employer/employee, landlord/tenant, buyer/seller, parent/child, teacher/student, husband/wife?

☐ Identify the place(s) where the facts arose.

Did the events occur in a public area, a private home, a school, a waterway, a farm?

☐ Identify whether objects or things were involved.

Was there a transaction involving the sale of goods?

Is the ownership of land or chattel in dispute?

☐ Identify the acts or omissions which form the basis of the action.

Was there a robbery, a breach of contract, an assault, an act of discrimination?

☐ Determine whether there is a defense to the action.

Is there a basis for self-defense, justification, privilege?

☐ Characterize the relief sought.

Are the parties seeking damages?

Are they monetary or equitable damages, or both?

7. Should I "Skip Around" on the MBE?

Some believe that the first twenty questions and the last twenty questions are "easier" and therefore, they should answer those first and then go back to the others. Since MBE questions appear in completely random order, both in terms of subject matter and complexity, there is no benefit from jumping around but quite possibly there is a detriment: you can lose your place on the answer sheet and enter your selections incorrectly.

Also, it takes time to read a question, decide to skip it, and then return to read it again later. You simply don't have this extra time. However, if you find that you must skip some questions to return later, leave the appropriate spaces on your answer sheet so that you don't mismark subsequent answer choices.

8. Should I "Skip Around" When Answering the Essay Questions?

Generally, there's no rule that says you must answer the questions in the order in which they are presented as long as you mark your answer booklets appropriately. If you find that your reading of the first question is fruitless, then you might consider moving on to another question so as not to lose time or create anxiety. Chances are that once you're operating in "exam mode," when you return to the skipped question, you'll be able to answer it.

Be very careful—there are notable exceptions such as Connecticut where applicants must answer the questions in order because questions are collected every hour.

C. MASTERING ANXIETY

1.   What If I Am Feeling Anxious?

Pre-exam jitters are absolutely normal and very necessary. You should expect to feel anxious. It's also useful because the adrenaline ensures that you'll operate at peak performance. The problem occurs when it interferes with your performance. It should subside once you start working.

Take a moment to think about all the work you've done to prepare. In fact, you've over-prepared. It's the best way to provide the confidence necessary to ward off the usual exam jitters.

2.   Is There Anything Else I Can Do If I'm Feeling Anxious?

Try to recall past experiences of success. You've taken tests all your life and you've done well or you wouldn't be here now sitting for the bar exam. Just think of all the college exams you've taken and the LSAT itself. These were tough exams and you managed quite nicely. There's something to be said about the value of past experience—if you've done it before, you can do it again. And remember it's only an exam. In the general scheme of things, it's still only an exam.

Conjure a "negative" role-model. This worked nicely for me. I knew several people from high school and college who were living full and productive lives as lawyers. I had not considered them particularly exceptional. I thought to myself "if so-and-so could pass the bar exam, then so could I." I'm sure you know someone who can serve as your own negative role model. Just never tell them.

Begin the exam and work your way through, one question after another. As you move forward, your exam preparation will take over and you'll soon be thinking of the questions and nothing else.

CHAPTER 11

ADVICE FOR THE RE–TAKER

A. IF AT FIRST YOU DIDN'T SUCCEED

Of all bar-takers, it might be said that you face the most daunting task of all: overcoming your fear of failure. My heart is with you. But I know that you can pass the bar exam because I've worked with so many re-takers to know that it's possible. It's possible because you're going to follow the plan this time.

There are any number of reasons candidates don't pass the bar exam: the reasons are almost as varied as the test takers themselves. There are always a small minority of candidates who walk into the exam unprepared, knowing that they're unprepared. But this isn't typical. The vast majority work hard in preparing for the exam but working hard is not the same as working smart.

It won't be easy to pick up your books once again, but pick them up you must if you want to be the attorney you went to law school to become. Allow yourself some time to regroup emotionally and physically before taking up the task of bar preparation once again. But once you do, don't look back! You're not the same person you were the first time around, and now you're going to do things very differently.

And you must proceed differently to achieve a different result. Some re-takers erroneously believe that if they had simply spent more time on their studies, they would have passed. However, I can practically guarantee that spending more time doing what you've done before will do nothing to change the outcome. A different result requires a different approach, not more of the same. It also requires that you be brutally honest with yourself: you have to face the truth about you did or did not do. For example, if you did not learn the black letter law— really learn it so that you could recite it automatically—then no study schedule or checklist will compensate for this deficiency, no matter how elaborate or comprehensive.

Before we get involved in an intense examination of your test-taking skills and substantive knowledge, we need to consider some of the more basic issues. The most difficult part will be getting through the first few weeks after learning the results. You won't feel like doing much of anything— least of all looking over the materials sent to you by the bar examiners. But you must. There are some time-sensitive matters that require your attention and you may not be thinking all too clearly at the moment.

Here is where I can do the thinking for you—if you let me. I've tried to make it as painless as possible. Let the following series of questions do the thinking for you.

B.   WHERE TO START?

After allowing yourself a brief cooling off period, it's time to get moving. The steps outlined below provide a place for you to begin.

1.   Look to Your Jurisdiction

What information does your state release to failing examinees? You must consider each of the following:

- Are copies of your exam answers available?

- Are the test questions available?

- Are representative good answers or model answers available?

- Is there a fee?

- Is there a deadline?

- Is there someone who can help explain what you have received?

Make every effort to get your hands on your essays. Some jurisdictions make them available to the re-taker. The availability of such materials is typically included in your application for re-examination. But since the application arrives with the failure notification, it's easy to overlook in the misery of the moment. Still, you must be strong and read through all the materials sent to you by your state's bar examiners and see if they make copies of your own essay answers available. If no mention is made of this option either in the application papers or on the website, you must contact their office immediately and inquire directly. You must not lose this opportunity because once you have your hands on your essays, you can immediately apply the IRAC self-diagnostic. This gives your study program a dramatic shot forward and it's what you need at this point.

2. Know Your State's Regrading Procedure

You may want to have your exam regraded:

- Is there an automatic regrading process or must you petition the bar examiners myself?

- Is there a fee?

- Is there a deadline?

- Can you have the MBE answer sheet re-scored by hand? Is this information available from your local jurisdiction or must you contact the National Conference of Bar Examiners?

Answer sheets are scored electronically and I don't know about you, but I don't trust machines to always do the right thing. Maybe the machine counted an erasure instead of your correct answer choice. Don't take any chances when there exists a single possibility that you can avoid doing this again. However, you must be realistic. If your MBE score was very low and there's no way a couple of correct answer choices would make a difference between passing and failing, then you can't expect miracles. Face the facts, harden your resolve, and move on.

3. Find Someone to Talk to About the Exam

It often helps to speak with someone about your experience. It may not be easy for you to talk about it, but it can be incredibly helpful to speak with someone who has experience with the bar exam and can be objective. Consider contacting someone from your bar review course or the bar examiners from your jurisdiction. They are the experts on the bar exam and are in the best position to offer useful advice.

Also, you might want to reach out to your law school. While most schools do not offer formal programs to graduates retaking the bar exam, some provide informal counseling or other assistance. I would recommend contacting the Dean of Students or Director of Academic Support.

C. SELF–REFLECTION QUESTIONS

Before you begin a substantive review and work with MBE and essay questions, you should consider some of the other factors involved in the preparation process to see where you might have gone wrong. The first step is answer the following questions openly and honestly.

1. Did you study for the MBE and forget about the essays because you wrongly believed that if you got a high enough MBE score the bar examiners would not read your essays?

2. Did you get so distracted by concerns about the technicalities and procedures of the bar exam

(timing considerations, scoring, format, length, and pass rates) that you lost sight of the law?

3. Did you fail to reach "automaticity" by memorizing the black letter law, relying instead on only a general familiarity with concepts?

4. Were you overwhelmed by the subject matter outlines from the bar review course?

5. Did you work with released bar exam essays from your jurisdiction?

6. Even if you purchased or downloaded these essays, did you *really* work with them by

☐ actually writing out answers?

☐ writing answers under timed conditions?

☐ comparing what you wrote to the model/sample answer and appreciating the differences?

7. Did you practice with actual, released MBE questions?

8. Did you practice MBE questions correctly by

☐ answering one question at a time?

☐ reading the explanation even when you answered the question correctly?

☐ de-constructing each of the answer choices and asking,

☐ Do I know why each of the incorrect answer choices is incorrect?

☐ Can I fully articulate the reasoning to support the correct answer choice?

☐ Did I check my notes if I could not recall the specific language of the rule?

☐ Did I check my notes if I wasn't sure of related sub-issues, even if not necessary to answer the question?

9. If you answered a question incorrectly, did you go back over the question and try to determine where you made a wrong turn

☐ was it a problem with how I read the question?

☐ was it a problem with my knowledge of the black letter law?

10. Did you include a timed practice session to see whether you could answer between 16 and 17 questions in 30 minutes?

11. Did you include at least one practice session to simulate a six-hour test period of 200 questions?

D. ADOPT A TWO–PRONGED APPROACH

Once again, because you're a re-taker, your preparation will follow a different course than a first time test-taker. Your situation is unique because you have a "baseline." This means that you have some idea of your strengths and weaknesses in the Multistate subjects and the essays in terms of hard, real numbers. While you might wish that you didn't have the experience it took to acquire a baseline, you're going to make the best of the situation by using it to your advantage.

You must keep two objectives in mind as your prepare: first, to preserve the general knowledge base you acquired as a result of your earlier studies; and second, to increase your mastery of the specific subjects and sections of the bar exam that caused you difficulty.

1. Preserving Your Substantive Knowledge

The bar exam tests the black letter law to a level of specificity that doesn't stay with you for too long. You'll need to make a complete review of all subjects. What is the best way to cover all the necessary material?

a. Consider Re-taking a Bar Review Course

1. Can you afford to take another course?

Bar review courses are expensive and even with the reduced fee some offer to re-takers, they can still be expensive and not necessarily the best use of your time. Unless you fall into one of the categories in question 2 below, I'd suggest you forgo a course.

2. How long has it been since you've graduated law school?

If it has been more than 18 months since you've graduated from law school or taken your last bar exam, then I strongly recommend a review course. You may not think it necessary but it's essential for two reasons:

- To make sure you are studying current law

  Bar review courses continuously update their materials so candidates have access to the current law in preparing for the exam. While your notes from one bar administration to the next will still be timely, you should not take chances with study materials older than that.

- To get back into the routine

  It is not easy to get back into the habit of studying and if you've been away from it for a while, it might be best to commit to a structured program. The set schedule of classes and assignments might be just what you need to re-acclimate yourself to the process.

If you fall within this category, ask:

☐ Should you repeat the course you've already taken?

Some candidates like to sit through the same course a second time because they receive a reduced rate and don't have to take any new notes. If you are an "oral" learner, then hearing the material again may be very helpful.

On the other hand, you might want to take a different course: the change in approach, focus, sequence, and study materials may be necessary to keep you engaged and lead to a different result.

☐ Should you take a different, but still traditional bar review course?

☐ Should you take one of the "abbreviated" courses offering targeted reviews of substance and skills training? There are a number of short-term bar review courses that offer intense re-taker classes. These are often ideal for those pressed for time and money who still need the direction that only a structured study environment can provide.

☐ Should you take an on-line course? Finally, there are a number of on-line programs available that allow you to work from home and still receive valuable feedback. If you are pressed for time because of work or other commitments during the bar preparation period, this is a viable option.

b. *Do It On Your Own If You're Disciplined*

If you're a conscientious worker and a recent re-taker, it's possible, even preferable to work on your own. There is no need to sit through lectures and gather the material again. Instead, you can use these precious hours to study the material and practice questions.

If you plan to work on your own, then follow the schedule from your prior bar review course to make sure that you cover all the topics. However, be sure to adapt the schedule so that you spend more time where you need it. This assumes you've kept your bar review materials. If not, get in touch with a law school buddy and see if you can borrow them.

2. Increasing your Mastery of Individual Subjects and Sections

By taking a targeted approach to the topics and areas of the bar exam that caused you difficulty, you can concentrate your efforts where they're needed most and will do the most good. How do you determine what and where your weaknesses lie?

a. What Can You Learn From Your MBE Scores?

The NCBE urges jurisdictions to provide examinees with only the MBE total scaled score because it is not affected by the difficulty of the questions on the particular exam. The concern is that raw subscores may provide misleading information for the following reasons:

☐ "Because raw scores are simple counts of the questions answered correctly, they are not scaled to take into account the difficulty of the questions on the particular form of the exam that was taken. A low raw score in a subject might not in fact be the result of adequate or even good performance if the questions in that subject were more difficult than those in other subjects."

☐   "Because there are relatively few questions in each subject area, raw scores in individual subjects are not very reliable. If examinees were to take a second test with similar questions, the examinee score would likely fluctuate by five or so points (out of 31 or 33 points) just because of a different selection of questions."

☐   "Even if an examinee did in fact perform better in one area than another, that examinee might be better advised to devote additional study to the MBE content area of his or her intended practice, since improvement in any area will increase the total score on the next examination."[43]

So what does this mean? It means that the better you get at answering MBE questions, irrespective of subject area, the greater the likelihood of improving your overall MBE performance. Given this information, I would suggest that you pick your subjects and focus on increasing your score in the areas where you're most likely to have success. In addition to the subjects for which you have the greatest affection (if that's true of any of the subjects at this point), I'd suggest that you hone in on those topics which feature a more direct application of rule to fact, such as Torts, Criminal Law, and Constitutional Law.

43. Susan M. Case, Ph.D., "The Testing Column How to Help Repeaters Improve Their MBE Scores," *The Bar Examiner*, November 2007.

Then you must buckle down and practice, practice, practice.

On the other hand, if your jurisdiction provides a subject breakdown of your MBE scores, you can consider this information to target your study efforts.

1. How do you use the numbers to identify strengths and weaknesses?

   You can use the numbers to see if there are significant differences in your performance between individual subjects. For example, if you scored a "23" in Constitutional Law and only a "9" in Property, then you know you have a lot of work to do in that area.

2. What does it mean if the numbers are pretty consistent between all the MBE subjects?

   If the numbers are consistent, then you may have a reading comprehension problem in addition to a gap in substantive knowledge. You'll want to drill yourself on reading the questions and focusing on the bar examiners' very particular use of vocabulary. Your ability to identify signal words and legally significant phrases will help to compensate for some reading deficiencies.

3. What does it mean if the numbers vary widely from subject to subject?

   If there's a wide variation in scores between subjects, then it's not likely to be a reading comprehension problem, but a true subject-specific deficiency. In this case, you have to make some tough decisions. Some subjects are easier to master than others. Pick your subjects and focus on increasing your score in the areas where you're most likely to have success.

b. *What Can You Learn From Your Essays?*

1. What do the numbers mean?

If your jurisdiction breaks down your essay scores, then look for any significant differences between individual essays.

☐ Do your essays show a range of scores?

If you find a range of scores, including some rather high scores, then your problem is most likely a function of the subject matter and not your general essay writing skills. You need to concentrate on learning the substantive law in the low-scoring areas and practice the technique for constructing solid statements of the rule. Write sample answers and lean heavily on the "building block" approach by incorporating elements, definitions, exceptions, or distinctions, into your articulation of the rule. See Chapter 7.

☐ Are your essay scores consistent?

If your scores tend to be consistent, then you need to focus on both substance and form. You should work on improving your performance on each part of an essay, beginning with articulation of the issue and following through with a complete rule section and a thorough analysis of the applicable facts.

2. How do you use the copies of the exam answers you requested from the bar examiners?

    You are going to use "forensic IRAC" to identify the flaws in your work and correct them.

c. What Can You Learn From Your MPT Score?

Since the bar examiners give you the "law" on the MPT, how and where did you go wrong?

1. Did you finish the MPT?

    Typically, a low score on the MPT results from a lack of practice. It is not difficult "legally" but it can be a race against the clock. Adequate practice is essential to master the MPT. Your goal is to make your approach to the material so mechanical that come test day, it's purely automatic.

2. Did you use an outline to prepare your answer?

    The MPT includes so much material that it's easy to get lost. It is necessary to draft an outline before you write to organize your response.

3. Did you re-state the facts and background material instead of addressing the issues?

If you have the opportunity to review your MPT response, then look to see whether you included unnecessary background facts before finally getting to the issue. This just takes up your valuable time without adding any point-worthy material. Instead, practice beginning your response with a direct reference to the issue you're asked to resolve.

4. Did you include long, quoted passages from the cases?

Once again, this is a major time-waster. While you want to cite to the Library cases to support your rule statements, rely on quoting key phrases rather than copying whole passages.

E. GETTING BEYOND THE DISAPPOINTMENT

It's hard to understand how hundreds of hours spent attending bar review classes, reading outlines, studying notes, and taking practice exams could possibly result in a failing score, but it can and it does. I'm not about to minimize your dis-appointment—it really hurts—but what matters now is what you learn from the experience so your next attempt is successful. It won't be easy but it's essential if you're going to pass the bar exam. It's what you do when you realize that you've been traveling down the wrong road: you go back to where you made the wrong turn and proceed again. It's the going back and finding out where the wrong turn was taken that's our job.

Hopefully, this discussion has demystified the bar exam for you and at the same time provided you with a solid work plan to follow as you prepare. If you follow the advice and strategies offered in this book, seize the opportunity to practice from previous exams, and take advantage of the guidance your own jurisdiction provides, you'll be in a most favorable position on exam day.

Good luck on the bar exam and in your future endeavors as a practicing attorney.

†